Y0-BRT-710

© 2003 Algrove Publishing Limited
ALL RIGHTS RESERVED.
No part of this book may be reproduced in any form, including photocopying, without permission in writing from the publishers, except by a reviewer who may quote brief passages in a magazine or newspaper or on radio or television.

Algrove Publishing Limited
36 Mill Street
Almonte, Ontario
K0A 1A0

National Library of Canada Cataloguing in Publication Data

William Bullock & Co
    William Bullock & Co. : Spon Lane Iron Foundry, West Bromwich, Staffordshire.

(Classic reprint series)
Includes index.
ISBN 1-894572-77-7

    1. Spon Lane Iron Foundry--Catalogs. 2. Ironwork--England--West Bromwich--Catalogs.
3. Iron industry and trade--England--West Bromwich--Catalogs. I. Title. II. Series: Classic reprint series (Ottawa, Ont.)

HD9521.9.W54W5 2003   739.4'8'029442494   C2003-901450-9

Printed in Canada
#10703

Publisher's Note

If the title page and printing information had not been available, it would have been possible to determine the country of origin of this catalog just by the selection of products. In what other country would a manufacturer offer 75 styles of umbrella stand and some 245 different boot scrapers? It had to come from a country renowned for rain and, by implication, mud. Regrettably, we were unable to pin down the exact date of original publication. Informed opinion puts it early in the 1800's.

Leonard G. Lee, Publisher
July 2003
Almonte, Ontario

WILLIAM BULLOCK & Co.

SPON LANE IRON FOUNDRY,
WEST BROMWICH,
STAFFORDSHIRE.

MANUFACTURERS OF THE IMPROVED
CAST KITCHEN FURNITURE.

COFFEE MILLS, HINGES, PULLIES, CASTORS
LATCHES, ITALIAN IRONS, MAN TRAPS,
SHOE SCRAPERS, GARDEN LABELS,
SAD IRONS, THREE LEGED POTS,
LATH NAILS, SHOE BILLS,
WHEEL AND TOE TIPS, &c. &c.

T.H. SMITH
ENGRAVER   STATIONER
LITHOGRAPHIC   PRINTER
NEWHALL ST BIRMINGHAM

☞ The long Numbers affixed to each Article will be sufficient to order by.

FOR EXAMPLE:

In page 29 A is **No. 282**, which number will do instead of writing, "*Hot-house Pullies, strong, with Brass Wheels, ⅝ thick.*"

IMPROVED TINNED
CAST IRON KITCHEN FURNITURE.

The Engravings are to a scale of one-tenth of an Inch.

100 BELLIED   **101** UPRIGHT   **102** LIP'D

100. SAUCEPANS, with Round Handles.

No.			Tinned. s. d.	Untinned. s. d.	Covers. s. d.	
00 Saucepans			0 7	0 5	0 4	each.
0	½	pint	0 8	0 6	0 4	
1	1	,,	0 10	0 8	0 4	
2	1½	,,	1 0	0 9	0 4	
3	2	pints	1 2	0 10	0 5	
3x	2½	,,	1 4	0 11	0 5	
4	3	,,	1 6	1 0	0 5	
4x	3½	,,	1 8	1 2	0 5	
5	4	,,	1 9	1 3	0 5	Tin
5¼	4½	,,	1 10	1 4	0 5	Steamers,
5x	5	,,	1 11	1 5	0 6	nett.
5xx	5½	,,	2 1	1 7	0 6	s. d.
6	6	,,	2 2	1 8	0 6 ... 1 1	each.
6¼	6½	,,	2 4	1 9	0 6 ... 1 2	
6x	7	,,	2 5	1 10	0 6 ... 1 3	
7	8	,,	2 7	2 0	0 6 ... 1 3	
7x	9	,,	2 10	2 2	0 6 ... 1 4	
8	5	quarts	3 0	2 4	0 6 ... 1 4	
9	6	,,	3 6	2 9	0 7 ... 1 6	
10	7	,,	3 9	3 0	0 7 ... 1 10	
11	8	,,	4 0	3 3	0 7 ... 2 2	
11x	9	,,	4 3	3 6	0 7 ... 2 3	
12	10	,,	4 6	3 9	0 7 ... 2 4	
13	12	,,	5 0			

102. SAUCEPANS, WITH LIPS.

No.		s. d.	
No. 00		0 8	each.
0		0 9	
1		0 11	
2		1 1	
3		1 3	
3x		1 5	
4		1 7	
4x		1 9	
5		1 11	
5¼		2 0	
5x		2 2	
5xx		2 4	
6		2 5	
6¼		2 7	
6x		2 8	
7		2 11	
7x		3 2	
8		3 5	
9		3 11	
10		4 3	
11		4 6	
11x		4 9	
12		5 1	

101.—Upright Saucepans to nest, same prices as above.

103. FRONT HANDLE SAUCEPANS, AND COVERS.

		Tinned. s. d.	Untinned. s. d.	
2	quarts	2 8	2 3	each.
3	,,	3 2	2 9	
4	,,	3 10	3 3	
5	,,	4 3	3 9	
6	,,	4 10	4 3	
7	,,	5 3	4 6	
2	gallons	5 6	4 9	
2¼	,,	5 9	4 10	
2½	,,	6 0	5 0	
2¾	,,	6 3	5 3	
3	,,	6 6	5 6	
3¼	,,	6 9	5 9	
3½	,,	7 0	6 0	
4	,,	7 6	6 6	
4½	,,	8 3	7 0	
5	,,	9 0	7 6	

104. UPRIGHT ROUND POTS.
To 7 gals. same prices as below.

106. OVAL POTS, END HANDLES.
Same sizes and prices as below.

105. ROUND POTS AND COVERS.

No.			s.	d.	
1	1	pint	1	3	each.
2	1½	,,	1	6	
3	2	,,	1	9	
3x	2¼	,,	1	11	
4	3	,,	2	0	
4x	3½	,,	2	2	
5	2	quarts	2	3	
5¼	4½	pints	2	5	
5x	5	,,	2	6	
5xx	5½	,,	2	7	
6	3	quarts	2	8	
6¼	6½	pints	2	10	
6x	7	,,	2	11	
7	4	quarts	3	1	
7x	9	pints	3	4	
8	5	quarts	3	6	
9	6	,,	4	0	
10	7	,,	4	6	
11	2	gallons	4	9	
	2¼	,,	5	3	
	2½	,,	5	9	
	2¾	,,	6	0	
	3	,,	6	3	
	3¼	,,	6	7	
	3½	,,	6	10	
	4	,,	7	6	
	4½	,,	8	3	
	5	,,	9	0	
	5½	,,	9	9	
	6	,,	10	6	
	7	,,	11	6	
	8	,,	12	6	
	9	,,	13	6	
	10	,,	14	6	
	12	,,	18	0	
	15	,,	23	0	

107. OVAL POTS AND COVERS.

No.			s.	d.	
000000	2	quarts	3	0	each.
00000	3	,,	3	6	
0000	4	,,	4	0	
000	5	,,	4	6	
00	6	,,	4	9	
00x	7	,,	5	3	
0	2	gallons	5	6	
0¼	2¼	,,	5	9	
0x	2½	,,	6	0	
0xx	2¾	,,	6	3	
1	3	,,	6	6	
1x	3½	,,	7	6	
2	4	,,	9	0	
2x	4½	,,	9	9	
2xx	5	,,	10	6	
3	5½	,,	11	3	
3x	6	,,	12	0	
3xx	6½	,,	12	6	
4	7	,,	13	0	
4x	7½	,,	14	0	
5	8	,,	15	0	
5¼	8½	,,	15	9	
5x	9	,,	16	6	
6	10	,,	18	0	
7	12	,,	20	0	
8	14	,,	23	0	

108. UPRIGHT OVAL POTS AND COVERS.

With either Bails or Bow Handles.

		s.	d.	
1½	gallons	4	9	each.
2	... ,, ...	5	6	
3	... ,, ...	6	6	
3½	... ,, ...	7	6	
4	... ,, ...	9	0	
4½	... ,, ...	9	9	
5	... ,, ...	10	6	
6	... ,, ...	12	0	

Bail handle.

109. SOUP POTS AND COVERS.

With either Bails or Bow Handles.

					Steamers.		
			s.	d.		s.	d.
No. 000	2½	pints	...	1	10 each	1	0 extra.
00	2	quarts	...	2	3	1	0
0	3	... ,,	...	2	8	1	0
1	4	... ,,	...	3	0	1	2
2	5	... ,,	...	3	6	1 · 2
2x	6	... ,,	...	4	0	1	2
3	2	gallons	...	4	9	1	4
4	2½	... ,,	...	5	9	1	4
5	3	... ,,	...	6	3	1	4
6	4	... ,,	...	7	6	1	6
7	4½	... ,,	...	8	3	1	6
8	5	... ,,	...	9	0	1	6
9	6	... ,,	...	10	6	1	6

112. STOCK POTS, WITH BOW HANDLES AND COVERS.

					With tap.		
			s.	d.		s.	d.
3	gallons		6	3	...	10	0 each.
4	... ,, ...		7	6	...	12	6
5	... ,, ...		9	0	...	15	0
6	... ,, ...		10	6	...	16	6

111. UPRIGHT OVAL POTS AND COVERS.

With Saucepans fitted into the Covers.

				s.	d.	
4	gallons, complete			11	6	each.
4½	... ,,	...... ,,	...	12	3	
5	... ,,	...... ,,	...	14	3	
6	... ,,	...... ,,	...	16	0	

EXTRA STRONG.

110. OVAL BAKERS' POTS AND COVERS.

		Tinned.			Untinned.		
		s.	d.		s.	d.	
4	gallons	10	0	...	7	0	each.
5	... ,, ...	11	6	...	8	6	
6	... ,, ...	13	0	...	10	3	
7	... ,, ...	14	0	...	11	3	
8	... ,, ...	16	0	...	13	0	
9	... ,, ...	18	0	...	15	0	
10	... ,, ...	19	0	...	16	0	
12	... ,, ...	21	0	...	18	0	

STEAMER

TINNED

113. POTATO STEAMERS AND COVERS.

With Tinned Cylinder.

			s.	d.	
6	......	inch	......	4	6 each.
7	......	,,	......	5	6
8	......	.,	......	6	6
9	......	,,	......	7	6
10	......	,,	......	8	6

IMPERIAL TEA KETTLE
— WITH —
REGISTERED MALLEABLE HANDLE.

114W_WELL KETTLES

for close Fire Grates.

		s	d	
Nº 1 W	—	4	0	each
. 2 W	—	4	9	.
. 3 W	—	5	6	.
. 4 W	—	6	6	.
. 5 W	—	7	6	,
. 6 W	—	8	6	.

WELL TO 1 2 & 3. 4¾ × 2 In.

. . 4. 5 & 6. 6¼ × 2 .

Nº	Wrought Barrel	Brass Barrel	
0000_000_00_0	6ᵈ	8ᵈ	Extra
1 _ 2 _ 3 _3x	8ᵈ	10ᵈ	
4 _ 4x_ 5 _ 5x	9ᵈ	1/.	
6 _ 7 _ 8	10ᵈ	1/1	

Iron Handle

Fall Handle

Barrel Handle

114. ROUND TEA KETTLES, WITH SPOUTS CAST IN.

No.			Iron Handle. s. d.	Brass Handle. s. d.	Iron Drop Handle. s. d.	Brass Drop Handle. s. d.	Brass Barrel Handle. s. d.	Untinned Iron Handle. s. d.
No. 00000	2¼	pints	2 3					
0000	2⅜	..,,...	2 4	3 4	2 7	3 7	3 4	1 6 each.
000	2½	..,,...	2 6	3 6	2 9	3 9	3 6	1 8
00	2¾	..,,...	2 9	3 9	3 0	4 0	3 9	1 10
0	3	..,,...	3 0	4 0	3 3	4 3	4 0	2 0
1	4	..,,...	3 3	4 3	3 6	4 6	4 6	2 2
2	5	..,,...	3 9	4 9	4 0	5 0	5 0	2 9
3	6	.. ,,...	4 6	5 9	4 9	6 0	6 0	3 3
3x	7	..,,...	5 0	6 3	5 3	6 6	6 6	3 6
4	4	quarts	5 6	6 10	5 9	7 1	7 1	3 9
4x	9	pints	6 0	7 4	6 8	7 7	7 7	4 3
5	5	quarts	6 6	7 10	6 9	8 2	8 1	4 9
5x	11	pints	7 0	8 6	7 4	8 10	8 9	5 3
6	6	quarts	7 6	9 3	8 0	9 6	9 6	5 9
7	7	..,,..	8 6	10 3	8 9	10 6	10 6	6 6
8	8	..,,...	9 6	11 3	9 9	11 6	11 6	7 6
9	9	..,,...	10 6	12 3	10 9	12 6	12 6	8 6
10	10	.. ,,...	11 6	13 6	11 9	13 9	13 6	9 6
12	3	gallons	12 9	14 3	13 0	15 6	14 6	10 6

115. HARVEST CUP.

THE BRIM TINNED ON BOTH SIDES.

Half-pint, 8d. each.

117. DRINKING CUPS.

THE BRIM TINNED ON BOTH SIDES.

			s. d.	
No. 0	½ pint	...	0 9	each.
1	¾ ,,	...	0 11	
2	1 ,,	...	1 1	

116. OVAL TEA KETTLES, WITH SPOUTS CAST IN.

No.			Iron Handle. s. d.	Brass Handle. s. d.	Iron Drop Handle. s. d.	Brass Drop Handle. s. d.	Brass Barrel Handle. s. d.	Untinned Iron Handle. s. d.
No. 0	3	pints	3 6	4 6	3 9	4 9	4 9	2 0 each.
1	4	... ,, ...	3 9	4 9	4 0	5 0	5 0	2 2
2	5	... ,, ...	4 3	5 3	4 6	5 6	5 6	2 9
3	6	... ,, ..	5 0	6 3	5 3	6 6	6 6	3 3
3x	7	... ,, ...	5 6	6 9	5 9	7 0	7 0	3 6
4	4	quarts	6 0	7 4	6 3	7 7	7 7	3 9
4x	9	pints	6 6	7 10	6 9	8 1	8 1	4 3
5	5	quarts	7 0	8 4	7 3	8 8	8 8	4 9
5x	11	pints	7 6	9 0	7 9	9 4	9 3	5 3
6	6	quarts	8 0	9 9	8 6	10 0	10 0	5 9
7	7	... ,, ...	9 0	10 9	9 3	11 0	11 0	6 6
8	8	... ,, ...	10 0	11 9	10 3	12 0	12 0	7 6
9	9	... ,, ...	11 0	12 9	11 3	13 0	13 0	8 6
10	10	.. ,, ...	12 0	13 9	12 3	14 0	14 0	9 6

DIRECTIONS

THE DIGESTER.

The great importance and utility of this valuable Utensil, "THE DIGESTER," not only to poor Families but to the Public in general, in producing a larger quantity of wholesome and nourishing Food, by a much cheaper method than has ever been hitherto obtained, is a matter of such serious and interesting consideration, as cannot be too earnestly recommended to those who make Economy in the support of their Families an object of their attention.

The chief, and indeed the only thing necessary to be done, is to direct a proper mode of using it to most advantage ; and this mode is both simple and easy.

Care must be taken in filling the Digester, to leave room enough for the Steam to pass off through the Valve at the top of the Cover. This may be done by filling the Digester only three parts full of Water and bruised Bones or Meat, which it is to be noticed are all put in together. It must then be placed NEAR A SLOW FIRE SO AS ONLY TO SIMMER ; (more heat injures the quality) and this it must do for the space of Eight or Ten Hours. After this has been done, the Soup is to be strained through a hair sieve or cullender, in order to separate any bits of bones. The soup is then to be put into the Digester again, and after whatever Vegetables, Spices, &c., are thought necessary, are added, the whole is to be well boiled together for an hour or two, and it will then be fit for immediate use.

N.B.—In putting on the Lid of the Digester, take care that a Mark thus (X) on the Lid is opposite to a similar Mark (X) on the Digester.

118. TEA KITCHENS.

With Brass Tubes and best Patent Cocks.

No. 000	1½ gallons		s.	d.
No. 000	1½ gallons	10	3 each.
00	2 ... ,, ..	11	0
0	2½ ... ,, ..	12	0
1	3 ... ,, ..	13	3
1x	3½ ... ,, ..	14	0
2	4 ... ,, ..	14	9
2x	4½ ... ,, ..	15	6
3	5 ... ,, ..	16	3
4	6 ... ,, ..	18	9
5	7 .. ,, ..	21	0
6	8 ... ,, ..	23	0
7	9 ... ,, ..	26	0
8	10 ... ,, ..	28	0
9	12 ... ,, ..	33	0

If with Lock Cock, 1s. each extra.
If with Lock Cock and Lock Cover, 2s. each extra.

119. SAUCEPAN DIGESTERS.

		s.	d.
1	pint	2	3 each.
2	pints......	2	6
3	...,, ...	2	9
2	quarts ...	3	0
3	... ,, ...	4	0
4	... ,, ...	4	6
5	...,, ...	5	3
6	... ,, ...	6	0
7	... ,, ...	6	9
8	... ,, ...	7	6

120. STEWPAN DIGESTERS.

		s.	d.
No. 1	2½ pints ...	3	0 each.
2	3 ... ,, ...	3	6
3	3½... ,, ...	4	0
5	5½... ,, ...	5	6
6	7½... ,, ...	7	6

121. DIGESTERS.

		s.	d.
4	quarts ...	4	6
5	... ,, ...	5	3
6	... ,, ...	6	0
7	... ,, ...	6	9
2	gallons ...	7	6
2¼	... ,, ...	8	0
2½	... ,, ...	8	6
3	... ,, ...	9	6
3½	... ,, ...	11	0
4	... ,, ...	13	0
5	... ,, ...	14	6
6	... ,, ...	16	0
7	... ,, ...	19	0
8	... ,, ...	22	0
9	... ,, ...	24	0
10	.. ,, ...	26	0

122 RUMFORD POTS and COVERS.

		s.	d.
No. 00	....	2	6 each.
0	....	2	9
1	....	3	0
2	....	3	6
3	....	4	0
4	....	4	6
5	....	5	0
6	....	5	6
7	....	6	3
8	....	7	0
9	....	7	9
10	....	8	6
11	....	9	6
12	....	11	0
13	.. ..	12	0
14	....	13	0
15	....	14	0
16	....	15	0
17	....	16	0
18	....	17	0
19	....	18	0
20	....	19	0
21	....	21	6
22	....	23	0

With Digester Tops, if required.

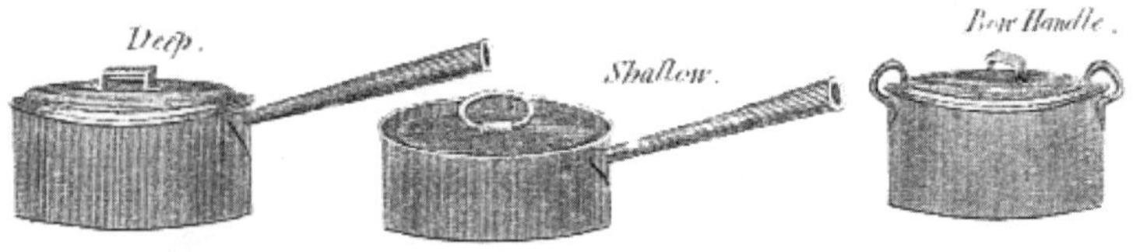

123. DEEP STEWPANS.

Measure	No.	Diam.	Round Bright Handles. s. d.	Flat Handles. s. d.
	0000	$5\frac{1}{4}$in.	0 11	... 1 3 ea.
	000	$5\frac{5}{8}$in.	1 1	... 1 5
$1\frac{1}{2}$ pints	00	$6\frac{1}{8}$in.	1 2	... 1 6
2 ... ,, ..	0	$6\frac{5}{8}$in.	1 4	... 1 8
$2\frac{1}{2}$... ,, ...	1	7 in.	1 6	... 1 10
3 ... ,, ...	2	$7\frac{1}{4}$in.	1 10	... 2 2
4 ... ,, ...	3	$8\frac{1}{8}$in.	2 3	... 2 6
$5\frac{1}{2}$... ,, ...	4	$8\frac{7}{8}$in.	2 9	... 3 0
6 ... ,, .	5	$9\frac{3}{8}$in.	3 3	... 3 6
7 ... ,, ...	6	$9\frac{7}{8}$in.	3 9	... 4 0
$8\frac{1}{2}$... ,, ...	7	$10\frac{1}{4}$in.	4 0	... 4 6
10 ... ,, ...	8	$10\frac{5}{8}$in.	4 3	... 5 0
$10\frac{1}{2}$... ,, ...	9	11 in.	4 9	... 5 6
12 ... ,, ...	10	$11\frac{3}{4}$in.	5 6	... 6 3
13 ... ,, ...	11	$12\frac{1}{8}$in.	6 3	... 7 3
16 . . ,, ...	12	$12\frac{3}{4}$in.	7 3	... 8 0
19 ... ,, ...	13	$13\frac{1}{2}$in.	8 3	... 9 3
22 ... ,, ...	14	$14\frac{1}{2}$in.	9 3	...10 0
23 ... ,, ...	15	$14\frac{3}{4}$in.	10 3	...11 0
26 ... ,, ...	16	$15\frac{3}{8}$in.	11 3	...12 0
	17	16 in.	13 6	...14 6
	18	$16\frac{7}{8}$in.	16 0	...17 0
	20	$18\frac{7}{8}$in.	20 0	...

124. SHALLOW STEWPANS.

No.	Round Bright Handles. s. d.	Flat Handles. s. d.
No. 0000	0 11	... 1 3 each.
000	1 1	... 1 5
00	1 2	... 1 6
0	1 4	... 1 8
1	1 6	... 1 9
2	1 9	... 1 11
3	2 0	... 2 3
4	2 3	... 2 6
5	2 9	... 3 0
6	3 0	.. 3 6
7	3 3	... 3 9
8	3 6	... 4 3
9	4 0	.. 4 6
10	4 3	... 5 0
11	4 9	.. 5 6
12	5 6	... 6 0
13	6 3	... 7 0
14	7 3	... 8 0
15	8 0	... 9 0
16	9 0	...10 0

Extra Shallow, only 2 inches deep, same prices and sizes.

DEEP STEWPANS

Bow Handles.

No.		s. d.
No. 0000	....	0 11 each.
000	....	1 1
00	....	1 2
0	....	1 4
1	....	1 6
2	....	1 10
3	....	2 3
4	....	2 9
5	....	3 3
6	....	3 9
7	....	4 0
8	....	4 3
9	....	4 9
10	....	5 6
11	....	6 3
12	....	7 3
13	....	8 3
14	....	9 3
15	....	10 3
16	....	11 3
17	....	13 6
18	....	16 0

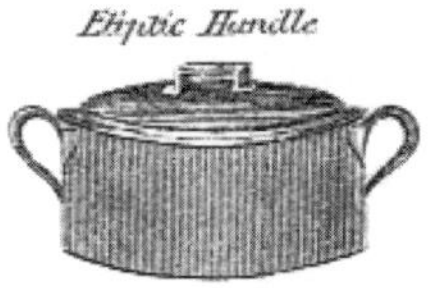

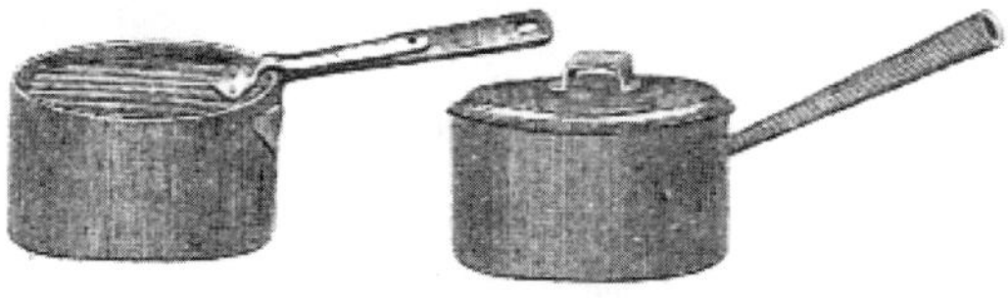

DEEP STEWPANS.

Eliptic Handles.

No.		s. d.
No. 0000	....	0 11 each.
000	....	1 1
00	....	1 2
0	....	1 4
1	....	1 6
2	....	1 10
3	....	2 3
4	....	2 9
5	....	3 3
6	....	3 9
7	....	4 0
8	....	4 3
9	....	4 9
10	....	5 6
11	....	6 3
12	....	7 3
13	....	8 3
14	....	9 3
15	....	10 3
16	....	11 3
17	....	13 6
18	....	16 0

125. FRENCH STEWPANS.

With Bright Handles and planished Covers.

No.	Measure	s. d.
No. 00000	......	1 8 each.
0000	......	1 10
000	......	2 0
00	......	2 2
0	......	2 4
1	3 pints	2 7
2	4 ,,	3 0
3	5 ,,	3 6
4	6 ,,	4 0
5	7 ,,	4 6
6	9 ,,	5 0
7	5 quarts	5 6
8	6 ,,	6 0
9	7 ,,	6 7
10	8 ,,	7 4
11	9 ,,	8 3
12	10 ,,	9 3
13	12 ,,	10 8
14	15 ,,	12 2
15	17 ,,	13 9

With Black Handles and Rim Covers.

No.		s. d.
No. 00000	......	1 0 each.
0000	......	1 2
000	......	1 4
00	......	1 6
0	......	1 9
1	......	2 0
2	......	2 6
3	......	3 0
4	......	3 6
5	......	4 0
6	......	4 6
7	......	5 0
8	......	5 6
9	......	6 0
10	......	6 6
11	......	7 3
12	......	8 3
13	......	9 0
14	......	10 6
15	......	12 0

 126. FISH KETTLES
AND COVERS.

		s.	d.	With Strainers.	s.	d.
No. 000	12 inches long	5	6	....	7	0 each.
00	13 ...... ,, ...	6	0	....	7	6
0	14 ...... ,, ...	6	6	....	8	0
0½	15 ...... ,, ...	7	0	....	8	8
1	16 ...... ,, ...	7	6	....	9	4
2	17 ...... ,, ...	8	6	....	10	8
3	18 ...... ,, ...	9	9	....	12	3
4	20 ...... ,, ...	11	3	....	14	0
5	22 ...... ,, ...	16	0	....	19	3
6	24 ...... ,,.	19	6	....	23	3
7	26 ...... ,, ...	22	3	....	26	6
3x	18½ inch by 10 inch, } straight sides .... {	10	0	....	12	6

127. TURBOT KETTLES AND COVERS.

		With Strainers.				
		s.	d.	s.	d.	
No. 0 ...	16 inches long.............................	11	0	... 13	6	each.
1 ...	18 inches long, by 14½ inches wide	12	0	... 14	6	
2 ... 20	...... ,, ... 15¼	... ,, ...	14	0	... 17	0	
3 ... 20	,....... ,, ... 16	... ,, ...	15	0	... 18	0	
4 ... 21	...... ,, ... 15¼	... ,, ...	16	0	... 19	6	
5 ... 22	...... ,, ... 15	... ,, .	18	0	... 21	6	
6 ... 22	...... ,, ... 17	... ,, ...	19	0	... 22	6	
7 ... 24	...... ,, ... 18½	... ,, ...	23	0	... 27	6	
8 . 24	...... ,, ... 20	... ,, ...	24	0	... 28	6	

If with End Handles same prices.

128. OVAL STEWPANS.
AND COVERS.
Round Bright Flat
Handles. Handles. Strainers.

			s.	d.		s.	d.		s.	d.	
No. 0	5 pints...		3	9	...	4	0	...	1	0	each.
0½	3 quarts		4	0	...	4	3	...	1	0	
1	4 ... ,,	...	4	3	...	4	6	...	1	2	
2	5 ... ,,	...	5	0	...	5	6	...	1	2	
3	6 ... ,,	...	6	0	...	6	6	...	1	6	
4	8 ... ,,	...	7	3	...	7	9	...	1	6	
5	10 ... ,,	...	8	3	...	9	0	...	1	9	
6	13 ... ,,	...	9	9	...10	9	...	1	9		
7	15 ... ,,	...11	6			....	1	9			
8	19 ... ,,	...14	0			....	1	9			
9	22 ... ,,	...16	0			....	1	9			

Larger if wanted. Bow Handles same price.

129. OVAL SAUCEPANS.
AND COVERS.
With Front Handle.

			s.	d.		s.	d.	
2	quarts.........		2	8	......	3	0	each.
3	... ,,	....	3	2	......	3	6	
4	... ,,	....	3	8	......	4	0	
5	... ,,	....	4	0	......	4	4	
6	... ,,	....	4	4	......	4	9	
7	... ,,	....	4	8	......	5	0	
2	gallons		5	1	......	5	6	
2¼	... ,,	....	5	3	......	5	9	
2½	... ,,	....	5	7	......	6	0	
3	... ,,	... .	6	0	......	6	6	
3½	... ,,	... .	7	0	......	7	6	
4	... ,,	....	8	6	......	9	0	
4½	... ,,	....	9	3	......	9	6	
5	... ,,	10	0		......	10	6	

WITH FLAT HANDLE

11 in

130. ROUND FRYING PANS.
With either Bail, Flat Handles, or Bow Handles.
Turned. Tinned.

			s.	d.		s.	d.		s.	d.	
6	inch	1	3	......	1	6	.....	1	11	each.	
7	,,	1	6	......	1	9	......	2	3		
8	,,	1	8	......	1	11	......	2	8		
9	,,	1	10	......	2	2	.....	3	0		
10	,,	2	0	.....	2	4	......	3	4		
11	,,	2	3	.....	2	8	......	3	9		
12	,,	2	6	......	3	0	...	4	1		
13	,,	3	0	......	3	6	......	4	10		
14	,,	3	6	...	4	1	......	5	6		
15	,,	4	0	......	4	8	......	6	3		
16	,,	4	6	......	5	3	...	7	0		

131. Oval Frying Pans, same sizes and prices.

WITH BAIL

10 in

WITH BOW HANDLES

132. IMPROVED GRIDIRONS.

	s.	d.
8 inch......	1	2 each.
9 "	1	4
10 "	1	5
11 "	1	7
12 "	2	2
13 "	2	7
14 "	3	0

𝔕ettie's 𝔓attern.
With Cell for Gravy.

	s.	d.
9 inch......	1	4 each.
11 "	1	9
12 "	2	4
14 "	3	3

133. STEAK PANS.

		ROUND.		OVAL.	
		s. d.		s. d.	
No. 1	8½ inch......	2 0	...	2 10 each.	
2	10 "	3 0	...	3 9	
3	11 "	3 9	...	4 9	
4	13 "	5 0	...		

134. PIKELET PANS, TURNED.

	s.	d.
8 inch...............	2	0 each.
9 "	2	3
10 "	2	6

137. MILK PANS, SHALLOW.

	s.	d.
10 inch diameter	1	6 each.
12 " ...... "	2	0
14 " ...... "	2	9
16 " ...... "	3	6

135. GLUE POTS.

	Tinned Pans.	Copper Pans.	Untinned Pans.
	s. d.	s. d.	s. d.
No. 8o's ...	0 11 ...	2 1 ..	0 8 each.
7o's ...	0 11 ...	2 1 ..	0 8
6o's ...	1 0 ...	2 2 ...	0 9
5o's ...	1 2 ...	2 4 ...	0 10
4o's ...	1 4 ...	2 6 ...	1 0
3o's ...	1 6 ...	2 9 ...	1 2
00 ...	1 8 ...	3 0 ..	1 4
0 ...	1 10 ...	3 3 ...	1 6
1 ...	2 1 ...	3 9 ...	1 8
2 ...	2 7 ...	4 6 ...	2 2
3 ...	3 2 ...	5 3 ...	2 8
4 ...	3 10 ...	6 0 ...	3 4
5 ...	4 6 ...	7 3 ...	3 8
6 ...	5 6 ...	8 3 ...	4 6
7 ...	6 0 ...	9 3 ..	5 0
8 ...	6 6 ...	10 3 ...	5 6

136. DINNER PLATES, TINNED.

	s.	d.
8 inch diameter	1	0 each.
9 " ... "	1	1
10 " ... "	1	2

138. IMPROVED MILK PANS.

WITH SPOUT.

No.					s. d.	s. d.
0	4 quarts	12½ in. diameter			3 3 ...	each.
1	6 "	14½ "	"		4 0 ...	4 6
2	8 "	15½ "	"		4 6 ...	5 0
3	10 "	17¾ "	shallow		5 6 ...	6 0
3x12	"	17¾ "	deep		6 6 ...	7 0
4	12 "	19¾ "	shallow		7 0 ...	7 6
5	18 "	19¾ "	deep		8 0 ...	8 6
6	24 "	22 "	shallow		8 6	

139. PRESERVING PANS.

			s.	d.	
11 inches	......	...	4	6	each.
12 ,,	......		5	0	
13 ,,	......		5	6	
14 ,,	......		6	0	
15 ,,	......		7	0	
16 ,,	......		8	0	
18 ,,	......		9	0	
20 ,,	......		11	0	
22 ,,	......		14	0	

140. BOWL BASINS.

			s.	d.	
No. 0	...	7½ inch diameter...	2	0	each.
1	...	8¼ ,, ... ,, ...	2	4	
2	...	9 ,, ... ,, ...	2	7	
3	...	9¾ ,, ... ,, ...	2	11	
4	...	10½ ,, ... ,, ...	3	3	
5	...	11½ ,, ... ,, ...	3	7	

141. BOWL BASINS, FOR PLUG AND WASHER.

Diameter.	s.	d.		Diameter	s.	d.	
8½ inch	2	8	each.	11½ inch	5	0	each
9½ ,,	3	0		14 ,,	6	6	
10½ ,,	3	4		16 ,,	8	6	

BRASS PLUG AND WASHER,
FOR BASINS.
s. d.
1 10 each nett.

142.

MASLIN KETTLES,
WITH BAIL.

With three feet, if required.

					Tinned		With Bow Handles and Rim Covers.	
					s.	d.	s.	d.
No. 1	...	2½ pints	......		1	1	2	0 each.
2	...	3 ,,	......		1	3	2	2
3	...	3½ ,,	......		1	5	2	4
4	...	4½ ,,	......		1	7	2	6
5	...	5½ ,,	......		1	9	2	9
6	...	6 ,,	......		1	11	3	0
7	...	7 ,,	......		2	1	3	3
8	...	4 quarts	......		2	4	3	6
9	...	5 ,,	......		2	7	3	10
10	...	6 ,,	......		2	10	4	3
11	...	7 ,,	......		3	3	4	8
12	...	2 gallons	......		4	0	5	4
13	...	2½ ,,	......		4	9	6	3
14	...	3 ,,	......		5	9	7	0
15	...	3½ ,,	......		7	0	8	6
16	...	4 ,,	......		9	0	10	0
17	...	4½ ,,	......		9	6		
18	...	5 ,,	......		10	0		
19	...	5½ ,,	......		11	0		
20	...	6 ,,	......		12	0		

143. SHALLOW BASINS.

						s.	d.	
No. 0	...	6¾ inch diameter...				0	10	each.
1	...	8 ,,	...	,,	...	1	1	
2	...	8¾ ,,	...	,,	...	1	4	
3	...	9¾ ,,	...	,,	...	1	8	
4	...	10⅜ ,,	...	,,	...	2	0	
5	...	10¾ ,,	...	,,	...	2	6	
6	...	11¼ ,,	...	,,	...	3	0	

144. DEEP BASINS.

						s.	d.	
No. 0	...	8¼ inch diameter...				1	1	each.
1	...	8½ ,,	...	,,	...	1	4	
2	...	9 ,,	...	,,	...	1	8	
3	...	10 ,,	...	,,	...	2	0	
4	...	10½ ,,	...	,,	...	2	5	
5	...	11 ,,	...	,,	...	2	10	
6	...	12 ,,	...	,,	...	4	0	
7	...	15 ,,	...	,,	...	5	6	
8	...	16 ,,	...	,,	...	6	0	

146. DOUBLE MORTARS,

AND PESTLES.

Turned......... 3s. 0d. | Tinned......3s. 6d. each

145. MORTARS, BELL SHAPED,

AND PESTLES.

No.	Diameter.			Black. s. d.	Turned. s. d.	Tinned. s. d.
0	3½ inch			0 11	... 1 1	... 1 4 each.
1	4 ,,	¼ pint		1 1	... 1 3	... 1 6
2	4½ ,,	¾ ,,		1 6	... 1 9	... 2 0
3	5 ,,	1 ,,		1 9	... 2 0	... 2 3
4	5½ ,,	1½ ,,		2 3	... 2 6	... 2 9
5	6 ,,	2 ,,		2 9	... 3 0	... 3 6
6	6½ ,,	3 ,,		3 6	... 3 9	... 4 3
7	7 ,,	4 ,,		4 2	... 4 6	... 5 0
8	8 ,,	5 ,,		5 0	... 5 6	... 6 3
9	9 ,,	3 qrts.		6 6	... 7 0	... 8 0
10	10 ,,	4 ,,		7 9	... 8 6	... 9 9
11	11 ,,	5 ,,		9 6	...11 8	...12 0
12	12 ,,	6 ,,		12 0	...13 0	...15 0
13	13 ,,	7 ,,		18 0	...20 6	...23 0
14	14 ,,	9 ,,		23 0	...26 0	.. 29 0
15	15 ,,	12 ,,		28 0	...31 0	...34 0
16	16 ,,	13 ,,		33 0	...36 0	...40 0
17	17 ,,	,,		38 0	...42 0	...48 0
18	18 ,,	,,		44 0	...49 0	...55 0

147. MORTARS, MARBLE SHAPED,

AND PESTLES.

No.			Black. s. d.	Turned. s. d.	Tinned. s. d.
1	...	½ pint	1 7	... 1 9	... 2 3 each.
1½	...	¾ ,,	2 3	... 2 6	... 3 0
2	..	1 ,,	3 0	... 3 3	... 3 10
3	...	2 ,,	4 0	... 4 3	... 5 0
4	...	3 ,,	4 6	... 4 9	... 5 6
5	...	3½ ,,	5 6	... 6 0	... 7 6
6	...	4½ ,,	6 6	... 7 0	... 8 6

148. LIGHT MORTARS,

AND PESTLES, MARBLE SHAPE.

No.			Black. s. d.	Turned. s. d.	Tinned. s. d.
1	...	¾ pint	1 6	... 1 9	... 2 0 each.
2	...	1 ,,	2 0	... 2 4	... 2 8
3	...	1½ ,,	2 6	... 3 0	... 3 5
4	...	2 ,,	3 0	... 3 6	... 4 0
5	...	2½ ,,	3 9	... 4 3	... 4 9
6	...	3 ,,	4 6	... 5 0	... 5 6

TOBACCO POTS, IF BRONZED 6D. EACH EXTRA.

150. OCTAGON.　149. OVAL, TINNED.

150. OCTAGON.

s. d.
No. 1................... 3 6 each.
2................. 4 3

149. OVAL, TINNED.

s. d.　s. d.
No. 1...... 2 6 ... 3 0 each.
2...... 3 6 ... 4 0

150A. ROUND.

s. d.
Untinned .... 3 3 each.
Tinned............... 3 9

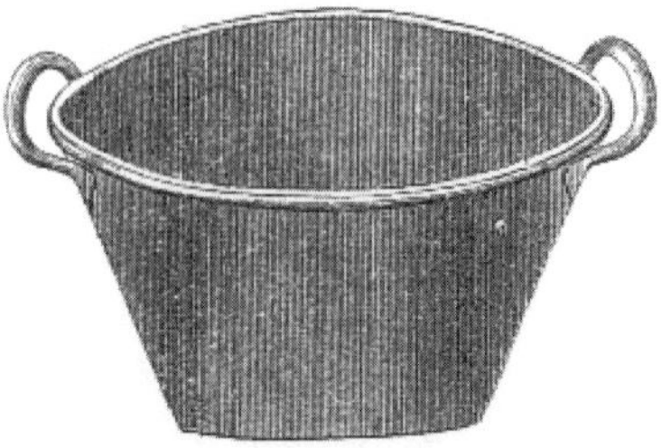

160. DEEP MILK PANS, TINNED.

No.		s.	d.	
7	13in. wide 10 in. deep...12 quarts	6	0	each
8	15in. wide 7¼in. deep...12 quarts	6	0	

161. ARNOTT SHOVELS

Japanned, wood handles.

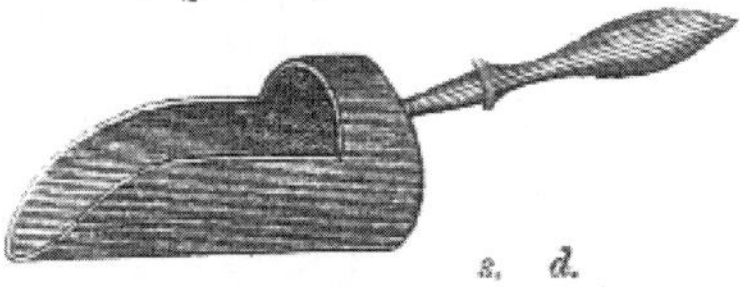

		s.	d.	
6	inch long inside......	10	0	doz.
7	,, ... ,, ... ,, ...	11	0	
7½	,, ... ,, ... ,, ...	12	0	
8	,, ... ,, ... ,, ...	13	0	

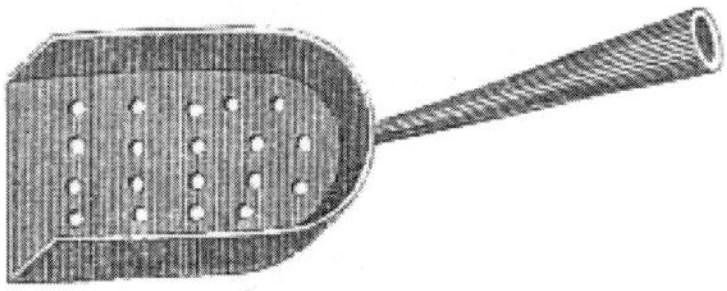

162. ROUND BACK SIFTERS.

Japanned

No.	Bottom.	s.	d.	
00	7½ by 4¾ inch	7	6	doz.
0	8 ,, 5 ,,	8	0	
1	8½ ,, 5⅜ ,,	8	6	
2	9 ,, 5¾ ,,	9	0	
3	9½ ,, 6⅛ ,,	10	0	
4	10 ,, 6¼ ,,	11	0	
5	11 ,, 6½ ,,	13	0	

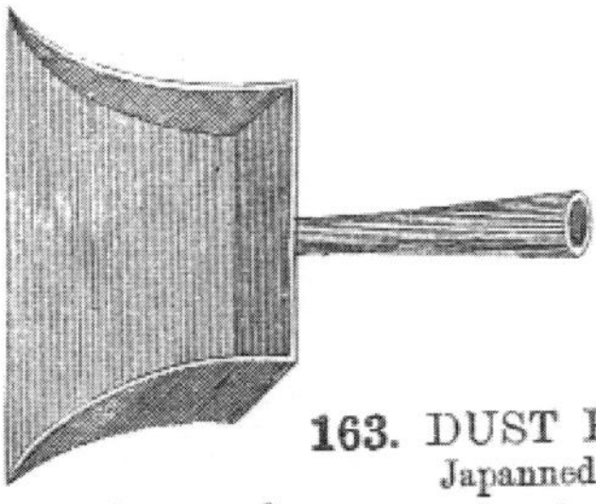

163. DUST PANS.

Japanned.

	s. d.	s. d.	s.	s. d.	s.	s.	s.	s.
	6 9	7 3	8	8 6	10	11	12	15 doz.
No.	000...	00	0 ...	1 ...	2...	2x ...	3 ...	4
	7	8	8½	9	10	10½	11¼	12½in. across

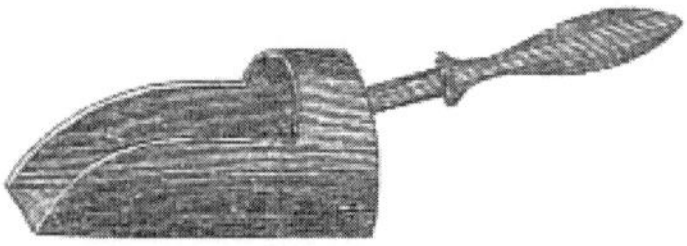

164. COAL BOX SHOVELS.

Japanned wood handles.

	s.	d.	
6 inch long inside	10	0	doz.
7 ,, ... ,, ... ,, ...	11	0	
7½ ,, ... ,, ... ,, ...	12	6	
8 ,, ... ,, ... ,, ...	13	0	

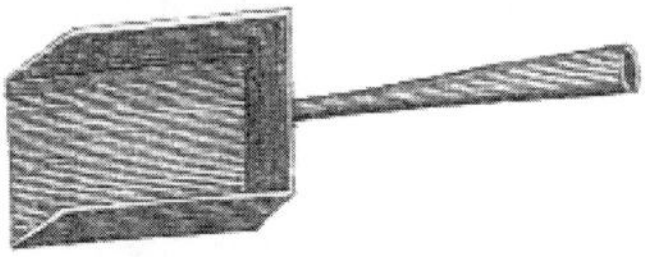

165. COPPER HOLE SHOVELS.

Japanned.

No.		s.	d.	
0	3¾ inches across front	5	6	doz.
1	4 ,, ... ,, ... ,, ...	6	6	
2	4½ ,, ... ,, ... ,, ...	7	6	
2x	4¾ ,, ... ,, ... ,, ...	8	0	
3	5 ,, ... ,, ... ,, ...	8	6	
3x	5¼ ,, ... ,, ... ,, ...	9	3	
4	5½ ,, ... ,, ... ,, ...	10	0	

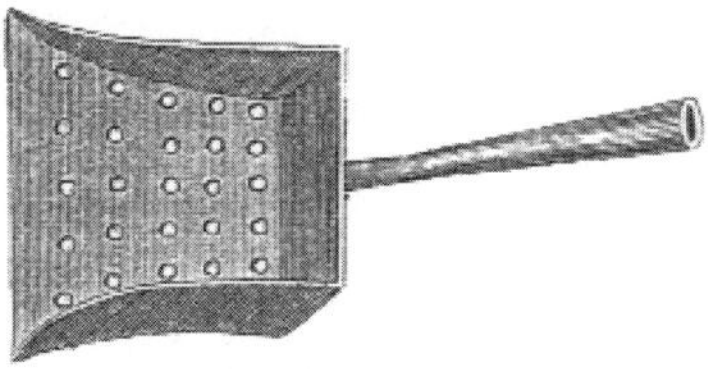

166. CINDER SIFTERS.

Japanned.

No.		s.	d.	
0000	6 inches deep......	6	3	doz.
000	7 ,, ... ,, ...	6	9	
00	7½ ,, ... ,, ...	7	3	
0	8 ,, ... ,, ...	8	0	
1	8½ ,, ... ,, ...	8	6	
2	9 ,, ... ,, ...	10	0	
3	9½ ,, ... ,, ...	12	0	
4	10½ ,, ... ,, ...	15	0	

If with wood handles, 1s. per doz. extra.

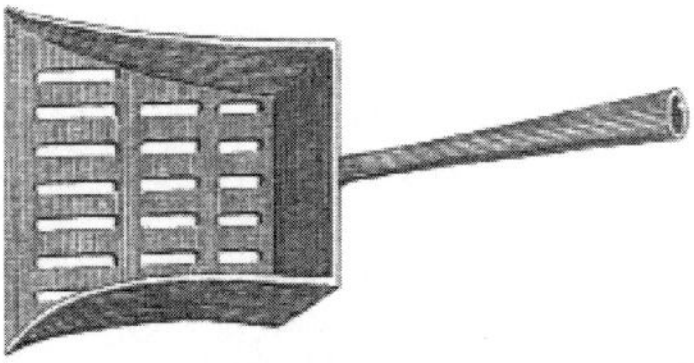

167. CINDER SIFTERS, with long holes.

Japanned.

Same sizes and prices as above.

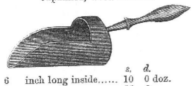

171. BELLIED COFFEE POTS.

No.			s.	d.	
000	1	pint	1	0	each.
00	1¼	"	1	1	
0	1½	"	1	2	
1	1¾	"	1	3	
2	2	"	1	6	
3	2¼	"	1	9	
4	2½	"	2	1	
5	3	"	2	5	
6	3½	"	2	10	

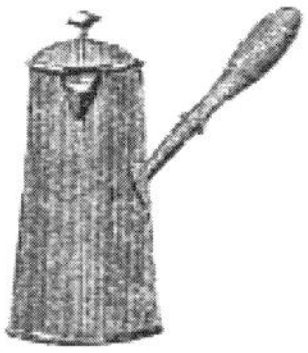

172. UPRIGHT COFFEE POTS.

No.		s.	d.
00	....	1	1
0	....	1	3
1	....	1	5
2	....	1	8
3	....	2	0
4	....	2	6
5	....	3	0

173. BELLIED CHOCOLATE POTS.

No.		s.	d.	
0	....	1	2	each.
1	....	1	3	
2	....	1	6	
3	....	1	9	
4	....	2	1	
5	....	2	5	
6	....	2	10	

174. COFFEE POTS.
NEW PATTERN.

		s.	d.	
2 pints	....	2	1	each.
2½ "	....	2	3	
3 "	....	2	6	
3½ "	....	2	10	
4 "	....	3	2	
5 "	....	3	8	
6 "	....	4	2	
8 "	....	4	8	

175. UPRIGHT CHOCOLATE POTS.

No.		s.	d.	
00	....	1	0	each.
0	....	1	2	
1	....	1	4	
2	....	1	7	
3	....	2	0	
4	....	2	6	
5	....	3	0	

176. CHOCOLATE POTS, NEW PATTERN.

		s.	d.	
2 pints	....	2	0	each.
2½ "	....	2	2	
3 "	....	2	4	
3½ "	....	2	8	
4 "	....	3	0	
5 "	....	3	6	
6 "	....	4	0	
8 "	....	4	6	

179. SKILLETS.

No.			s.	d.	
1	2 pints	...	1	2	each.
2	2½ ,,	...	1	3	
3	3 ,,	...	1	8	
4	4 ,,	...	1	10	
5	5½ ,,	...	2	0	
6	6 ,,	...	2	5	
7	7 ,,	...	2	7	
8	4 quarts		2	10	
9	5 ,,	...	3	3	
10	6 ,,	...	3	9	
11	7 ,,	...	4	0	
12	8 ,,	...	4	7	

177. BELLIED COFFEE POTS
With Hinge to the cover.
Cover tinned inside.

No.			s.	d.	
000	1	pint	1	4	each.
00	1¼	"	1	5	
0	1½	"	1	6	
1	1¾	"	1	7	
2	2	"	1	10	
3	2¼	"	2	1	
4	2½	"	2	6	
5	3	"	2	10	
6	3½	"	3	3	

178. UPRIGHT COFFEE POTS.
With Hinge to the cover.
Cover tinned inside.

No.		s.	d.	
00	....	1	5	each.
0	....	1	7	
1	....	1	9	
2	....	2	0	
3	....	2	4	
4	,.........	2	10	
5	....	3	4	

181A ROUND BOW HANDLE POTS. WITH DIGESTER COVERS TINNED.

X —— X

		WITH FLANCH.
	S D	S D AS X
No 6 _ 3 QUARTS	4.6	5.0 EACH
. 7 _ 4 _ . _	5.3	5.9 _ .
. 8 _ 5 _ . _	6.0	6.6 _ .
. 9 _ 6 _ . _	6.6	7.0 _ .
.10 _ 7 _ . _	7.3	7.9 _ .
.11 _ 2 GALLONS	8.0	8.6 _ .
.12 _ 2½ _ . _	9.6	10.3 _ .
.13 _ 3 _ . _	11.0	11.9 _ .
.14 _ 3½ _ . _	13.0	13.9 _ .
.15 _ 4 _ . _	15.0	15.9 _ .
.15x 4½ _ . _	17.0	17.9 _ .
.16 _ 5 _ . _	19.0	19.9 _ .
.16x 5½ _ . _	21.0	21.9 _ .
.17 _ 6 _ . _	23.0	23.9 _ .

121A DIGESTERS TINNED COVERS WITH FLANCH.

	S D
1 QUART	3.0 EACH.
2 QUARTS	3.6 _ . _
3 _ . _	4.6 _ . _
4 _ . _	5.0 _ . _
5 _ . _	5.9 _ . _
6 _ . _	6.6 _ . _
7 _ . _	7.3 _ . _
8 _ . _	8.0 _ . _
2¼ GALLONS	8.9 _ . _
2½ . . _	9.3 _ . _
3 _ . _	10.3 _ . _
3½ _ . _	11.9 _ . _
4 _ . _	13.9 _ . _
4½ . _	14.6 _ . _
5 . _	15.3 _ . _
6 _ . _	16.9 _ . _
7 _ . _	19.9 _ . _
8 _ . _	22.9 _ . _
9 _ . _	24.9 _ . _
10 _ . _	26.9 _ . _

181 ROUND BOW HANDLE POTS, AND COVERS.

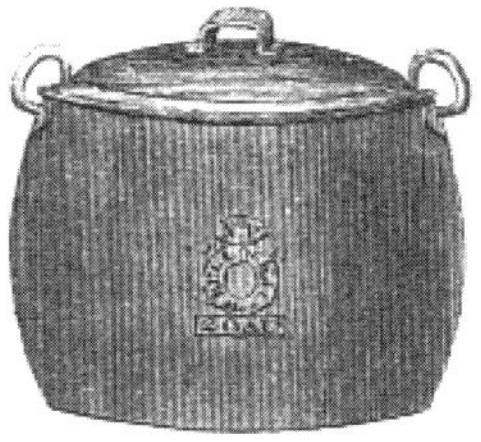

No.	Size	s.	d.	No.	Size	s.	d.
No. 1	1 pint	1	3 ea.	No. 11	2 gall.	4	9 ea.
2	1½ ,,	1	6	11x	2¼ ,,	5	3
3	2 ,,	1	9	12	2½ ,,	5	9
3x	2½ ,,	1	11	12x	2¾ ,,	6	0
4	3 ,,	2	0	13	3 ,,	6	3
4x	3½ ,,	2	2	13x	3¼ ,,	6	7
5	4 ,,	2	3	14	3½ ,,	6	10
5¼	4½ ,,	2	5	15	4 ,,	7	6
5x	5 ,,	2	6	15x	4½ ,,	8	3
5xx	5½ ,,	2	7	16	5 ,,	9	0
6	6 ,,	2	8	16x	5½ ,,	9	9
6¼	6½ ,,	2	10	17	6 ,,	10	6
6x	7 ,,	2	11	18	7 ,,	11	6
7	8 ,,	3	1	19	8 ,,	12	6
7x	9 ,,	3	4	20	9 ,,	13	6
8	5 quarts	3	6	21	10 ,,	14	6
9	6 ,,	4	0	22	12 ,,	18	0
10	7 ,,	4	6	23	15 ,,	23	0

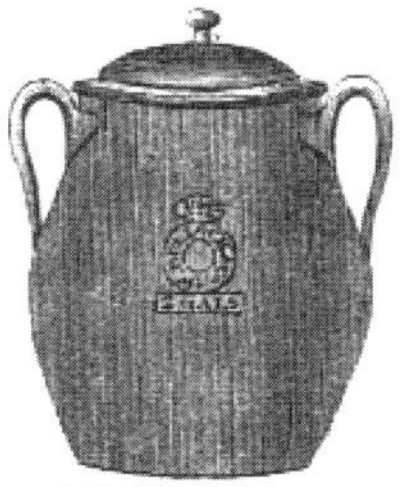

182. DEEP ROUND POTS,

With elliptic handles and covers.

Size	s.	d.
2 quarts	2	6 each.
3 ,,	3	0
4 ,,	3	6
5 ,,	4	0
6 ,,	4	6
7 ,,	5	0
2 gallons	5	6
2½ ,,	6	0
3 ,,	6	9
3½ ,,	7	4
4 ,,	8	0

184. PORRINGERS, TINNED.

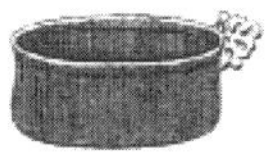

Size	Open. s.	Open. d.	Cover. s.	Cover. d.
½ pint	0	8	0	4 each.
1 ,,	0	10	0	4
1½ ,,	1	0	0	5
2 ,,	1	2	0	5

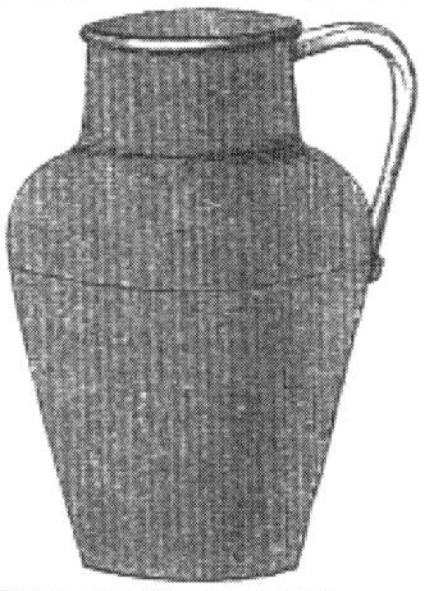

186. WATER JUGS, TINNED.

s. d.	s. d.	s. d.	s. d.	s.
1 6	1 10	2 2	2 7	3 each.
1	2	3	4	5 quarts.

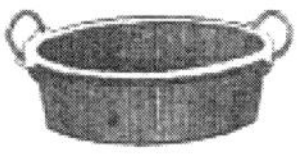

185. RICE PANS, TINNED.

Shallow, with wire handles.

Size	s.	d.	Size	s.	d.
4½ in. diam.	0	7	9½ in. diam.	1	4½ ea.
5 ,,	0	8	10 ,,	1	6
5½ ,,	0	8½	10½ ,,	1	7½
6 ,,	0	9	11 ,,	1	9
6½ ,,	0	9½	11½ ,,	1	11
7 ,,	0	10	12 ,,	2	1
7½ ,,	0	11	12½ ,,	2	4
8 ,,	1	0	13 ,,	2	6
8½ ,,	1	1½	13½ ,,	3	0
9 ,,	1	3	14 ,,	3	6

Covers, 4*d.* to 1*s.* 1*d.* each.

183. GROG, or STEWPOTS.

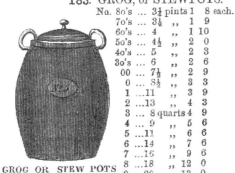

No.	Size	s.	d.
No. 8o's	3¼ pints	1	8 each.
7o's	3½ ,,	1	9
6o's	4 ,,	1	10
5o's	4½ ,,	2	0
4o's	5 ,,	2	3
3o's	6 ,,	2	6
00	7½ ,,	2	9
0	8½ ,,	3	3
1	11 ,,	3	9
2	13 ,,	4	3
3	8 quarts	4	9
4	9 ,,	5	6
5	11 ,,	6	6
6	14 ,,	7	6
7	16 ,,	9	6
8	18 ,,	12	0
9	20 ,,	13	0
10	24 ,,	14	0

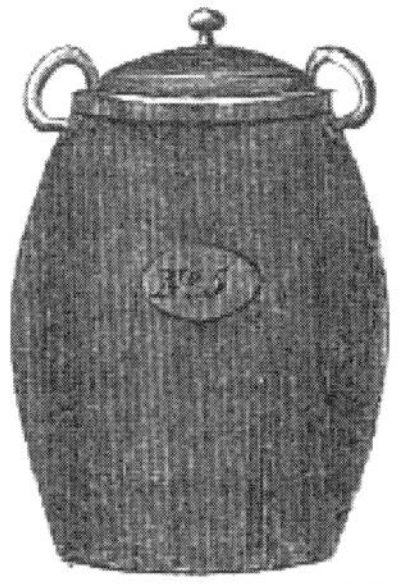

GROG OR STEW POTS *with Bow Handles & Covers*

15

Coved 151

N°00 ____ 6/ Doz.
. 0 ____ 6/6 ,,
. 1 ____ 7/6 ,
. 2 ____ 8/6 ,

Upright 152

Open   With Plain Covers
N°0. 6/ _____ 8/ Doz
,, 1. 6/6 _____ 9/6 ,,
,, 2. 7/6 _____ 11/ ,,
,, 3. 8/6 _____ 12/6 ,,

Octagon 154

N° 0 ____ 6/ Doz.
,, 1 ____ 6/6 ,,
,, 2 ____ 7/6 ,,
,, 3 ____ 8/6 ,,

N°10 ____ 8/6 Doz,
Bronzd 14/.

Open   Cover'd
N° 6 __ 8/. __12/ Doz.
,, 6 × __10/ __14/. ,,
,, 7 __12/ __16/. ,,

WhiteInside   Bronz'd
N° 8 ____ 12/ _____ 17/6 Doz
,, 9 ____ 14/ _____ 19/6 ,,

N°11 ____ 8/6 Doz.
Bronzd 14/. .

Deep 156

Brown with Covers
N° 0 _____ 13/ Doz.
,, 1 _____ 15/. ,,
,, 2 _____ 18/. ,,

N°12 ____ 8/6 Doz.
Bronzd 14/. .

N°13 ____ 8/6 Doz
Bronz'd __14/ .

N° 14 ___ 8/6 Doz.
Bronzed 14/. ,

Open Cover'd
N° 15 __10/. 14/. Doz.
Bronz'd 15/6 19/6 ,,

N°16 ____ 8/6 Doz
Bronzd 14/. ,

Open Cover'd
N°17 __10/. 14/. Doz.
Bronz'd 15/6 19/6

Open __Cover'd
N° 18 __11/6 __15/6 Doz.
Bronz'd 17/. __21/. , ,

Open Cover'd
N°19 10/. 15/6 Doz.
Bronzd 15/. 21/. ,,

Open Cover'd
N° 20 __ 10/. __15/6 Doz.
Bronzed __15/. __21/. ,

Open __Cover'd
N° 21 __ 8/6 __ 13/. Doz.
Bronz'd 14/. __18/6 ,,

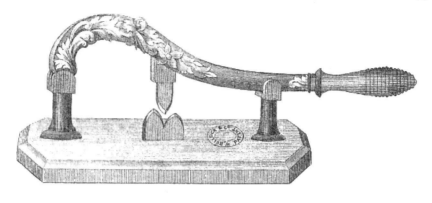

PATENT SUGAR NIPPERS. 187

Japanned. Bronzed. Bright.

		s	d.	s.	d.	s.	d.	
No. 1		3	. 6	4	. 0	4	. 6	each.
No. 2	LARGE	6	. 0	6	. 6	7	. 6	
	For Grocers use.							

Open for Grinding.   When closed 4½ by 3 in.

CAMP COFFEE MILL. 188 REGISTERED.

s. d.

Nº 1, Complete with Block Tin Cases 3. 6 ea.

„ 2 „ with Cast Cases to Screw 4. 6 „

„ 3 „ with Lacqᵈ Brass Cases 11. 0 „

FOR USE   CLOSED

PORTABLE COFFEE MILL 194
s d
3 . 6 Each

190 VERTICAL COFFEE MILL
BRONZED

Nº 1 ____ 5/6

„ 2 ____ 6/6

„ 3 ____ 7/6 EACH

192. ROUND COFFEE MILLS, IMPROVED SHAPE.

No.	s.	d.
9	2	9 each.
10	3	0
11	3	3
12	3	8
13	4	0

193. SQUARE COFFEE MILLS.

No.	s.	d.
000	3	0 each.
00	3	3
0	3	6
1	4	0
2	4	6
3	5	0
4	5	9
5	6	6

189. TABLE MILLS, BRONZED, IMPROVED.

No.	s.	d.
1	5	0 each.
2	6	0
3	7	0
4	8	6

195. FLANCH COFFEE MILLS.

No.	s.	d.
0	4	0 each.
1	4	6
2	5	6
3	6	6
4	8	0
4x	9	0
5	10	0
6	12	0
7	15	0
8	18	0

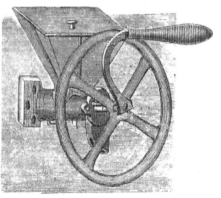

196. GROCERS' MILLS, WITH WHEELS.

No.	s.	d.		No.	s.	d.
13	8	0 each.		18	20	0 each.
14	10	0		20	25	0
15	12	0				
16	14	0				
17	17	0				

197. COUNTER MILLS.

No.	s.	d.
1	4	6 each.
2	5	6
3	6	6
4	8	0

198. ROUND MILLS, With Brass Hoppers.

No.	s.	d.
110	3	0 each.
111	4	0
112	4	6
113	5	0

199. ROUND COFFEE MILLS.

No.	s.	d.
00	2	9 each.
0	3	0
1	3	3
2	3	8
3	4	0

N.B.—Any of the above made to grind Pepper if required.

Nº 0 _ 18 ⁰ each.

Nº 1 _ 21 ⁰ „

Nº 2 _ 38 ⁰ „

HAT AND UMBRELLA STANDS
Nº 200A.

5 Fᵗ. 1 In

4 Fᵗ. 4 In

LOOSE PAN

LOOSE PAN

Japand. Bronz'd

Nº 16 _ 4 Pegs _ 5 Fᵗ 1 in 28/ _ 30/6 Ea.

„ 16 A _ 6 „ 5 _ 6 „ 32/ _ 34/6 „

Nº 17 Japanned 28/. Ea
„ Bronzed } 32/.
or Berlin }

HAT & COAT STANDS.
201

6.Ft. 4.In

5.Ft. 7.In

LOOSE PAN

s d
Nº18. Japanned 72.0 ea.
Bronzed 76.0 „

s d
Nº19. Japanned 35.0 ea.
Bronzed 39.0 „

Nº 35

Nº 25

Nº	Pegs	high	Japanned	— Bronzed
33	4	5 Feet 7 in.	35/6	39/- ea
34	6	6 . 1 in	37/6	41/6 .
35	8	6 . 7 in	39/6	44/6 .

With wrought Iron pegs

Nº	Pegs	high	— Japanned	-Green	_Bronzed
20	4	5 Feet	20/-	21/6	23/- ea
21	6	5 . 8 in	30/-	31/6	34/- "
22	8	6 . 2 in	33/-	34/6	37/- "
23	10	6 . 9 in	36/-	37/6	40/- "

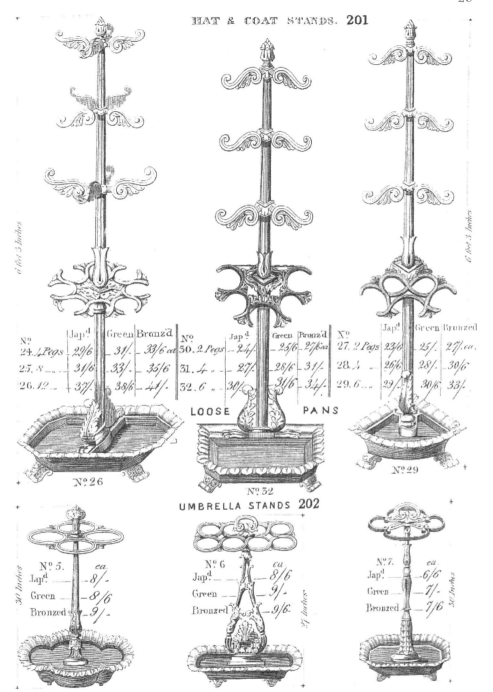

6 feet 3 Inches

6 feet 3 Inches

Nº		Jap.d	Green	Bronz'd
24.	4 Pegs	29/6	31/.	33/6 ea
25.	8 "	31/6	33/.	35/6
26.	12 "	37/.	38/6	41/.

Nº		Jap.d	Green	Bronz'd
30.	2 Pegs	24/.	25/6	27/6ea
31.	4 "	27/.	28/6	31/.
32.	6 "	30/.	31/6	34/.

Nº		Jap.d	Green	Bronzed
27.	2 Pegs	23/6	25/.	27/.ea.
28.	4 "	26/6	28/.	30/6
29.	6 "	29/.	30/6	33/.

LOOSE   PANS

Nº 26

Nº 32

Nº 29

UMBRELLA STANDS 202

Nº 5.	ea
Jap.d	8/.
Green	8/6
Bronzed	9/.

30 Inches

Nº 6	ea
Jap.d	8/6
Green	9/.
Bronzed	9/6

27 Inches

Nº 7.	ea
Jap.d	6/6
Green	7/.
Bronzed	7/6

30 Inches

No.	Japanned. Each.	Bronzed. Each.	No.	Japanned. Each.	Bronzed. Each.	No	Japanned. Each.	Bronzed. Each.
0	5/-	6/-	24	16/-	17/-	49	8/6	9/6
1	7/3	8/3	25	6/-	7/-	50	8/-	9/-
2	10/6	11/6	26	17/-	18/-	51	9/-	10/-
3	8/-	9/-	27	4/3	5/3	52	8/-	9/-
4	8/-	9/-	28	10/-	11/-	53	5/6	6/6
4L	6/6	7/6	29	7/6	8/6	54	8/-	9/-
5	8/-	9/-	30	9/6	10/6	55	3/3	4/3
6	8/6	9/6	31	5/6	6/6	56	13/6	14/6
7	6/6	7/6	32	8/3	9/3	57	6/-	7/-
8	6/6	7/6	33	6/-	7/-	58	5/6	6/6
9	8/3	9/3	34	7/6	8/6	59	10/-	12/-
10	8/-	9/-	35	13/-	14/-	60	8/6	9/6
11	6/-	7/-	36	11/6	12/6	61	3/9	4/9
12	5/9	6/9	37	4/6	5/6	62	12/6	13/6
13	7/6	8/6	38	8/6	9/6	63	4/9	5/9
14	6/6	7/6	39	4/-	5/-	64	7/-	8/-
15	8/3	9/3	40	7/3	8/3	65	7/-	8/-
16	8/9	9/9	41	10/-	11/-	66	8/-	9/-
17	9/9	10/9	42	9/-	10/-	67	9/6	10/6
18	8/6	9/6	43	4/6	5/6	68	8/6	9/6
19	13/6	15/6	44	7/-	8/-	69	14/-	16/-
20	20/-	22/-	45	7/-	8/-	70	11/8	12/8
21	7/6	8/6	46	7/6	8/6	71	15/8	16/8
22	8/6	9/6	47	8/6	9/6	72	11/-	12/-
23	15/-	16/-	48	8/9	9/9	73	13/-	14/-

UMBRELLA STANDS. 202

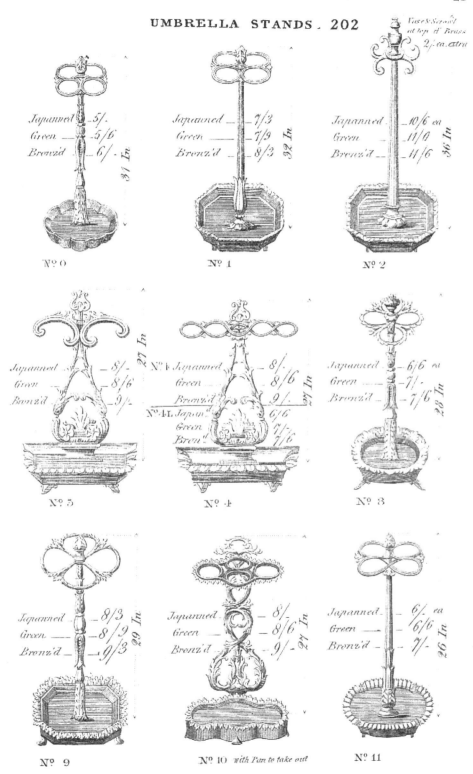

Vase & Scroll at top of Brass 2/- ea. extra

Nº O
Japanned — 5/.
Green — 5/6
Bronz'd — 6/.
31 In

Nº 1
Japanned — 7/3
Green — 7/9
Bronz'd — 8/3
32 In

Nº 2
Japanned — 10/6 ea
Green — 11/0
Bronz'd — 11/6
36 In

Nº 5
Japanned — 8/-
Green — 8/6
Bronz'd — 9/-
27 In

Nº 4
Japanned — 8/-
Green — 8/6
Bronz'd — 9/-
Nº 4L
Japan. — 6/6
Green — 7/-
Bron. — 7/6
27 In

Nº 3
Japanned — 6/6 ea
Green — 7/-
Bronz'd — 7/6
28 In

Nº 9
Japanned — 8/3
Green — 8/9
Bronz'd — 9/3
29 In

Nº 10 with Pan to take out
Japanned — 8/-
Green — 8/6
Bronz'd — 9/-
27 In

Nº 11
Japanned — 6/- ea
Green — 6/6
Bronz'd — 7/-
26 In

22

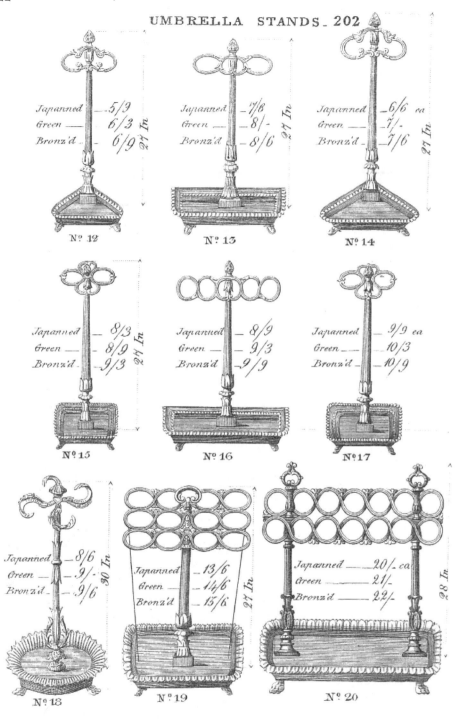

Nº 12
Japanned — 5/9
Green — 6/3
Bronz'd — 6/9
24 In

Nº 13
Japanned — 7/6
Green — 8/-
Bronz'd — 8/6
24 In

Nº 14
Japanned — 6/6 ea
Green — 7/-
Bronz'd — 7/6
24 In

Nº 15
Japanned — 8/3
Green — 8/9
Bronz'd — 9/3
24 In

Nº 16
Japanned — 8/9
Green — 9/3
Bronz'd — 9/9

Nº 17
Japanned — 9/9 ea
Green — 10/3
Bronz'd — 10/9

Nº 18
Japanned — 8/6
Green — 9/-
Bronz'd — 9/6
30 In

Nº 19
Japanned — 13/6
Green — 14/6
Bronz'd — 15/6
27 In

Nº 20
Japanned — 20/- ea
Green — 21/-
Bronz'd — 22/-
28 In

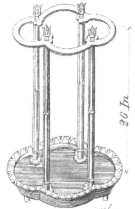

Nº 21. *Japanned* 7/6 *ea.*
Bronzed 8/6

Nº 22. *with loose pan*
Japanned 8/6 | *Bronzed* 9/6

Nº 23. *with loose pans*
Japanned 15/- | *Bronzed* 16/*ea*

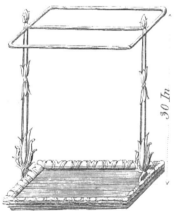

Nº 24.
24 *inch by* 15½ *in.*
Japanned 16/- | *Bronzed* 17/-

Nº 25. *Japanned* 6/-
Bronzed — 7/-

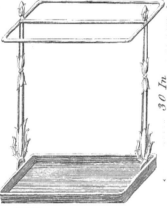

Nº 26.
30 *inch by* 16 *in.*
Japanned 17/- | *Bronzed* 18/- *ea*

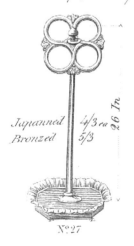

Japanned 4/3 *ea*
Bronzed 5/3

Nº 27

Japanned 10/- *ea*
Bronzed 11/-

Nº 28

Japanned 7/6 *ea*
Bronzed 8/6

Nº 29

30 In.

UMBRELLA STAND

With Pan to take out. 1/ ea extra.
Japd. Bronzed
Nᵒ 50.   9/6 10/6 ea.

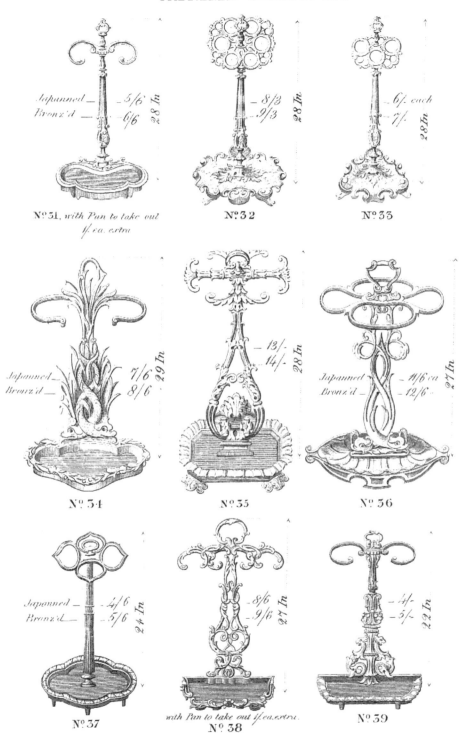

Japanned — 5/6
Bronz'd — 6/6
28 In

Nº 31, with Pan to take out
1/ ea. extra

— 8/3
— 9/3
28 In

Nº 32

6/. each
7/-
28 In

Nº 33

Japanned — 7/6
Bronz'd — 8/6
29 In

Nº 34

13/-
14/-
28 In

Nº 35

Japanned — 11/6 ea
Bronz'd — 12/6
27 In

Nº 36

Japanned — 4/6
Bronz'd — 5/6
24 In

Nº 37

— 8/6
— 9/6
27 In

with Pan to take out 1/ ea. extra.
Nº 38

— 4/-
— 5/-
22 In

Nº 39

UMBRELLA STANDS 202

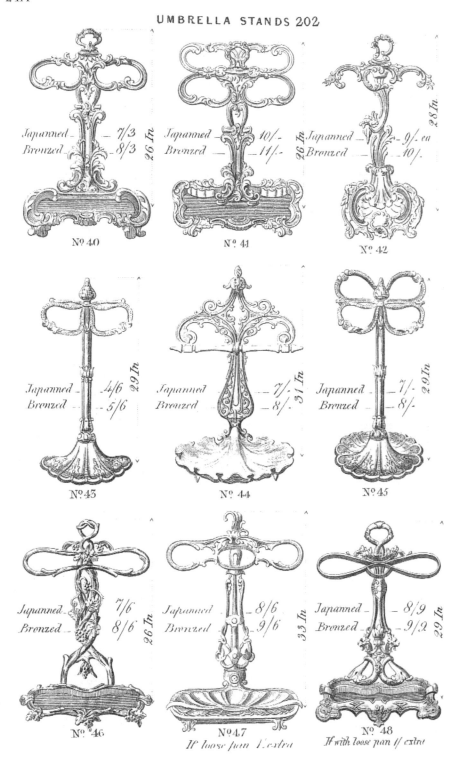

Japanned — 7/3
Bronzed — 8/3
26 In.
№ 40

Japanned — 10/-
Bronzed — 11/-
26 In.
№ 41

Japanned — 9/- ea
Bronzed — 10/-
28 In.
№ 42

Japanned — 4/6
Bronzed — 5/6
29 In.
№ 43

Japanned — 7/-
Bronzed — 8/-
31 In.
№ 44

Japanned — 7/-
Bronzed — 8/-
29 In.
№ 45

Japanned — 7/6
Bronzed — 8/6
26 In.
№ 46

Japanned — 8/6
Bronzed — 9/6
33 In.
№ 47
If loose pan 1/ extra

Japanned — 8/9
Bronzed — 9/9
29 In.
№ 48
If with loose pan 1/ extra

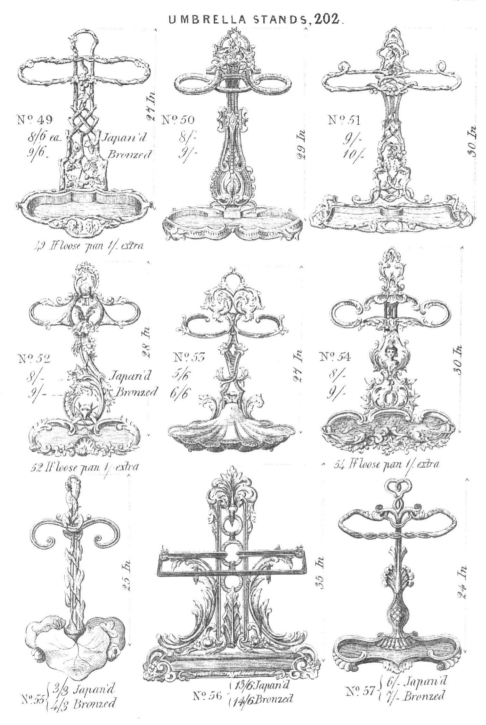

Nº 49 8/6 ea. Japan'd 9/6. Bronzed 27 In.
49 If loose pan 1/. extra

Nº 50 8/- 9/- 29 In.

Nº 51 9/- 10/- 30 In.

Nº 52 8/- 9/- Japan'd Bronzed 28 In.
52 If loose pan 1/ extra

Nº 53 5/6 6/6 27 In.

Nº 54 8/- 9/- 30 In.
54 If loose pan 1/ extra

Nº 55 { 3/3 Japan'd 4/3 Bronzed 25 In.

Nº 56 { 13/6 Japan'd 14/6 Bronzed 35 In.

Nº 57 { 6/- Japan'd 7/- Bronzed 24 In.

24C

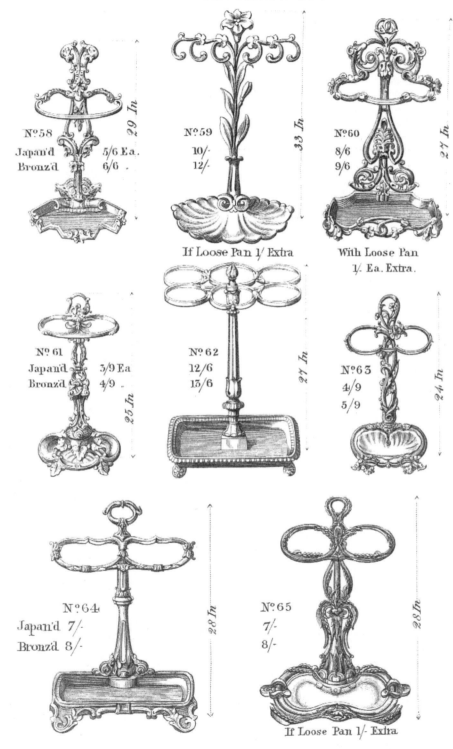

Nº 58
Japan'd   5/6 Ea.
Bronz'd   6/6 .

29 In

Nº 59
10/-
12/-

33 In

If Loose Pan 1/ Extra

Nº 60
8/6
9/6

27 In

With Loose Pan
1/. Ea. Extra.

Nº 61
Japan'd   3/9 Ea
Bronz'd   4/9 .

25 In

Nº 62
12/6
13/6

27 In

Nº 63
4/9
5/9

24 In

Nº 64
Japan'd 7/-
Bronz'd 8/-

28 In

Nº 65
7/-
8/-

28 In

If Loose Pan 1/- Extra

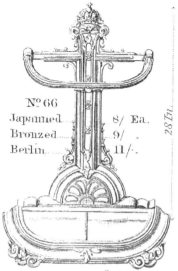

Nº 66
Japanned........ 8/ Ea.
Bronzed......... 9/ -
Berlin.......... 11/ -.

28 In.

If Loose Pan 1/8 Ea. extra

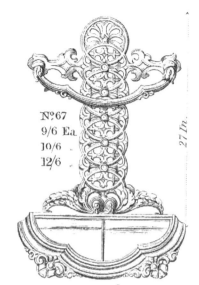

Nº 67
9/6 Ea
10/6
12/6

27 In.

If Loose Pan 1/8 Ea extra

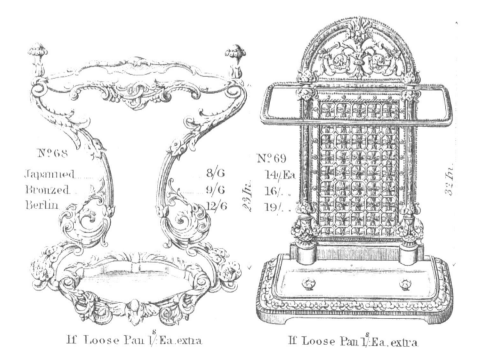

Nº 68
Japanned........ 8/6
Bronzed......... 9/6
Berlin.......... 12/6

23 In.

Nº 69
14/ Ea
16/ -
19/ -.

32 In.

If Loose Pan 1/8 Ea. extra

If Loose Pan 1/8 Ea. extra

202 UMBRELLA STANDS

31 IN HIGH
24 . WIDE

30 IN HIGH
24 . WIDE

Nº 70 WITH LOOSE PAN JAPᴰ 11/8
BRONZED 12/8

Nº 71 WITH LOOSE PAN JAPᴰ 15/8 EA
BRONZED 16/8 .

31 IN HIGH
21 . WIDE

33 IN HIGH
23 . WIDE

Nº 72 WITH LOOSE PAN JAPᴰ 11/-
BRONZED 12/- EA

Nº 73 WITH LOOSE PAN JAPᴰ 13/-
BRONZED 14/- EA

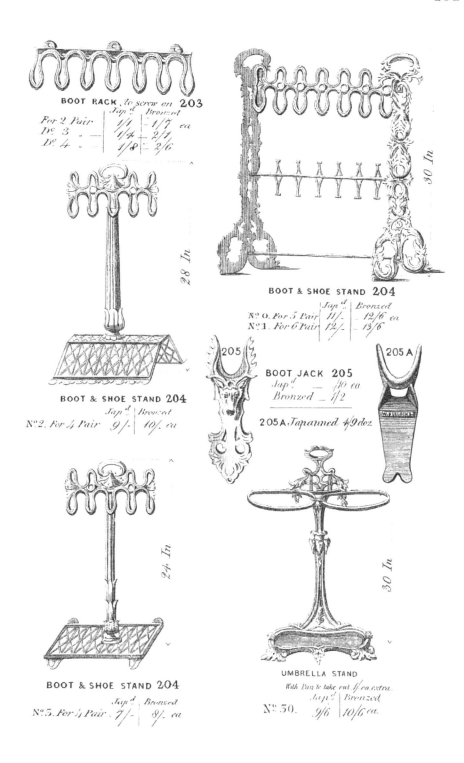

BOOT RACK *to screw on* **203**

For 2 Pair	Jap.d	Bronzed
D.o 3	—	1/1 — 1/7 ea
D.o 4	—	1/4 — 2/1
		1/8 — 2/6

BOOT & SHOE STAND 204

28 In

30 In

BOOT & SHOE STAND 204

	Jap.d	Bronzed
N.o O. For 5 Pair	11/-	12/6 ea
N.o 1. For 6 Pair	12/-	13/6

BOOT & SHOE STAND 204

	Jap.d	Bronzed
N.o 2. For 4 Pair	9/-	10/- ea

205

BOOT JACK 205

	Jap.d	—	/10 ea
	Bronzed	—	1/2

205 A *Tapanned* **4/9 doz.**

205 A

24 In

30 In

BOOT & SHOE STAND 204

	Jap.d	Bronzed
N.o 3. For 4 Pair	7/-	8/- ea

UMBRELLA STAND

With Pan to take out 1/ ea.extra.

	Jap.d	Bronzed
N.o 30.	9/6	10/6 ea.

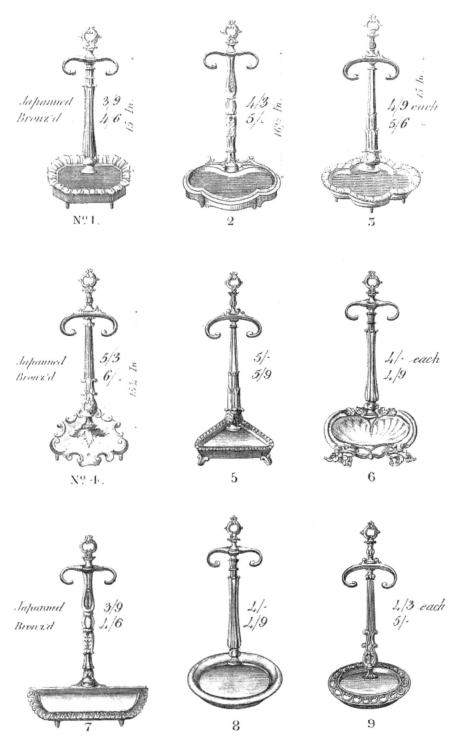

Japanned
Bronz'd
3/9
4/6
15 In.

N°. 1.

4/3
5/.
16½ In.

2

4/9 each
5/6
15 In.

3

Japanned
Bronz'd
5/3
6/.
15½ In.

N°. 4.

5/.
5/9

5

4/. each
4/9

6

Japanned
Bronz'd
3/9
4/6

7

4/.
4/9

8

4/3 each
5/.

9

	Discount.
No. 230. PATENT BUTTS, warranted made with Wired Joints, *polished.* 1/3 1/6 1/9 2/1 2/6 2/10 3/2 3/8 4/2 4/9 5/3 5/10 6/6 9/6 12/ 14/6 17/ doz. 1 1¼ 1½ 1¾ 2 2¼ 2½ 2¾ 3 3¼ 3½ 3¾ 4 4½ 5 5½ 6 inch.	
240 STRONG PATENT BUTTS, warranted made with Wired Joints. Same prices as 230 above. Polished.	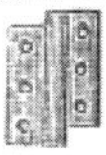
Polished. 8/6 10/- 12/6 15/6 19/- 24/- doz. **241** SKEW BUTTS, 2½ ... 3 ... 3½ ... 4 ... 4½ ... 5 *inch.*	
233 IRON-FRAMED PULLEYS. 1/8 1/10 2/1 2/4 2/6 3/- 3/4 4/4 5/4 doz. 1¼ ... 1⅜ ... 1½ ... 1⅝ ... 1¾ ... 1⅞ ... 2 ... 2¼ ... 2½ inch.	
234 BRASS-FRAMED PULLEYS. 3/2 3/6 4/1 4/8 5/3 5/9 6/6 7/6 9/6 doz. 1¼ ... 1⅜ ... 1½ ... 1⅝ ... 1¾ ... 1⅞ ... 2 ... 2¼ ... 2½ inch.	
243 IRON-FRAMED AXLE PULLEYS. 5/6 6/- 6/6 7/- 7/6 8/3 9/6 doz. 1½ ... 1⅝ ... 1¾ ... 1⅞ ... 2 ... 2¼ ... 2½ inch.	
244 BRASS-FRAMED AXLE PULLEYS. 8/- 9/- 10/- 11/- 12/- 14/- 16/- doz. 1½ ... 1⅝ ... 1¾ ... 1⅞ ... 2 ... 2¼ ... 2½ inch.	
0/8 0/8½ 0/9 0/10 0/11 1/1 1/2 1/4 doz. **231** SURPLICE PINS. 2½ ... 3 ... 3½ ... 4 ... 4½ ... 5 ... 5½ ...6 inch.	
1/6 1/7 1/10 2/1 2/4 doz. **231A** HAT AND COAT PINS. No. 0 ... 1 ... 2 ... 3 ... 4	
235 CUPBOARD BUTTONS. 7/- 7/- 8/- 9/- 10/- 12/- 14/- 16/- gross. 1¼ ... 1½ ... 1¾ ... 2 ... 2¼ ... 2½ ... 2¾ ...3 inch.	
242 THREE-WHEEL CASTORS. IRON OR WOOD BOWLS. 8/6 9/6 10/6 11/6 13/- 14/6 18/- 20/- 23/6 30/- doz. set. No. 1 ... 2 ... 3 ... 4 ... 5 ... 6 . . 7 ... 8 ... 9 ... 10	
236 FRENCH CASTORS. 6/9 7/3 7/9 8/- 9/- 10/- 11/- 11/9 12/3 12/9 13/6 set. 6 ... 7 ... 8 ... 9 ... 10 ... 11 ... 12 ... 13 ... 14 ... 15 ... 16 inch.	
232 ITALIAN IRONS AND HEATERS. 7/9 8/- 8/6 9/- 10/- 11/- 12/- doz. 3¼ ... 3½ ... 4 ... 4½ ... 5 ... 5½ ... 6 inch.	
2/2 2/2 2/2 2/4 2/6 2/9 3/- 3/6 each. **524** IMPROVED BOX IRONS. 3...3½...4...4½...5...5½.. 6...6½ inch	
3/3 3/6 4/- 4/6 5/- 5/9 6/6 each **237** SQUARE COFFEE MILLS. No. 00...0...1...2.. 3.. 4...5	
4/- 4/6 5/6 6/6 8/- 10/- each. **238** FLANCH COFFEE MILLS. No. 0 ...1... 2 ...3...4 ...5	
96 CHEAP SAD IRONS. No. 1 to 10 ...... *Nett, per Cwt.*	
239 DITTO, WITH BARREL HANDLES. No. 1 to 10. *Nett, per Cwt.*	
570 BEST SAD IRONS. No. 1 to 10......... *Nett, per Cwt.*	
96A CHEAP M IRONS. No. 1 to 6 .... *Nett, per Cwt.*	
239A DITTO, WITH BARREL HANDLES. No. 1 to 6 *Nett, per Cwt.*	

BEST CAST IRON HINGES.

250. EDGE BUTTS.

POLISHED 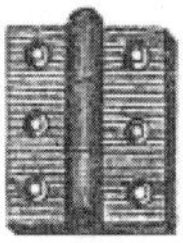 JOINTS.

	s.	d.	
1 inch............	1	3	dozen pair.
1¼ ,, ...	1	6	,,
1½ ,, ...	1	9	,,
1¾ ,, ...	2	1	,,
2 ,, ...	2	6	,,
2¼ ,, ...	2	10	,,
2½ ,, ...	3	2	,,
2¾ ,, ...	3	8	,,
3 ,, ...	4	2	,,
3¼ ,, ...	4	9	,,
3½ ,, ...	5	3	,,
3¾ ,, ...	5	10	,,
4 ,, ...	6	6	,,
4¼ ,, ...	8	0	,,
4½ ,, ...	9	6	,,
5 ,, ...	12	0	,,
5¼ ,, ...	13	3	,,
5½ ,, ...	14	6	,,
6 ,, ...	17	0	,,
6½ ,, ...	20	0	,,
7 ,, ...	23	0	,,
7½ ,, ...	30	0	,,
8 ,, ...	36	0	,,
8½ ,, ...	42	0	,,

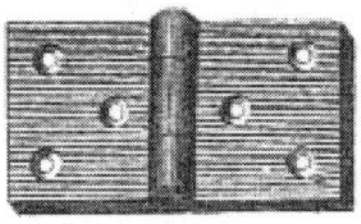

251. SQUARE BUTTS.

POLISHED JOINTS.

1 inch	1s.	6d.	doz.
1¼ ,, ...	1	8	
1½ ,, ...	2	0	
1⅝ ,, ...	2	6	
1¾ ,, ...	3	0	
1⅞ ,, ...	3	6	
2 ,, ...	4	0	
2¼ ,, ...	4	6	
2½ ,, ...	5	6	
3 ,, ...	8	0	

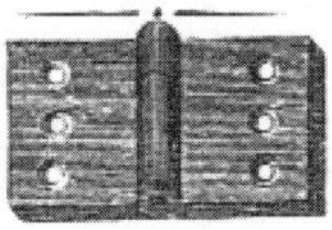

252. PEW BUTTS.

JAPANNED.

	s.	d.	
1¾ inch...........	4	0	doz
2 ,, ...	5	0	
2¼ ,, ...	5	6	
2½ ,, ...	6	0	
2¾ ,, ...	6	9	

253. SKEW BUTTS.

Left hand 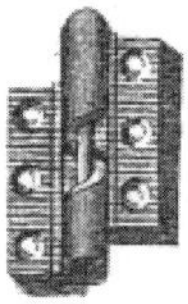

	s.	d.		BROAD SKEWS.	s.	d.
2 inch	7	6	doz.			
2¼ ,, ...	7	9				
2½ ,, ...	8	6				
2¾ ,, ...	9	3				
3 ,, ...	10	0	......	3 by 3½	13	0
3¼ ,, ...	11	3				
3½ ,, ...	12	6	......	3½ by 4	17	0
3¾ ,, ...	14	0				
4 ,, ...	15	6	......	4 by 4½	21	0
4½ ,, ...	19	0				
5 ,, ...	24	0				
6 ,, ...	30	0				

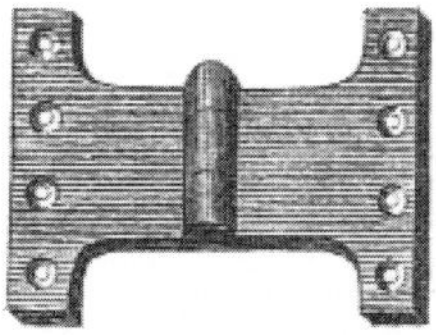

254. PARLIAMENT HINGES.

Joint.	Open.	doz. s.	d.	Joint.	Open.	doz. s.	d.
1¼ in....	2½ in....	4	9	2 in....	3 in....	7	0
1½ ,, ...	2 ,, ...	5	3	2 ,, ...	3½ ,, ...	7	3
1½ ,, ...	3 ,, ..	5	6	2 ,, ...	4 ,, ...	7	6
1¾ ,, ...	2 ,, ...	6	3	2¼ ,, ...	4 ,, ...	8	6
1¾ ,, ...	2½ ,, ...	6	6	2¼ ,, ...	4½ ,, ...	9	6
1¾ ,, ...	3 ,, ...	6	9	2½ ,, ...	5 ,, ...	10	6
1¾ ,, ...	3½ ,, ...	7	0	2½ ,, ..	6 ,, ...	12	0
2 ,, ...	1½ ,, ...	6	3	2½ ,, ...	7 ,, ...	16	0
2 ,, ...	2 ,, ...	6	6	2¾ ,, ...	5½ ,, ...	12	6
2 ,, ...	2½ ,, ...	6	9	3 ,, ...	6 ,, ...	15	0

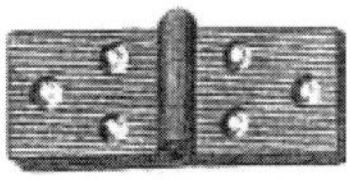

255. BACK FLAPS.

POLISHED JOINTS.

	s.	d.	
¾ inch	1	1	doz.
⅞ ,, ...	1	3	
1 ,, ...	1	5	
1⅛ ,, ...	1	7	
1¼ ,, ...	1	9	
1⅜ ,, ...	2	0	
1½ ,, ...	2	4	
1⅝ ,, ...	2	9	
1¾ ,, ...	3	3	
2 ,, ...	3	9	
2¼ ,, ...	4	6	
2½ ,, ...	6	6	

Turned Ends

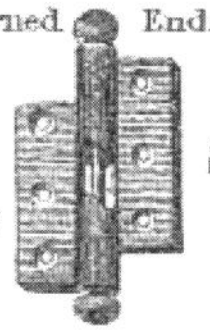

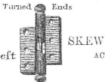

256. NEW SKEW BUTTS.

DOUBLE Left ACTION.

	s.	d.		Broad high rise. s.	d.	
2½ inch………	10	6 doz.				
3 ,, ………	12	6				
3½ ,, ………	16	0	………	20	6	doz.
4 ,, ………	20	0	………	25	0	
4½ ,, ………	24	0	………	30	0	
5 ,, ………	28	0	………	35	0	
6 ,, ………	35	0	………	42	0	

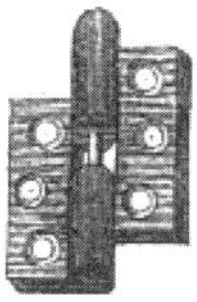

Left

257. LOOSE BUTTS.

Turned Ends

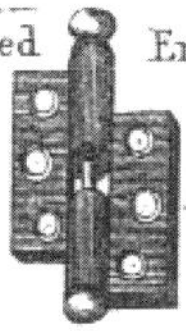

Right

	s.	d.	Turned Ends. s.	d.		s.	d.	Turned Ends. s.	d.	
1 in.	1	9 …	2	9	2¾ in.	4	6 …	6	3	doz. pair
1¼ ,,	2	0 …	3	1	3 ,,	5	3 …	7	0	
1½ ,,	2	3 …	3	5	3¼ ,,	6	0 …	7	9	
1¾ ,,	2	6 …	3	9	3½ ,,	7	0	8	9	
2 ,,	3	0 …	4	6	4 ,,	9	0 …	10	9	
2¼ ,,	3	6 …	5	3	4½ ,,	12	0 …	13	9	
2½ ,,	4	0 …	5	9	5 ,,	16	0 …	17	9	

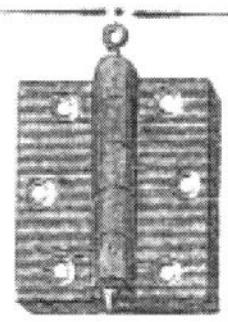

258. LOOSE PIN BUTTS.

	s.	d.
1½ inch………	2	0 dozen pair.
1¾ ,, ………	2	3
2 ,, ………	2	9
2¼ ,, ………	3	3
2½ ,, ………	3	9
2¾ ,, ………	4	3
3 ,, ………	4	9
3½ ,, ………	6	6
4 ,, ………	8	6
4½ ,, ………	10	6
5 ,, ………	14	0

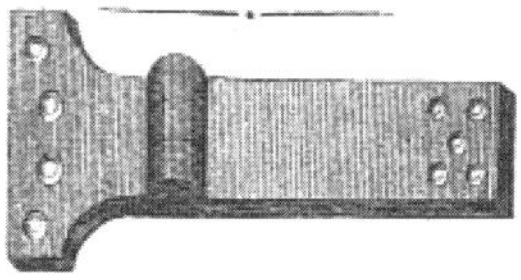

259. LONG STRAP PARLIAMENTS.

Joint.	Strap.	s.	d.
2 inch …	4¾ inch …	9	6 doz.
2¼ ,, …	5¾ ,, …	11	6
2½ ,, …	6¼ ,, …	12	6
2¾ ,, …	7 ,, …	15	0

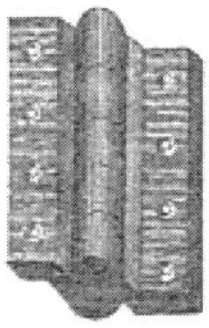

260. STRONG KNEE'D BUTTS.

		s.	d.
2½ inch…	½ inch joint…	9	0 doz.
3 ,, …	⅝ ,, bare …	11	0
3½ ,, …	⅝ ,, ………	12	6
4 ,, …	⅝ ,, ………	14	6
4 ,, …	⅞ ,, ………	18	0
4¼ ,, …	1 ,, ………	20	0
4½ ,, …	⅝ full ………	17	0
4½ ,, …	1 inch ………	22	0

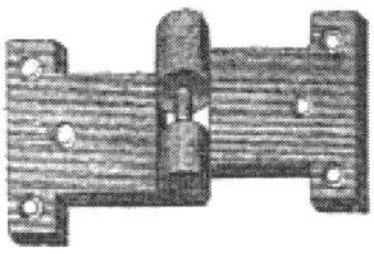

261. STRONG LOOSE JOINT PARLIAMENTS.

To rise	s.	d.	To rise	s.	d.
1½ inch …	4	9 doz.	3¼ inch …	8	9 doz.
1¾ ,, …	5	0	3½ ,, …	9	6
2 ,, …	5	6	4 ,, …	10	6
2¼ ,, …	6	0	4½ ,, …	11	6
2½ ,, …	6	6	5 ,, …	12	6
2¾ ,, …	7	0	5½ ,, …	13	6
3 ,, …	8	0	6 ,, …	14	6

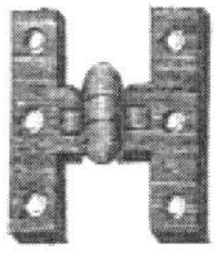

262. EGG HINGES.

JAPD.

	s.	d.
1⅛ inch in the clear	4	6 doz.
1¼ ,, ……… ,,	4	6
1½ ,, ……… ,,	4	6
1⅝ ,, ……… ,,	4	8
1¾ ,, ……… ,,	4	10
2 ,, ……… ,,	5	0
2¼ ,, ……… ,,	5	6
2½ ,, ……… ,,	6	0
2¾ ,, ……… ,,	6	6
3 ,, ……… ,,	7	0

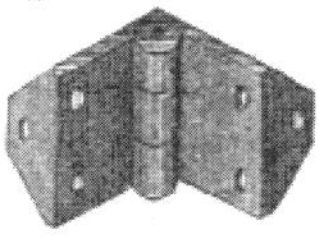

263. PEW HINGES.

JAPD.

Joint.	Open.	s.	d.
1 inch……	2 inch……	3	0 doz.
1½ ,, ……	2½ ,, ……	3	6
1¾ ,, ……	2¾ ,, ……	4	0
2 ,, ……	3 ,, ……	5	0
2 ,, ……	3½ ,, ……	5	3
2¼ ,, ……	2½ ,, ……	5	0
2¼ ,, ……	3½ ,, ……	5	6
2½ ,, ……	3½ ,, ……	6	0
2¾ ,, ……	4 ,, ……	6	9

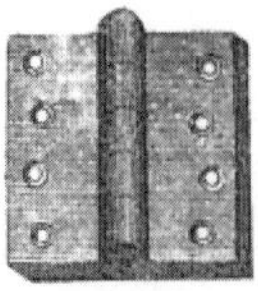

EDGE HOLE.    ZIG ZAG.

POLISHED JOINTS.

265. BEST BROAD BUTTS.

Size.		s.	d.	Size.		s.	d.
2 by	2 open	2	9	3½ by	4½ open	9	6
2	2¼ „	3	3	3½	5 „	10	6
2	2½ „	3	6	3¾	3 „	7	6
2¼	2¼ „	3	9	3¾	3¼ „	8	0
2¼	2½ „	4	0	3¾	3½ „	8	6
2½	2¼ „	3	9	3¾	3¾ „	9	0
2½	2½ „	4	3	3¾	4 „	9	6
2½	2¾ „	4	6	3¾	4¼ „	10	3
2½	3 „	4	9	3¾	4½ „	11	0
2½	3¼ „	5	3	4	3 „	8	6
2¾	2½ „	4	6	4	3¼ „	8	9
2¾	2¾ „	5	0	4	3½ „	9	0
2¾	3 „	5	6	4	3¾ „	9	6
3	2½ „	5	0	4	4 „	10	0
3	2¾ „	5	6	4	4¼ „	10	6
3	3 „	6	0	4	4½ „	11	0
3	3¼ „	6	6	4	4¾ „	11	9
3	3½ „	7	0	4	5 „	12	6
3	3¾ „	7	6	4	6 „	16	0
3	4 „	8	3	4¼	3¾ „	10	6
3¼	2¾ „	6	0	4¼	4 „	11	0
3¼	3 „	6	6	4¼	4¼ „	11	6
3¼	3¼ „	7	0	4¼	4½ „	12	6
3¼	3½ „	7	6	4¼	5 „	13	6
3¼	3¾ „	8	0	4½	3½ „	12	0
3¼	4 „	8	6	4½	3¾ „	12	6
3½	3 „	7	0	4½	4 „	13	0
3½	3¼ „	7	6	4½	4¼ „	13	6
3½	3½ „	8	0	4½	4½ „	14	0
3½	3¾ „	8	6	4½	4¾ „	14	6
3½	4 „	8	9	4½	5 „	15	0
3½	4¼ „	9	3	4½	5¼ „	15	9

BEST BROAD BUTTS, CONTINUED.

Size.		Dozen. s.	d.	Size.		Dozen. s.	d.
4½ by 5½ open		16	6	5 by 6 open		22	0
4¾	4 „	14	0	5½	4 „	17	0
4¾	4¼ „	15	0	5½	4½ „	18	0
4¾	4½ „	16	0	5½	5 „	19	6
4¾	4¾ „	17	0	5½	5½ „	21	6
4¾	5 „	18	0	5½	6 „	24	0
4¾	5½ „	19	0	5½	6½ „	27	0
5	3½ „	15	0	6	4½ „	20	0
5	4 „	16	0	6	5 „	21	6
5	4½ „	17	0	6	5½ „	23	6
5	5 „	18	6	6	6 „	26	0
5	5½ „	20	0	6	6½ „	29	0

266 COTTAGE HINGES. Jap.d

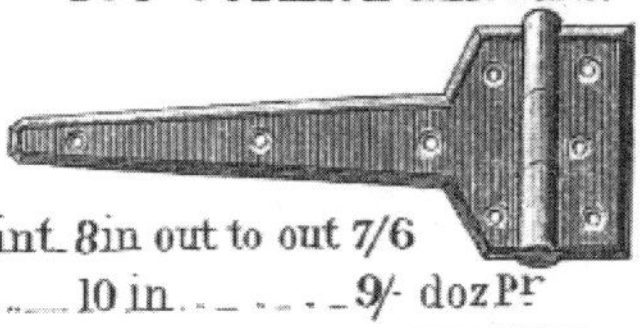

3 in Joint 8in out to out 7/6
3½ in ___ 10 in ___ 9/- doz Pr

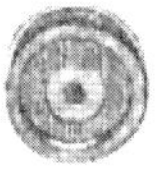

270. PULLEY WHEELS.

Turned and drilled. Pins, if required.

	Iron. s.	Iron. d.	Brass. s.	Brass. d.			Iron. s.	Iron. d.	Brass. s.	Brass. d.	
½ inch	0	6	0	10	doz.	2¼ inch	1	10	5	0	doz.
⅝ ,,	0	6	0	10		2½ ,,	2	0	6	6	
¾ ,,	0	6	0	10		2¾ ,,	2	3	8	6	
⅞ ,,	0	7	1	0		3 ,,	2	6	10	6	
1 ,,	0	8	1	6		3¼ ,,	3	3			
1¼ ,,	0	10	1	9		3½ ,,	3	6			
1⅜ ,,	0	11	1	11		3¾ ,,	4	0			
1½ ,,	1	0	2	0		4 ,,	5	0			
1⅝ ,,	1	2	2	4		4½ ,,	6	0			
1¾ ,,	1	4	2	9		5 ,,	8	0			
1⅞ ,,	1	6	3	3		6 ,,	9	6			
2 ,,	1	8	3	9							

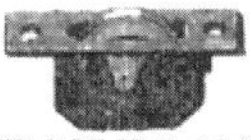

271. BEST IRON-FRAME PULLEYS.

	s.	d.	
1¼ inch	1	8	doz.
1⅜ ,,	1	10	
1½ ,,	2	1	
1⅝ ,,	2	4	
1¾ ,,	2	6	
1⅞ ,,	3	0	
2 ,,	3	4	
2¼ ,,	4	4	
2½ ,,	5	4	

272. BEST IRON-FRAME PULLEYS.

With Brass Wheels.

	s.	d.	
1¼ inch	2	8	doz.
1⅜ ,,	3	0	
1½ ,,	3	4	
1⅝ ,,	3	10	
1¾ ,,	4	4	
1⅞ ,,	4	9	
2 ,,	5	6	
2¼ ,,	6	8	
2½ ,,	8	6	

273. BEST BRASS-FRAME PULLEYS.

	s.	d.	
1¼ inch	3	2	doz.
1⅜ ,,	3	6	
1½ ,,	4	1	
1⅝ ,,	4	8	
1¾ ,,	5	3	
1⅞ ,,	5	9	
2 ,,	6	6	
2¼ ,,	7	6	
2½ ,,	9	6	

Any of the above Pulleys, with T Ends, 3*d.* dozen extra.

274. BEDSTEAD JOINTS.

JAPANNED.

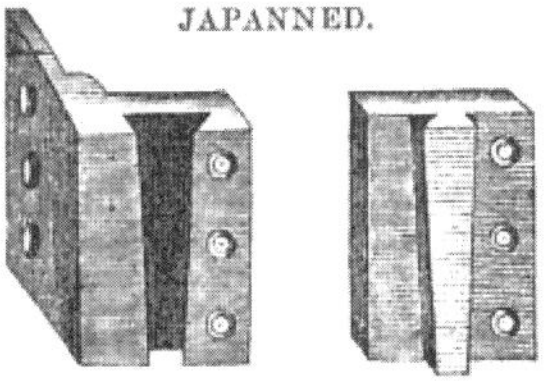

4¼ inch by 2¼ inch .... 15*s.* 0*d.* doz.

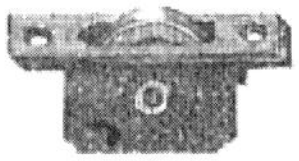

275. BRASS-FRAME AXLE PULLEYS.

	BRASS WHEELS. s.	d.	BRASS BUSHED. s.	d.	IRON WHEELS. s.	d.	FLAT BRASS WHEELS. s.	d.	
1¼ inch	7	0	8	0	6	6	9	0	doz.
1½ ,,	7	9	8	6	7	0	10	3	
1⅝ ,,	9	0	9	6	8	3	10	9	
1¾ ,,	10	3	11	3	9	3	11	6	
1⅞ ,,	11	0	12	0	10	0	12	9	
2 ,,	11	6	12	6	10	6	14	6	
2¼ ,,	14	6	16	0	13	0	17	6	
2½ ,,	17	0	18	6	15	0	20	0	
3 ,,	21	0	23	0	19	0	24	0	
3¼ ,,	24	0	26	0					
3½ ,,	28	0	30	0					
4 ,,	34	0	36	0					

276. IRON-FRAME AXLE PULLEYS.

	IRON WHEELS. s.	d.	BRASS BUSHED. s.	d.	BRASS WHEELS. s.	d.	FLAT IRON WHEELS. s.	d.
1¼ inch	5	0	6	0	6	3 doz.		
1½ ,,	5	6	6	6	6	9	6	6 doz.
1⅝ ,,	6	0	7	0	7	9	7	0
1¾ ,,	6	6	7	6	8	9	7	6
1⅞ ,,	7	0	8	0	9	6	8	0
2 ,,	7	6	8	6	10	6	9	0
2¼ ,,	8	3	9	6	12	0	10	0
2½ ,,	9	6	11	0	14	0	11	0
3 ,,	11	0	12	6	16	0	12	6

277. AXLE PULLEYS, SOLID BRASS FRONTS.

BUSHED WITH BRASS.

	s.	d.	
1½ inch	12	0	doz.
1¾ ,,	15	0	
2 ,,	18	0	
2¼ ,,	23	0	
2½ ,,	28	0	
3 ,,	38	0	

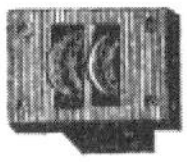

278. SHOWER BATH PULLEYS.

JAPANNED.

	Single. s.	d.	Double. s.	d.	
1½ inch	2	6	5	0	doz.
1¾ ,,	3	0	7	0	

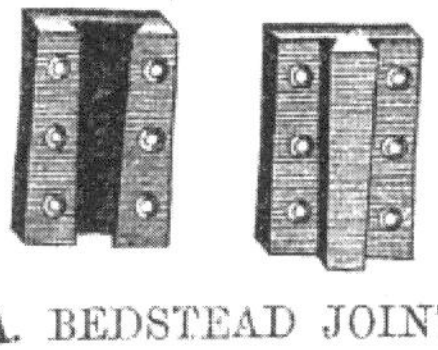

274A. BEDSTEAD JOINTS.

JAPANNED.

No.	Size	s.	d.	
No. 1	3½ by 2¼ inch	8	6	doz.
2	3½ ,, 2½ ,,	9	0	

281. HOT-HOUSE PULLEYS.
Brass wheels, $\frac{1}{2}$ in. thick.

	Single.		Double.		Treble.		
	s.	d.	s.	d.	s.	d.	
2 inch	11	0	17	0	25	0	doz.
2¼ ,,	14	0	22	0	30	0	
2½ ,,	17	0	27	0	38	0	

282. HOT-HOUSE PULLEYS.
STRONG.
Brass wheels, $\frac{5}{8}$ in. thick.

	Single.		Double.		
	s.	d.	s.	d.	
2 inch	12	0	19	0	doz.
2¼ ,,	15	0	23	0	
2½ ,,	18	0	28	0	

Bevil   Right angle

283. STRONG SINGLE HOT-HOUSE PULLEYS.
Brass wheels, $\frac{3}{4}$ in. thick.

	Bevil.		Angle.		
	s.	d.	s.	d.	
2 inch	13	0	12	6	doz.
2¼ ,,	16	0	15	6	
2½ ,,	19	6	19	0	

If solid brass wheels, 6d. each extra.

284. HOT-HOUSE LATCHES.
With latch plate.
20 in. long .... 22s. 6d. doz.

Nº 1   Nº 2   Nº 3

287. SIGNAL PULLEYS.
With 2 inch Wheels and Brass Pins.

	4/6	5/-	5/6 doz.
No. 1	2		3

2½ in   2½ in
291 GOTHIC STAPLES
Nº 1 _4/- ———— Nº 2 _5/- DOZ

288. HOT-HOUSE RACK ROLLER.
	s.	d.	
No. 1	9	0	each.
Windlass ...	1	0	

289. HOT-HOUSE RACK ROLLER.
Brass Bushed.
	s.	d.	
No. 2	10	0	each.
Windlass ...	1	0	

285 CASEMENT STAYS

Nº 1   8½ INCH   JAPᴰ 6   BRONZED. 8/- Doz.

Nº 2   8½ INCH   6/-   8/-

Nº 3   11 INCH   8/-   10/-

Nº 4

5/9	6/-	6/3	6/6	7/6
8	9	10	12	15 INCH.

IF BRONZED 2/- DOZ. EXTRA.

286. LAZY PULLEY.
3s. 0d. doz.

290. STANHOPE DOOR SPRING.
4s. 2d. each.

267. STROP SCREW PULLEY.

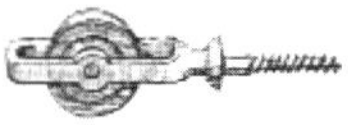

1 IN.	2/3 DOZ.
1¼.	2/8 .
1½.	3/2 .
1¾.	3/8 .
2 .	4/6 .
2½.	6/6 .

268. ANGLE SCREW PULLEY.

1½ IN.	3/ DOZ.
1¾.	3/6 „
2 „	4/3 „
2¼	5/3 „
2½	6/3 „

268A. SINGLE GUARDED PULLEY.

3/2	3/8	4/6	5/6	6/6	7/9 DOZ.
1½IN.	1¾	2	2¼	2½	3 IN.

354A LIGHT CUPD KNOBS.

6½D	7D	8½D	11D	1/3	2/1 Doz.
½	¾	1	1¼	1½	1¾ INCH.

G:G APRON KNOBS 1/ DOZ.

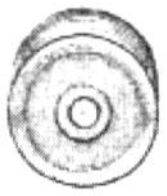

269 EXTRA STRONG PULLEY WHEELS
TURNED AND DRILLED

		s d				s d
1½ IN x $7/16$		1_6	3½ IN x $11/16$		5_3	DOZ
1¾ . x $7/16$ FULL		1_9	3¾ x $11/16$ FULL		6_0	
2 . x ½		2_0	4 x ¾		6_9	.
2¼ . x ½ FULL		2_4	4¼ x $3/4$ FULL		7_6	.
2½ . x $9/16$		2_9	4½ x 7/8		8_3	.
2¾ . x $9/16$ FULL		3_3	4¾ x 7/8 FULL		9_0	.
3 . x 5/8		3_9	5 x 1 IN		10_0	.
3¼ . x 5/8 FULL		4_6	5½ x 1 IN		_	

HARNESS HOOK.

Nº 9 8/ Doz.

BRIDLE HOLDER.

Nº 10 WITH 1 GIRTH HOOK 8/6 Doz.
„ „ 2 „ 9/ „

294. SCREW PULLEYS.

If wood bowls, 4*d.* and 6*d.* per doz. extra.

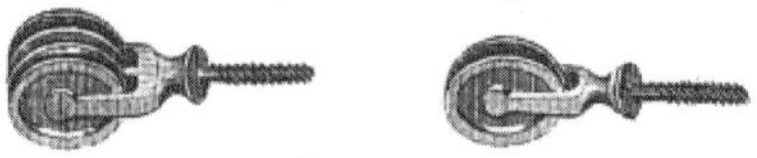

	Single. s.	d.	Extra strong. s.	d.	Double. s.	d.	Single brass wheels. s.	d.	
¾ inch	1	8			3	0	2	3	doz.
⅞ ,,	1	10			3	6	2	6	
1 ,,	2	0	3	6	4	0	3	0	
1¼ ,,	2	4	4	0	4	6	3	9	
1½ ,,	2	8	4	6	5	0	4	9	
1¾ ,,	3	2	5	3	6	0	5	9	
2 ,,	3	8	6	0	7	0	7	6	
2¼ ,,	4	6	7	0	8	0	8	9	
2½ ,,	5	6	8	0	10	0	9	9	
2¾ ,,	6	6	9	0	12	0	11	0	
3 ,,	7	6	10	0	14	0	13	0	
3½ ,,	9	6	11	0			15	0	
4 ,,			12	0			17	0	

295. SIDE PULLEYS.

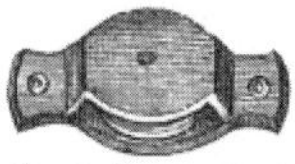

	Single. s.	d.	Brass wheels. s.	d.	Double. s.	d.	
¾ inch	1	4	2	0			doz.
1 ,,	1	6	2	6			
1¼ ,,	1	8	3	0	3	6	
1½ ,,	2	0	4	0	4	0	
1¾ ,,	2	6	5	3	5	0	
2 ,,	3	0	6	9	6	0	
2¼ ,,	3	9	7	9			
2½ ,,	4	6	9	0			
3 ,,	5	6	12	0			
4 ,,	8	6	17	0			

296. UPRIGHT PULLEYS.

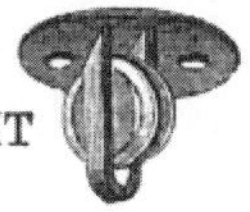

	Single. s.	d.	Double. s.	d.	Single brass wheels. s.	d.	
1 inch	1	6	3	0	2	6	doz.
1¼ ,,	1	8	3	6	3	0	
1½ ,,	2	0	4	0	4	0	
1¾ ,,	2	6	5	0	5	3	
2 ,,	3	0	6	0	6	9	
2¼ ,,	3	9	7	0	7	9	
2½ ,,	4	6	8	0	9	0	
3 ,,	5	6	11	0	12	0	

297. SPECTACLE PULLEYS.

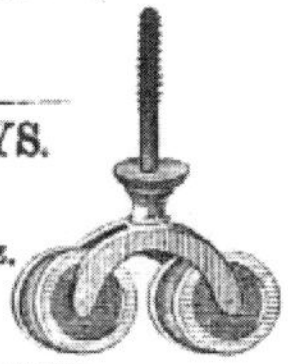

	Iron wheels. s.	d.	Brass wheels. s.	d.	
1¼ inch	12	0	16	0	doz.
1½ ,,	14	0	18	0	
1¾ ,,	17	0	22	0	

298. GUARDED SCREW PULLEYS.

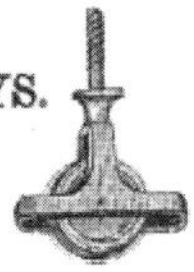

	Single. s.	d.	Double. s.	d.	
¾ inch	2	3	4	6	doz.
1 ,,	2	6	5	0	
1¼ ,,	3	0			
1½ ,,	3	6			
1¾ ,,	4	3			
2 ,,	5	0			
2¼ ,,	6	0			
2½ ,,	7	0			

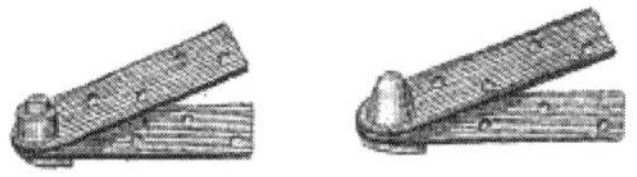

299. DOOR CENTRES.

⅞ inch wide 1*s.* 3*d.* set. | 1⅛ inch wide 1*s.* 6*d* set.

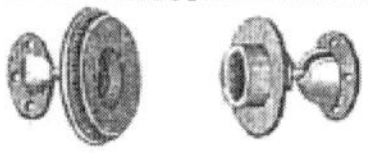

300. ROLLER BLIND ENDS.

JAPD., OR PAINTED WHITE.

3*s.*	3*s.* 3*d.*	3*s.* 6*d.*	4*s.*	5*s.* doz. set.
1¼ inch.	1½ inch.	1¾ inch.	2 inch.	2¼ inch.

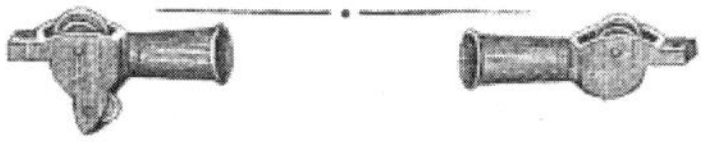

301. FRENCH CURTAIN ROD ENDS.

	Painted white. s.	d.	Tinned and lacquered. s.	d.	
⅝ inch	8	0	15	0	doz. pair.
¾ ,,	9	0	18	0	

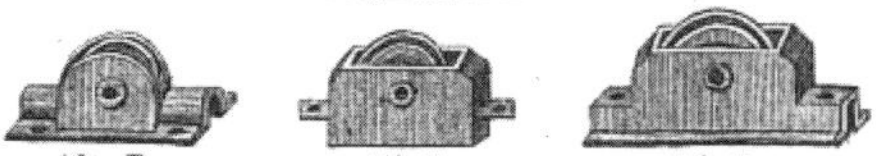

1⅜ In. *1½ In.* *1¾ In.*

302. IRON AXLE ROLLERS.

FOR SHOP PARTITIONS.

	Iron bowls. s.	d.	Brass bowls. s.	d.	
1¼ by 9/16 inch	7	6	11	6	doz.
1⅜ ,, ¼ ,, full	6	6	8	6	
1½ ,, ⅜ ,,	7	6	10	0	
1¾ ,, 7/16 ,,	8	6	11	6	
2 ,, 7/16 ,,	9	6	13	0	
2 ,, ½ ,,	10	6	14	6	

303. CENTRE HINGES.

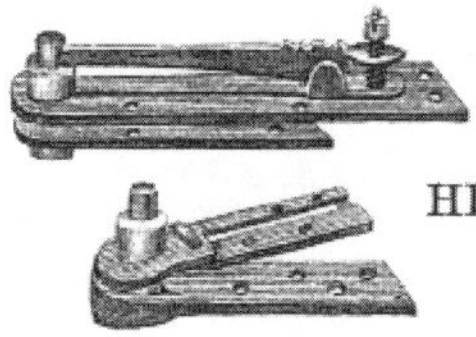

With roller to shut the door.

	s.	d.	
No. 0 for 1¼ inch doors	4	3	per set.
1 ,, 1½ ,, ,,	4	6	
2 ,, 1¾ inch & above	5	0	

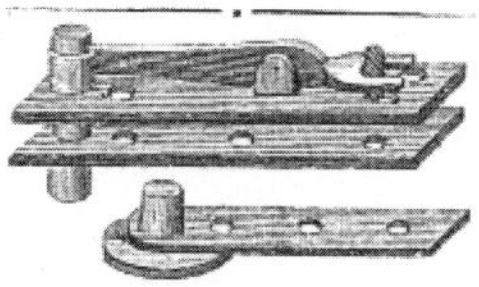

304. NEW DOOR CENTRES.

	s.	d.	
No. 3 for 1½ inch doors	3	6	per set.
4 ,, 1¾ ,, ,,	4	0	

306. NEW CENTRE CASTORS, JAPD.

WOOD BOWLS.

			s.	d.	
No. 1	1¾ in. plate	4	0	set.
2	2 ,, ,,	4	6
3	2½ ,, ,,	5	0

308. FOUR-WHEEL CASTORS.

	3s.	4s.	5s. 6d.	7s. 6d.	10s. set.
No. 1	2	3	4	5

309. STRONG PIVOT CASTORS, JAPD.

WOOD BOWLS.

			s.	d.	
No. 00	2 in. plate	5	6	set.
0	2¼ ,, ,,	6	0
1	2⅜ ,, ,,	6	6
2	2¼ ,, ,,	7	0
3	2⅜ ,, ,,	7	6
3A	3 in. bowl	8	0
3B	4 in. bowl ⎰	9	6
	2½ in. plate ⎱

307. IRON BEDSTEAD CASTORS, JAPD.

	Iron bowls.	Wood bowls.	Brass bowls.	
	s. d.	s. d.	s. d.	
No. 00	13 0	13 0	28 0	doz. set.
0	14 0	14 0	30 0
1	15 0	15 0	33 0
2	17 0	17 0	36 0
3	19 0	19 0	40 0

310. BEST THREE-WHEEL CASTORS.

No.	No.	Iron bowls. s. d.	Large wood bowls. s. d.	Brass bowls. s. d.	White bowls. s. d.	No.	No.	Iron bowls. s. d.	Large wood bowls. s. d.	Brass bowls. s. d.	White bowls. s. d.
116B or 000		8 0	9 6	10 0	11 6 doz.	123 or	7	18 0	19 6	33 0	20 6 doz.
116A ... 00		8 0	9 6	10 0	11 6	124 ...	8	20 0	22 0	42 0	23 0
116 ... 0		8 0	9 6	10 0	12 0	125 ...	9	23 6	26 0	51 0	25 0
117 ... 1		8 6	10 6	11 0	12 6	126 ...	10	30 0	32 0	60 0	30 0
118 ... 2		9 6	11 6	14 0	13 6	126A ...	11	36 0	38 0	63 0	36 0
119 ... 3		10 6	12 6	16 0	14 6	126B ...	12	42 0	44 0	70 0	42 0
120 ... 4		11 6	13 6	20 0	15 6	126C ...	13	57 0	59 0		
121 ... 5		13 0	15 0	24 0	16 6	126D ...	14	67 0	69 0		
122 ... 6		14 6	16 6	28 0	18 6						

White bowls to any of the other Castors, if required.

311. BEST FRENCH CASTORS, JAPD.

312. If stronger, and with ¾ inch pins, 1s. per set extra.

	s.	d.		s.	d.		s.	d.		s.	d.
4 inch	7	0	9 inch	9	0	14 inch	13	3	19 inch	16	9 set.
5 ,,	7	6	10 ,,	10	0	15 ,,	13	9	20 ,,	17	3
6 ,,	7	6	11 ,,	11	0	16 ,,	14	6	22 ,,	18	3
7 ,,	8	0	12 ,,	12	3	17 ,,	15	6			
8 ,,	8	9	13 ,,	12	9	18 ,,	16	3			

313. ONE WHEEL CASTORS.

JAPD. STRONG.

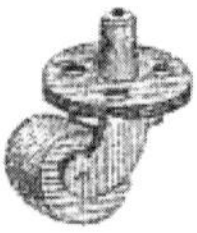

WOOD BOWLS.

No.	Plate	s.	d.	
No. 0	$1\frac{3}{4}$ inch plate	2	6	set.
1	2 ,, ... ,,	2	9	
2	$2\frac{1}{4}$,, ... ,,	3	0	
3	$2\frac{3}{8}$,, ... ,,	3	3	
4	$2\frac{1}{2}$,, ... ,,	3	6	
5	$2\frac{1}{2}$ full ... ,,	3	9	
6	$2\frac{5}{8}$ full .. ,,	4	0	

314. TWO-WHEEL CASTORS.

JAPD.

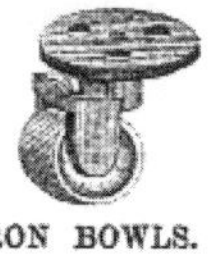

IRON BOWLS.

No.	Plate	s.	d.	
No. 0	$1\frac{1}{2}$ inch plate	8	6	doz. set.
1	$1\frac{5}{8}$,, ... ,,	9	6	
2	$1\frac{3}{4}$ bare ,,	10	6	
3	$1\frac{3}{4}$ full ,,	12	0	
4	$1\frac{7}{8}$,, ... ,,	14	0	
5	2 ,, ... ,,	16	0	
6	$2\frac{1}{8}$,, ... ,,	18	0	
7	$2\frac{1}{4}$,, ... ,,	20	0	
8	$2\frac{3}{8}$,, ... ,,	23	0	
9	$2\frac{1}{2}$,, ... ,,	27	0	
10	$2\frac{5}{8}$,, ... ,,	32	0	

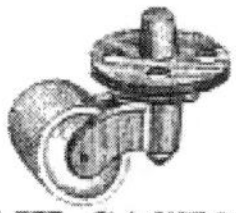

315. CLAW CASTORS, JAPD.

No.	Plate	Iron bowls. s.	d.	Brass bowls. s.	d.	
000	... $1\frac{1}{2}$ in. plate	15	0	... 19	0	doz. set.
00	... $1\frac{5}{8}$,, ,,	15	6	... 20	0	
0	... $1\frac{7}{8}$,, ,,	16	0	... 21	0	
1	.. $1\frac{3}{4}$,, ,,	17	6	... 24	0	
2	... 2 ,, ,,	23	0	... 36	0	
2	... $2\frac{1}{8}$,, ,,	30	0	... 50	0	

ROUND

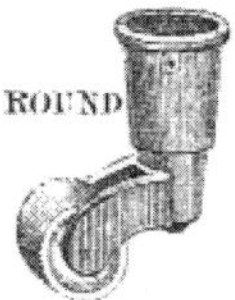

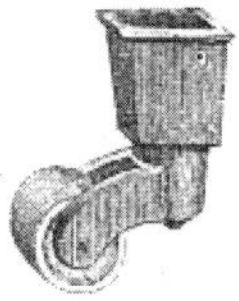

SQUARE

316. SOCKET CASTORS, JAPD.

Size	Iron bowls. s.	d.	High wood bowls. s.	d.	
$\frac{5}{8}$ inch	1	4	 1	6	set.
$\frac{3}{4}$,, ...	1	6	 1	8	
$\frac{7}{8}$,, ...	1	8	 1	10	
1 ,, ...	1	10	 2	0	
$1\frac{1}{8}$,, ...	2	0	 2	3	
$1\frac{1}{4}$,, ...	2	2	 2	6	
$1\frac{3}{8}$,, ...	2	6	 2	9	
$1\frac{1}{2}$,, ...	2	9	 3	0	
$1\frac{5}{8}$,, ...	3	2	 3	5	
$1\frac{3}{4}$,, ...	3	6	 3	9	

317. PIVOT CASTORS, JAPD.

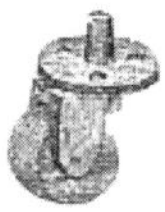

WOOD BOWLS.

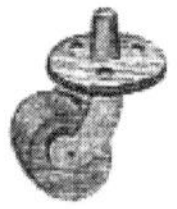

No.	Upright horn.	s.	d.	No.	Bent horn.	s.	d.	
40	$1\frac{1}{4}$ inch	30	6	40B	$1\frac{1}{4}$...	30	6	doz. set.
41	$1\frac{1}{2}$,,	32	0	41B	$1\frac{1}{2}$...	32	0	
42	$1\frac{3}{4}$,,	34	0	42B	$1\frac{3}{4}$...	34	0	
43	2 ,,	37	0	43B	2 ...	37	0	
44	$2\frac{1}{4}$,,	41	0	44B	$2\frac{1}{4}$...	41	0	
45	$2\frac{1}{2}$,,	45	0	45B	$2\frac{1}{2}$...	45	0	

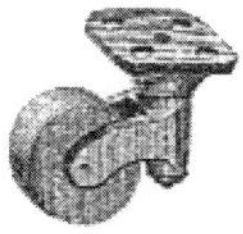

318. SQUARE PLATE CASTORS, JAPD.

WOOD BOWLS.

No.	Plate	s.	d.	
No. 46	... $1\frac{1}{2}$ in. plate	2	6	set.
47	... $1\frac{5}{8}$,, ,,	2	9	
48	... $1\frac{3}{4}$,, ,,	3	0	
49	... $1\frac{7}{8}$,, ,,	3	3	
50	... 2 ,, ,,	3	6	

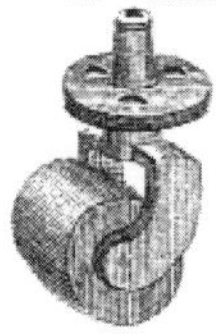

319. STRONG PIN CASTORS, JAPD.

WOOD BOWLS.

No. 20, plate $2\frac{3}{8}$ in., 3*s.* 6*d.* set.

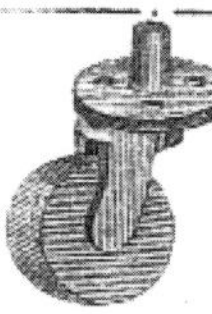

320. NEW PIVOT CASTORS, JAPD.

LARGE WOOD BOWLS.

No.	Plate	s.	d.	
No. 54	... $1\frac{3}{4}$ in. plate	3	0	set.
55	... $1\frac{7}{8}$,, ,, ...	3	3	
56	... 2 ,, ,, ...	3	6	
57	... $2\frac{1}{8}$,, ,, ...	3	9	
58	... $2\frac{1}{4}$,, ,, ...	4	0	
59	... $2\frac{3}{8}$,, ,, ...	4	4	
60	... $2\frac{1}{2}$,, ,, ...	4	9	
58A	... 3 in. bowl $2\frac{1}{4}$ plate	5	6	
58B	... $3\frac{1}{2}$ in. bowl $2\frac{1}{4}$ plate	6	0	

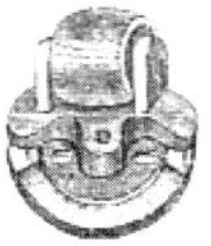

321. PATENT CASTORS, BEVIL ROLLER.

REGISTERED.

No.		Iron bowls. s.	d.	Large Wood bowls. s.	d.	Brass bowls. s.	d.
1	1½ in. plate	10	0	12	6	13	0 doz
2	1⅝ ,,	11	0	13	6	16	0 set.
3	1¾ ,,	12	0	14	6	18	0
4	1⅞ ,,	13	0	15	6	22	0
5	2 ,,	15	0	17	6	27	0
6	2⅛ ,,	17	0	20	0	31	0
7	2¼ ,,	20	0	22	6	37	0
8	2⅜ ,,	23	0	26	0	44	0
9	2½ ,,	28	0	31	0	56	0
10	2⅝ ,,	36	0	38	0	66	0
11	2⅞ ,,	43	0	45	0		
12	3 ,,	50	0	52	0		

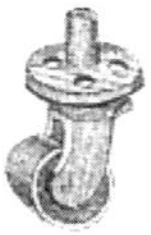

322. POMMEL CASTOR, JAPD.

IRON BOWLS.

	s.	d.
1½ inch plate	20	0 doz. sets.

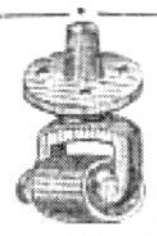

323. SINGLE PEG CASTORS.

No.		Iron bowls. s.	d.	Wood bowls. s.	d.
No. 141	1 inch plate	7	3	8	3 doz. set
142	1⅛ ,,	7	6	8	6
143	1¼ ,,	8	6	9	6
144	1⅜ ,,	9	6	10	9
145	1½ ,,	11	0	12	6
146	1⅝ ,,	13	0	14	6
147	1¾ ,,	15	0	16	6
148	1⅞ ,,	17	0	19	0
149	2 ,,	19	0	22	6

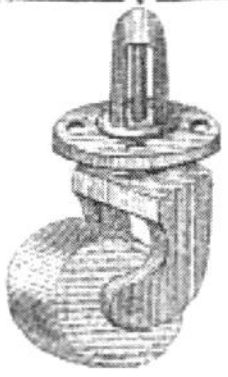

324. OPEN PIVOT CASTORS, JAPD.

WOOD BOWLS.

	s.	d.
1¼ inch plate	2	6 set.
1½ ,,	3	3
1¾ ,,	4	0
2 ,,	4	9
2¼ ,,	5	6
2½ ,,	6	3

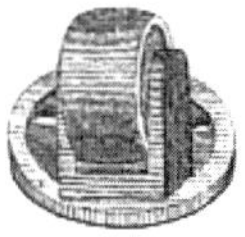

325. ONE-WHEEL CASTORS, JAPD.

	Iron bowls. s.	d.	Wood bowls. s.	d.
1½ inch plate	3	0	3	8 doz. sets, nett.
1⅝ ,,	3	3	4	0
1¾ ,,	3	7	4	4
1⅞ ,,	3	10	4	8
2 ,,	4	2	5	0
2⅛ ,,	4	6	5	4
2¼ ,,	5	0	5	9

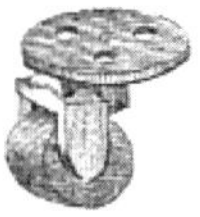

326. STRONG TWO-WHEEL CASTORS, JAPD.

WOOD BOWLS.

	s.	d.
1¼ inch plate	13	0 doz. sets.
1⅜ ,,	13	6
1½ ,,	14	6
1⅝ ,,	15	6
1¾ ,,	17	6
1⅞ ,,	20	0
2 ,,	23	0
2¼ ,,	26	0

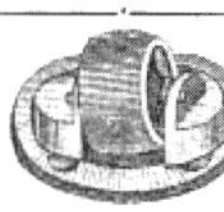

327. PATENT LOW CASTOR.

FOR PIANOS, IRON BOWLS.

No.		s.	d.
No. 5	2 inch plate	15	0 doz. sets.
6	2⅛ ,,	17	0
7	2¼ ,,	20	0

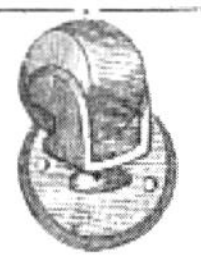

328. BALL PLATE CASTORS.

HIGH WOOD BOWLS, JAPD.

	s.	d.
1¾ inch plate	2	6 set.
1⅞ ,,	2	9
2 ,,	3	0
2⅛ ,,	3	3
2¼ ,,	3	6
2⅜ ,,	3	9
2½ ,,	4	0

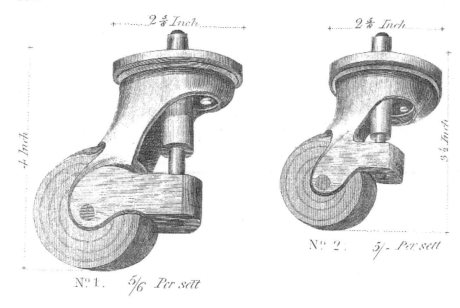

2⅝ Inch   2⅝ Inch

4 Inch   3½ Inch

Nº 1.   5/6 Per sett

Nº 2.   5/- Per sett

340

HUXLEY & HERIOT'S PATENT CASTORS.

Hard wood bowls
Calculated to carry heavy weights

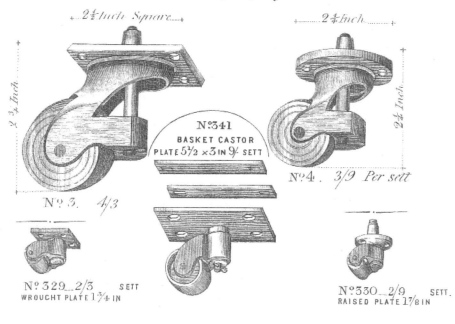

2½ Inch Square   2¼ Inch

2¾ Inch   2¼ Inch

Nº 341
BASKET CASTOR
PLATE 5½ × 3 IN 9/- SETT

Nº 3.   4/3   Nº 4.   3/9 Per sett

Nº 329 2/3 SETT
WROUGHT PLATE 1¾ IN

Nº 330 2/9 SETT.
RAISED PLATE 1⅞ IN

341. OVAL BELL PULLS.
Brass knob.

	s.	d.	s.	d.
No. 186	.. 3	6	... 6	0 doz.
186A	... 5	0	... 8	6

342. ROUND BELL PULLS.
Brass knob.

	s.	d.	s.	d.
No. 187	... 3	6	... 6	0 doz.
187A	... 5	0	... 8	6

343. SQUARE BELL PULLS.

No.	Flush.		With brass knob.	
	s.	d.	s.	d.
188	... 2¾ inch 5	0	.. 8	6 doz.
188A	... 3	,, 7	6	...12 0
188B	... 3½	,, 12	0	. 18 0
188C	... 4	,, 15	0	...22 0
188D	... 4½	,, 17	0	...24 0
188E	... 5	,, 19	0	...26 0
189	... 5½	,, 21	0	...28 0
189A	.. 6	,, 24	0	.. 32 0

No. 212 ... 5 inch,
s.	d.
Japanned 1	10 each.
Bronzed 2	2

No. 212A Offices, same price.

No. 213 ... 5 inch.
s.	d.
1	10 each.
2	2

No. 214 .. 5 inch.
s.	d.
1	10 each.
2	2

344. ROUND SUNK BELL PULLS, WITH LOOSE PLATE.
If with brass letters, 9d. each extra.

No. 215 ... 5 inch.
s.	d.
Japanned 1	11 each.
Bronzed 2	3

No. 216 ... 5 inch.
s.	d.
1	11 each.
Bronzed 2	3

No. 217 ... 5 inch.
s.	d.
1	11 each.
Bronzed 2	3

SUNK DOOR KNOB,
With loose plate.
No. 220 ... 5 inch.
s.	d.
Japanned ... 1	11 each.
Bronzed ... 2	3

345. BELL PULLS, PLAIN, WITH LOOSE PLATE.

	s.	d.			s.	d.
No. 201 ... 4 inch ... 15	0 doz.		No. 207 ... 4 inch ... 15		0 doz.
203 .. 5 ,, ... 19	0		209 ... 5 ,, ... 19		0
205 .. 6 ,, ... 24	0		211 ... 6 ,, ... 24		0

If bronzed, 4d. each extra.

FLUTED
346. GOTHIC DOOR KNOB
AND ROSE.
Hollow, with wrought shank.

	s.	d.
No. 9 Japanned ... 10	0 doz.
Bronzed ... 11	0
Solid ...,. ... 8	0

347. GOTHIC DOOR KNOBS
AND ROSES.

	Solid.		Hollow, with wrought shank.	
	s.	d.	s.	d.
No. 0 ... 5	6	 7	0 doz.
1 ... 6	0	 7	6
2 ... 7	0	 8	6
3 ... 8	0	 9	6

Bronzed, 1s. doz. extra.

OPEN
348. GOTHIC DOOR KNOB
AND ROSE.

	Solid.		Hollow, with wrought shank.	
	s.	d.	s.	d.
2⅜ inch 8	0	 10	0 doz.
2¼ ,, 7	6	 9	6
2 ,, 7	0	 9	0

Bronzed, 1s. doz. extra.

350. DOOR HANDLES.

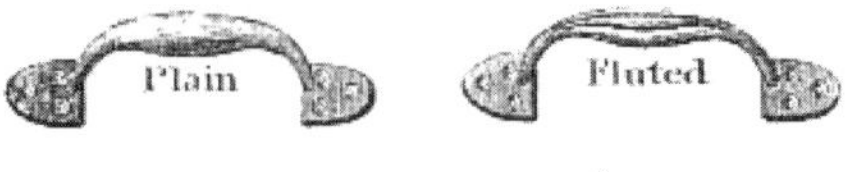
Plain
Fluted

	s.	d.	
No. 74B	1	3	doz.
74	1	6	
74A	1	9	
75	2	0	
76	2	6	
77	3	0	
77A	3	6	

Fluted the same prices.

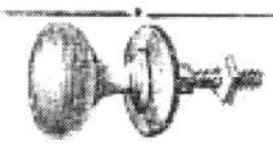

351. DOOR KNOBS AND ROSES.

No. 96B	$1\frac{5}{8}$ inch	3*s.* 6*d.*	doz.
96A	$1\frac{3}{4}$,,	3 9	
96	$1\frac{7}{8}$,,	4 0	
97	$2\frac{1}{8}$,,	5 0	
97A	$2\frac{3}{8}$,,	7 0	
97B	$2\frac{1}{2}$,,	8 0	
97C	$2\frac{3}{4}$,,	9 0	

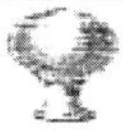

352. LOCK KNOBS.

		s.	d.	
No. 1	$1\frac{7}{8}$ inch	3	9	doz.
2	2 ,,	4	9	
3	$2\frac{1}{8}$,,	6	6	
4	$2\frac{3}{8}$,,	8	0	
5	$2\frac{3}{4}$,,	8	6	

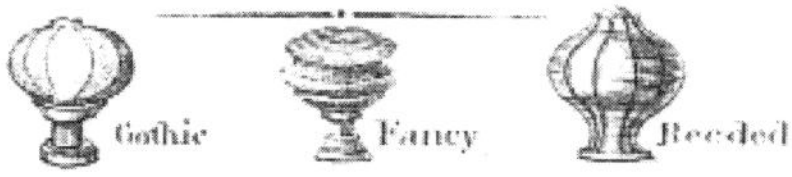
Gothic
Fancy
Reeded

353. NEW PATTERN LOCK KNOBS.

No	s.	d.	s.	d.	s.	d.	
0	4	6			4	6	doz.
1	5	0	5	0	5	0	
2	6	0	6	0	6	0	
3	8	0	8	0	8	0	

If with roses, 1*s.* doz. extra.

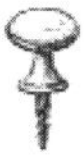

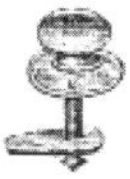

354. CUPBOARD KNOBS.

		s.	d.	
0000	$\frac{5}{8}$ in.	0	10	doz.
000	$\frac{3}{4}$,,	0	10	
00	$\frac{7}{8}$,,	0	11	
0	1 ,,	1	0	
1	$1\frac{1}{8}$,,	1	3	
2	$1\frac{1}{4}$,,	1	6	
3	$1\frac{3}{8}$,,	1	10	
4	$1\frac{1}{2}$,,	2	3	
5	$1\frac{5}{8}$,,	3	0	

If screwed shanks and nuts, 8*d.* doz. extra.

355. CUPBOARD TURNS AND ROSES.

	s.	d.	
$\frac{7}{8}$ in. clear	2	6	doz.
1 ,, ,,	2	6	
$1\frac{1}{8}$,, ,,	2	8	
$1\frac{1}{4}$,, ,,	2	10	
$1\frac{3}{8}$,, ,,	3	0	
$1\frac{1}{2}$,, ,,	3	2	
$1\frac{5}{8}$,, ,,	3	3	
$1\frac{3}{4}$,, ,,	3	4	
$1\frac{7}{8}$,, ,,	3	5	
2 ,, ,,	3	6	

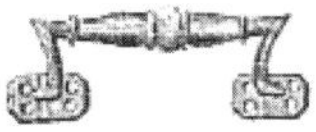

356. DOOR HANDLE.

	s.	d.	
Japanned	5	0	doz.
Bronzed	7	0	

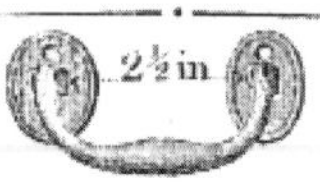
2½ in.

357. LIFTING HANDLES, JOINTED.

	Inside of handle.	s.	d.	
No. 78D	$2\frac{1}{8}$ inch	2	0	doz. pair.
78C	$2\frac{1}{4}$,,	2	0	
78B	$2\frac{3}{8}$,,	2	6	
78	$2\frac{1}{2}$,,	2	9	
78A	$2\frac{3}{4}$,,	3	0	
79	3 ,,	3	6	
79A	$3\frac{1}{4}$,,	4	0	
80	$3\frac{1}{2}$,,	4	6	
80A	$3\frac{3}{4}$,,	5	0	
81	4 ,,	5	6	
81A	$4\frac{1}{4}$,,	6	3	
81B	$4\frac{1}{2}$,,	7	0	
81C	5 ,, strong	10	0	
81D	6 ,, ,,	12	0	

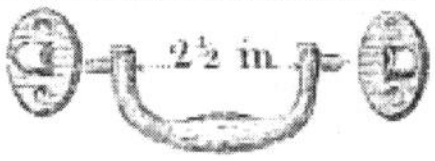
2½ in.

358. LIFTING HANDLES LOOSE.

	Inside of handles.	s.	d.	
No. 000	$2\frac{1}{8}$ inch	2	0	doz. pair.
00	$2\frac{1}{4}$,,	2	0	
0	$2\frac{3}{8}$,,	2	6	
1	$2\frac{1}{2}$,,	2	9	
2	$2\frac{3}{4}$,,	3	0	
3	3 ,,	3	6	
4	$3\frac{1}{4}$,,	4	0	
5	$3\frac{1}{2}$,,	4	6	
6	$3\frac{3}{4}$,,	5	0	
7	4 ,,	5	6	
8	$4\frac{1}{4}$,,	6	3	
9	$4\frac{1}{2}$,,	7	0	

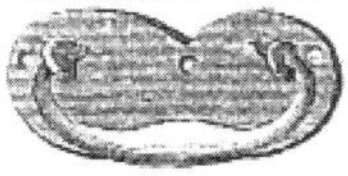

359. TRUNK HANDLES.

WITH WROUGHT IRON HANDLES.

	Inside of handle.	s.	d.	
No. 00	$2\frac{1}{4}$ inch	2	0	doz. pair.
0	$2\frac{3}{8}$,,	2	6	
1	$2\frac{1}{2}$,,	2	9	
2	$2\frac{3}{4}$,,	3	0	
3	3 ,,	3	6	
4	$3\frac{1}{4}$,,	4	0	
5	$3\frac{1}{2}$,,	4	6	
6	$3\frac{3}{4}$,,	5	0	
7	4 ,,	5	6	
8	$4\frac{1}{4}$,,	6	3	
9	$4\frac{1}{2}$,,	7	0	

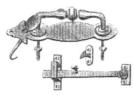

360. GATE LATCH.
With screws and nuts, wrought furniture.
19s. doz.

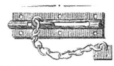

361. DOOR CHAINS.

	s.	d.			s.	d.
3½ inch	8	0	8 inch		12	0 doz.
4 ,,	8	0	9 ,,		15	0
5 ,,	8	6	10 ,,		18	0
6 ,,	9	6	11 ,,		22	0
7 ,,	10	6	12 ,,		26	0

361A. DOOR CHAINS WITH BRASS FRONTS
12/6 — 13/6 — 14/6 — 15/6 — 17/- DOZ
5 — 6 — 7 — 8 — 9 INCH
ALL IRON 7/6 — 8/6 — 9/- — 10/- — 12/6 DOZ

362 COMMON THUMB LATCHES
WITH WROUGHT FURNITURE
2/3 2/6 2/9 3/3 3/9 4/ DOZ
Nᵒ 132A 132 133 134 135 135A

363. NEW THUMB LATCHES.
With wrought furniture.

		s.	d.
No. 136		4	6 doz.
137		5	6
138		6	6
139		8	0
140		10	0

349. RING BELL PULL.
2s. doz.

364. NORFOLK LATCHES.
With wrought furniture.

No.	s.	d.	Wrought Plates. s.	d.
141B	4	8	5	6 doz.
141A	5	0	6	0
141	5	6	6	9
141½	6	6	7	9
142	7	6	8	9
143	9	0	10	3
144	11	0	12	6
144A	13	0	14	6

365. FLUSH LATCHES.
With wrought furniture.
5s. doz.

366. NIGHT BOLTS.

No.		s.	d.
182B	4 inch	12	0 doz.
182A	5 ,,	13	0
182	6 ,,	15	0
183	7 ,,	17	0
184	8 ,,	20	0

Side   End

367. BELL CRANKS.
No. 1	1s. 9d. doz.
2	2 0

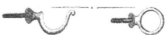

368. SECURE GUN HOOKS.
No. 1 ... 5s. No. 2 ... 5s. 6d. doz. pair.
N.B.—These are to lock.

369. GUN HOOKS.
2s. 6d. per doz. pair.

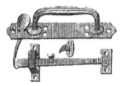

370. FLUTED NORFOLK LATCHES.
With wrought furniture.

	s.	d.	
No. 127B	5	6	doz.
127A	6	0	
127	8	0	
128	10	0	
129	12	0	

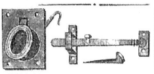

Nº 181 Nº 181C

371. STABLE LATCHES, FLUSH.
With wrought furniture.

	s.	d.	
No. 181A	9	0	doz.
181½	10	0	
181	12	0	
181B large	18	0	
181C	15	0	

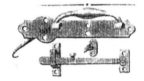

372. STABLE LATCH, JOINTED
HANDLE.
With Wrought furniture.
13s. 6d. doz.

373. PEW DOOR LATCH.
5s. 6d. doz.

374. SECRET LATCH.
FOR HALF DOORS.
10s. doz.

375. FLUSH PLATE AND RING.

	s.	d.	
No. 0	3	0	doz.
1	3	6	
2	4	0	
3	7	0	

376. SECRET LATCH.
With moving plate and wrought furniture.
No. 1 .... 17s. 6d. doz.

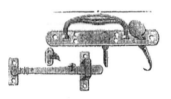

377. SECRET LATCH.
With wrought furniture.
No. 2 ...... 16s. doz.

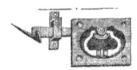

378. NEW STABLE LATCHES.
With wrought furniture.

	s.	d.	
Small	16	0	doz.
Large	24	0	

379. CABIN HOOKS.

	s.	d.			s.	d.	
2 inches	2	6	doz.	6 inches	3	10	doz.
2½ ,,	2	9		7 ,,	4	3	
3 ,,	3	0		8 ,,	4	9	
3½ ,,	3	2		9 ,,	5	6	
4 ,,	3	3		10 ,,	6	3	
4½ ,,	3	5		12 ,,	7	0	
5 ,,	3	6		Larger, if wanted.			

380. SECRET LATCH.
WITH DRAW-BACK BOLT ATTACHED.
With wrought furniture.
No. 3 .... 20s. doz.

381. SHUTTER LIFTS.

No.	s. d.	No.	s. d.	No.	s. d.
46A 2½in.	1 0	46 2 holes	0 8	47J…2½in.	1 6 doz.
		46½ ,,	0 9	47K 2¾	1 9
		47 3 ,,	0 10	47L 3 ,,	2 0

382. FLUSH SHUTTER LIFTS.

No.	s. d.	No.	s. d.	No.	s. d.
47A 2½in.	1 3	47C 2½in.	1 6	47E 2½in.	1 9 doz.
47B 3 ,,	1 6	47D 3 ,,	2 0	47F 3 ,,	2 0
				47G 3½,,	2 3

383. FLUSH SHUTTER LIFTS, NARROW.

No.	s. d.
25 2½ in.	1 2 per doz.
26 2¾ ,,	1 3
27 3 ,,	1 4

384. INSIDE SHUTTER LIFTS.

No.	s. d.
185 round	1 9 doz.
185A large for trap doors	5 0

385. SHUTTER SCREWS.

	s. d.
1¼ inch	2 4 doz.
1½ ,,	2 4
1¾ ,,	2 5
2 ,,	2 6
2¼ ,,	2 7
2½ ,,	2 8
2¾ ,,	2 10
3 ,,	3 0
3¼ ,,	3 2
3½ ,,	3 3
3¾ ,,	3 5
4 ,,	3 6
4¼ ,,	3 7
4½ ,,	3 8
4¾ ,,	3 9
5 ,,	3 10
5½ ,,	2 11
6 ,,	4 0

386.

SASH LIFT
9ᴰ doz

387 SASH PROPS.

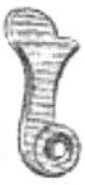

Nº 1. 10 d. | Nº 1x. 11 d. doz
| Nº 2, 1s. ,,

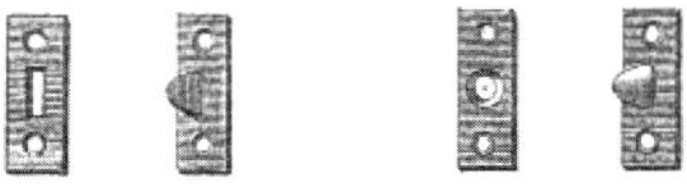

388. STUBS AND PLATES.

No.		s. d.	No.		s. d.
110	square	1 0	108	round	1 0 doz.
111	,,	1 3	109	,,	1 3
111A	,,	1 6	109A	,,	1 6
111B	,,	2 0	109B	,,	2 0

 Left Nº⊥   Right Nº1A

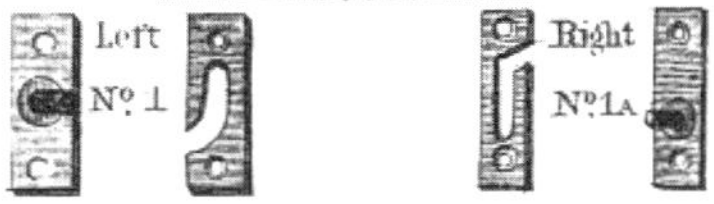

389. SASH PIVOTS.

		s. d.			s. d.
No. 0 strong		1 6	No. 0A narrow		1 2 doz.
1 ,,		2 0	1A ,,		1 4
2 ,,		3 0	2A ,,		1 6

With pin on the side, same price.

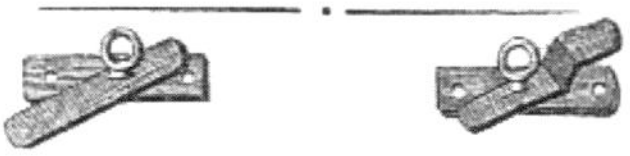

390. SHUTTER FASTENINGS.

	Straight.	Necked.
	s. d.	s. d.
No. 1	1 8	1 10 doz.
2	1 10	2 0

391. HOT BED FASTENINGS.

	s. d.		s. d.
8 inch	6 0 doz.	18 inch	15 0 doz.
11 ,,	6 6	24 ,,	20 0
15 ,,	10 0		

392. HOT BED HANDLES.

No.		s. d.	No.		s. d.
000	plain…	1 6 doz.	1	fluted…	3 0 doz.
00	,, …	2 0	2	,, …	4 0
0	,, …	2 6	3	,, …	5 0

393. DOOR SPRINGS, CIRCULAR.

	s d.		s. d.		s. d.		s. d.		s. d.
		3 …	3 6	4 …	4 9	5 …	5 6	6	6 each.
No. 00 …	0 …	1 …	2	… 3	… 4				

394. SASH ROLLERS.

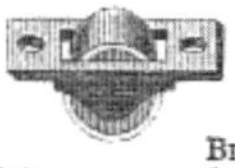

	Width of plate.		Iron s.	Iron d.	Brass bowls. s.	Brass bowls. d.
No. 82	½ inch		0	9	1	3 doz.
83	⅝ ,,		0	10	1	4
84	¾ ,,		1	0	1	7
85	¾ ,,	full	1	2	1	10
86	⅞ ,,		1	5	2	2
87	1 ,,		1	9	2	9
88	1⅛ ,,		2	3	3	6
89	1¼ ,,		3	6	4	9
90	1⅜ ,,		4	0	5	6
91	1½ ,,		4	6	7	6
92	1¾ ,,		5	6		
93	1⅞ ,,		7	0		
94	2 ,,		8	6		
95	2⅛ ,,		11	0		
95A	2½ ,,		15	0		

Square or round plates, same prices.

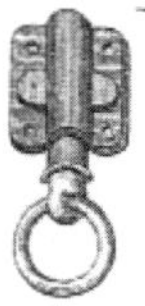

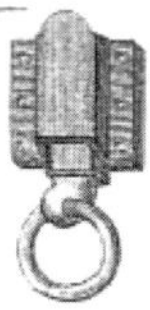

No. 98C ... 8s. 6d.   98D ... 10s. 6d.

395. MANGER RINGS.

WITH SPRINGS.

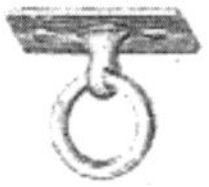

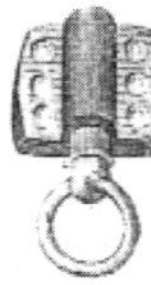

No. 98B plain 4s.   98 6s. 6d.   98X 9s. 6d. doz.

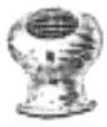

396. IRON COW KNOBS.

Japanned.

	s.	d.
No. 1	0	8 doz.
2	0	10
3	1	0
4	1	2
5	2	0
Ox Knobs	3	0

397. BRASS COW KNOBS.

	Hollow. s.	Hollow. d.	Solid. s.	Solid. d.
No. 1	3	0	4	0 doz
2	4	0	6	0
3	5	6	7	0
Ox Knobs	12	0		

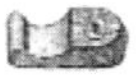

398. HALF BUTTONS.

		Broad. s.	Broad. d.	Narrow. s.	Narrow. d.
No. 101H	1¾ inch size	4	6	3	6 gross
102H	2 ,,	5	0	4	0
103H	2¼ ,,	6	0	5	0
104H	2½ ,,	7	0	6	0

400. CUPBOARD BUTTONS.

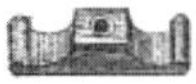

Narrow.

BROAD.	s.	d.	NARROW.	s.	d.
No. 0000...1 in.	3	9	No. 0000N...1 in.	3	9 gross.
000...1¼ ,,	4	0	000N...1¼ ,,	4	0
00...1⅜ ,,	6	0	00N...1⅜ ,,	5	0
0...1½ ,,	7	0	0N...1¾ ,,	5	6
101...1¾ ,,	8	0	101N...1¾ ,,	6	0
102...2 ,,	9	0	102N...2 ,,	7	0
103...2¼ ,,	11	0	103N ..2¼ ,,	9	0
104...2½ ,,	13	0	104N...2½ ,,	11	0
105 ..2¾ ,,	15	0	105N...2¾ ,,	13	0
106...3 ,,	16	0	106N...3 ,,	15	0
107...3¾ ,,	30	0			

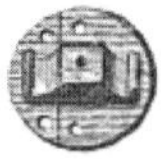

With Stop.

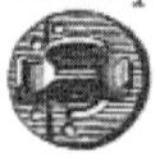

401. PEW BUTTONS.

	s.	d.
No. 1 ... 1¾ in.	1	2
2 ... 2 ,,	1	5
3 ... 2¼ ,,	1	7
4 ... 2½ ,,	1	9

402. PEW BUTTONS.

WITH STOP.

2in. ... 2s. 0d. doz.

403. MANGER ROLLERS.

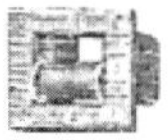

Single.

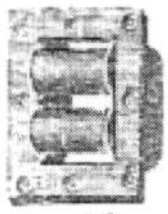

Double.

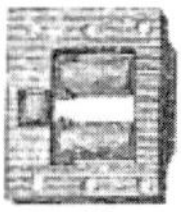

Treble

	Iron Bowls. s.	Iron Bowls. d.	Brass bowls. s.	Brass bowls. d.
Single	1	0	2	3 each.
Double	1	4	3	0
Treble	1	9	3	9
Four Rollers	2	3	4	3

For chain, same price as above.

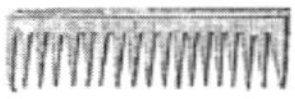

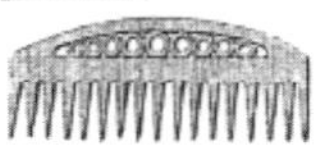

404. JOCKEY COMBS.

5in. or 6in....2s. 3d. doz. | 6in. arched...2s. 9d. doz.

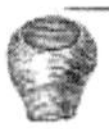

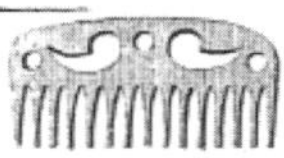

405. HALTER BALLS.

JAPD.

No.		s.	d.
1... ¾ lb. each		2	9 doz.
1x 1	,,	3	9
2...1¼	,,	4	6
3...1½	,,	5	6
4...1¾	,,	6	6
5 ..2	,,	7	6
6...	,,	8	6

406. MANE COMBS.

No.	s.	d.
000	0	6 doz.
00	0	8
0	0	10
1	1	0
2	1	3
3	1	6

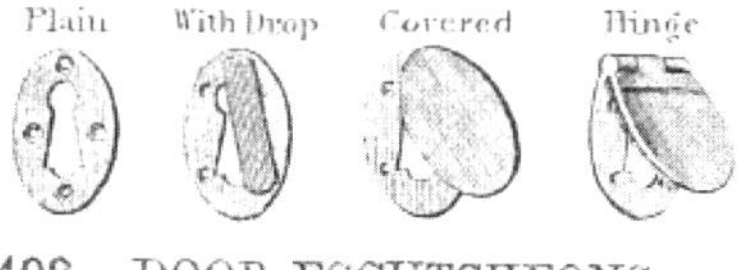

408. DOOR ESCUTCHEONS.

PER GROSS.

No.		Plain. s.	d.	Drop. s.	d.	Covered. s.	d.	Hinge. s.	d.
112A	5 inch	3	0	6	0	7	0	16	0
112	6 ,,	4	0	7	0	8	0	18	0
113	7 ,,	5	0	8	0	10	0	20	0
114	8 ,,	6	0	10	0	12	0	22	0
115	9 ,,	7	0	12	0	14	0	24	0
116	10 ,,	8	0	14	0	16	0	28	0
116A	11 ,,	10	0	16	0	18	0	32	0
116B	12 ,,	12	0	18	0	20	0	36	0

The hinge escutcheons have brass wires.

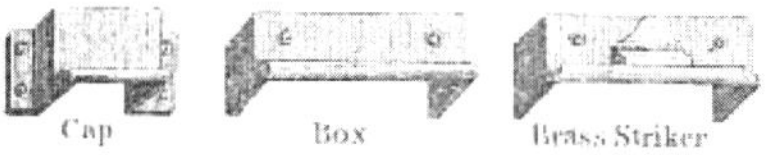

409. LOCK STAPLES.

CAP. No.	clear.	s.	d.	BOX. No.	for locks.	s.	d.	BRASS STRIKERS. s.	d.
190A	1 inch	1	1 doz.	195A	4 in	1	1	2	6 doz.
190	1⅛ ,,	1	2	195	5 ,,	1	3	3	0
191	1¼ ,,	1	4	196	6 ,,	1	6	3	6
192	1⅝ ,,	1	6	197	7 ,,	1	9	4	6
193	1⅞ ,,	1	10	198	8 ,,	2	0	5	6
194	2⅛ ,,	2	0	199	9 ,,	2	6	6	6
194A	2⅜ ,,	2	4	200	10 ,,	3	0	7	6
194B	2⅝ ,,	2	8	200A	11 ,,	3	6	8	6
194C	3 ,,	3	0	200B	12 ,,	4	0	9	6

Brass strikers to the cap staples, if wanted.

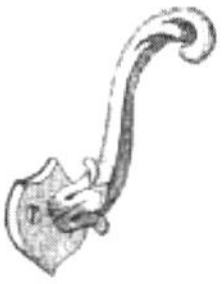

410. NEW SURPLICE PINS.

No.		s.	d.
No. 6	2½in.	0	10 doz.
7	3 ,,	0	11
8	3½ ,,	1	1
9	4 ,,	1	3
10	4½ ,,	1	5
11	5 ,,	1	8
12	5½ ,,	1	10

Bronzed, 1*s.* doz. extra.

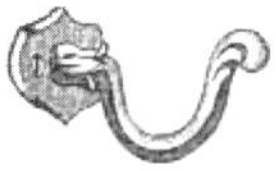

411. NEW COAT HOOK.

	s.	d.
No. 20	1	6 doz.

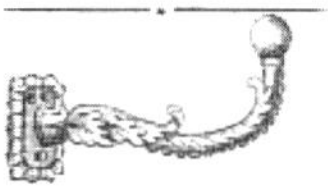

412. NEW HAT PIN.

No. 25...2*s.* 6*d.* doz.
Bronzed, 1*s.* doz. extra.

413. NEW HEAVY HAT PINS

	s.	d.
No. 26	5	6 doz.
Bronzed	6	6

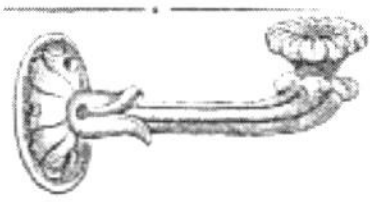

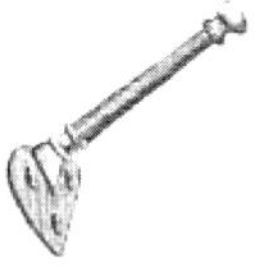

414. SURPLICE PINS.

	s.	d.
1¾ inch	0	7½ doz.
2 ,,	0	8
2½ ,,	0	8½
3 ,,	0	9
3½ ,,	0	10
4 ,,	0	11
4½ ,,	1	0
5 ,,	1	2
5½ ,,	1	4
6 ,,	1	6
7 ,,	2	0
8 ,,	2	6
9 ,,	3	0

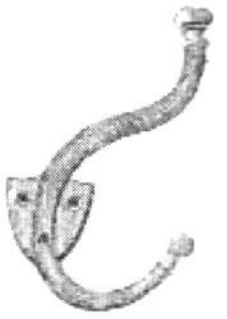

415. HAT AND COAT PINS.

No.	s.	d.	Extra strong. s.	d.
00	1	5	2	6 doz.
0	1	6	2	9
1	1	9	3	3
2	2	0	3	9
3	2	3	4	3
4	2	9	4	9
5	3	3	5	3

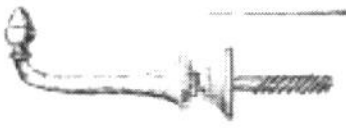

416. HAT HOOKS.

	s.	d.
1¼ inch	0	6 doz.
1¾ ,,	0	7
2 ,,	0	8
2½ ,,	0	9
3 ,,	0	10
3½ ,,	1	0
4 ,,	1	2
4½ ,,	1	4
5 ,,	1	6
5½ ,,	1	8
6 ,,	1	10

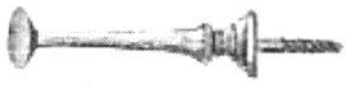

417. HAT PINS

	s.	d.
2 inch	0	8 doz.
2½ ,,	0	9
3 ,,	0	10
3½ ,,	1	0
4 ,,	1	2
4½ ,,	1	4
5 ,,	1	6
5½ ,,	1	8
6 ,,	1	10

418. With holes to screw on, same prices.

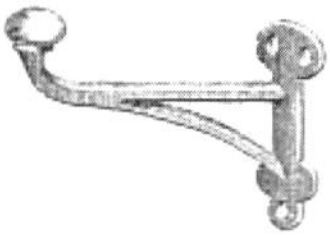

419. HAT BRACKETS.

	s.	d.
3 inch	1	5 doz.
3½ ,,	1	7
4 ,,	1	9
4½ ,,	2	0
5 ,,	2	3
5½ ,,	2	6
6 ,,	2	9
6½ ,,	3	0
7 ,,	3	3
8 ,,	4	0
Brass Knobs doz. extra	1	3

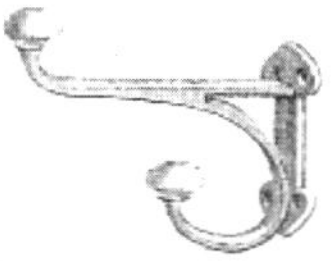

420. HAT AND COAT BRACKETS.

	s.	d.
4 inch	2	3 doz.
4½ ,,	2	6
5 ,,	2	9
5½ ,,	3	0
6 ,,	3	3
6½ ,,	3	6
Brass knobs doz. extra	2	6

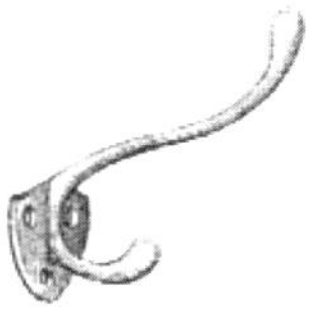

429. NEW HAT AND COAT PINS.

	s.	d.
No. 00N	1	5 doz.
0N	1	6
1N	1	9
2N	2	0
3N	2	3
4N	2	9
5N	3	3

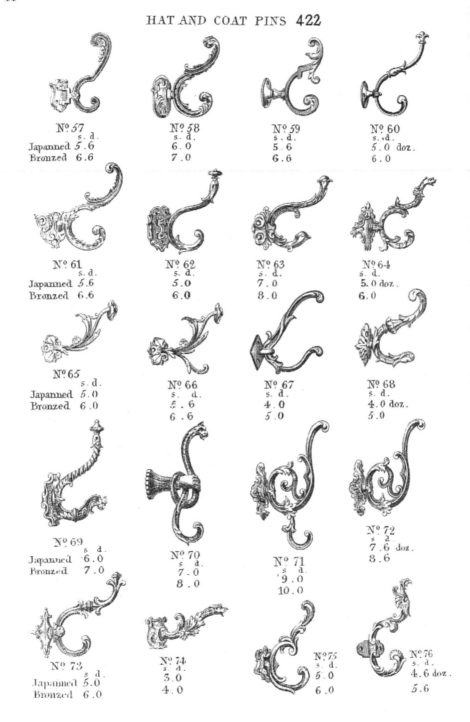

Nº 57
s. d.
Japanned 5.6
Bronzed 6.6

Nº 58
s. d.
6.0
7.0

Nº 59
s. d.
5.6
6.6

Nº 60
s. d.
5.0 doz.
6.0

Nº 61
s. d.
Japanned 5.6
Bronzed 6.6

Nº 62
s. d.
5.0
6.0

Nº 63
s. d.
7.0
8.0

Nº 64
s. d.
5.0 doz.
6.0

Nº 65
s. d.
Japanned 5.0
Bronzed 6.0

Nº 66
s. d.
5.6
6.6

Nº 67
s. d.
4.0
5.0

Nº 68
s. d.
4.0 doz.
5.0

Nº 69
s. d.
Japanned 6.0
Bronzed 7.0

Nº 70
s. d.
7.0
8.0

Nº 71
s. d.
9.0
10.0

Nº 72
s. d.
7.6 doz.
8.6

Nº 73
s. d.
Japanned 5.0
Bronzed 6.0

Nº 74
s. d.
3.0
4.0

Nº 75
s. d.
5.0
6.0

Nº 76
s. d.
4.6 doz.
5.6

COAT HOOKS. 423 AND 423 A
No. 00 _ 0.10 doz.

s. d.
„ 0 _ 1.0 „
„ 1 _ 1.2 „
„ 2 _ 1.4 „

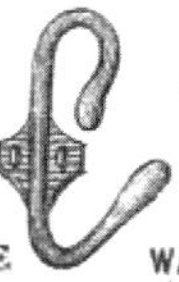

424
SECURE
HAT HOLDERS

s. d.
No. 1 _ 1.3 doz
„ 2 _ 1.6 „
„ 3 _ 1.9 „

424 A
WARDROBE HOOKS

SINGLE	DOUBLE
1/- _____	2/- doz.

No. 17
s. d.
Jap.d 2.0 doz
Bronz.d 3.6

CHIMNEY
HOOK. 425
s. d.
No. 3 _ 1.4 doz.

426
NAPKIN HOOKS.

s. d.	s. d.
No. 6 _ 1.2 doz.	No. 9 _ 1.6 doz.

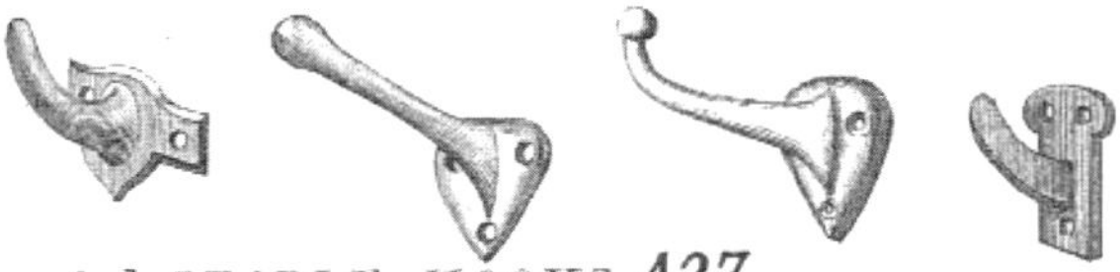

STABLE HOOKS. 427

s. d.
No. 12. 7.6
„ 12A. 6.0
„ 12B. 3.9
„ 12C. 2.6
„ 12D. 1.9

s. d.	s. d.	s. d.
No. 13. 8.6	No. 14. 5.0	No. 15 4.6 doz

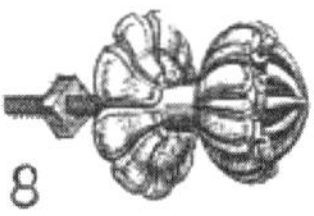

425. MELON KNOBS
With _ Square Hole
Japan.d _ Screw _ for Spindle

	s. d.	s. d.
1⅜ In	5.0 _	4.6 Doz.
1½ „	6.0 _	5.6 „
1¾ „	7.0 _	6.6 „
2 „	8.0 _	7.6 „

428
NEW DOOR KNOB & ROSE

	SOLID	HOLLOW
No. 1 _ 2¾ In	12.6 _	10.0 doz
„ 2 _ 3 _	13.6 _	11.0 _
„ 3 _ 3½ _	16.0 _	12.0 _

ALL WROUGHT SHANKS
BERLIN 2/. DOZ EXTRA.

421. CANDLE HOOKS

	s. d.	
3 In.	0.10	Doz
3½ „	1.0	„
4 „	1.2	„
4½ „	1.4	„
5 „	1.6	„

431 MORTICE LOCK FURNITURE JAP.d
If Knobs are Bronzed or Berlin 3/. doz. extra.
Wilkes Spindles Fitted 1/9 doz
Roses _____ 1/6 Jap.a 2/6 Bronz.d. Doz.
Drop Escutcheons 2/. ___ 3/

KNOB No. 30	31	32	33
1⅞ In ___ 4s. 0d.	1⅞ In ___ 4s. 0d.	2 In ___ 5s. 0d	2 In. ___ 5s. 0d Doz
2 „ ___ 5.0.	2⅛ „ ___ 5.0.	2¼ „ ___ 6.0.	2¼ „ ___ 6.0.
2¼ „ ___ 6.6.			

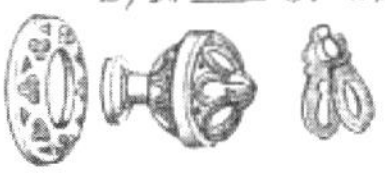

KNOB No. 34	35	36	37
1¾ In ___ 4s. 6d	2 In ___ 5s. 0d Doz.	2¼ In _ 6/-	2¼ In _ 6/- Doz
2 „ ___ 5.6.	2¼ „ ___ 6.0. „		
2¼ „ ___ 6.6.	2⅝ „ ___ 7.0. „		

S STABLE LATCHES 800

N.º 1 _ 2 _ 3. 4.
If Cast Latches ———— 14/. 18/. 22/. 26/- doz.
If Wrought D.º ———— 17/. 22/. 27/. 32/- .

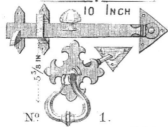

10 INCH

N.º 1.

GOTHIC LATCHES 801

With Cast Latch ——— 2/6 each.
With Wrought Latch 3/6 .

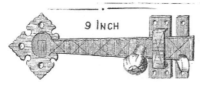

9 INCH

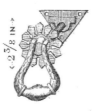

N.º 2. 1s. 10 d. ea. | N.º 3. 1s. 10 d. ea.
With Wrought Latch and Ketch 1s. ea. extra.
Berlin Black 1s. ea. extra.

N.º 4. 1s. 10 d. ea.

N.º 5. 2s. 0 d. ea.
With Wrought Latch and Ketch 1s. ea. extra.
Berlin Black 1s. ea. extra.

GOTHIC LATCHES 801

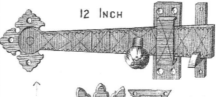

12 INCH

6½ IN ROSE

N.º 6. 3s. 0 d. ea.
With Wrought Latch and Ketch 1s. ea. extra.
Berlin Black 1s. ea. extra.

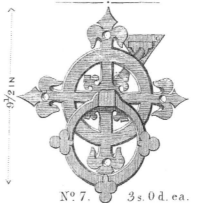

9½ IN

N.º 7. 3s. 0 d. ea.
With Wrought Latch and Ketch 1s. ea. extra.
Berlin Black 1s. ea. extra.

N.º 8. 2s. 9 d. ea.
With Wrought Latch and Ketch 1s. ea. extra.
Berlin Black 1s. ea. extra.

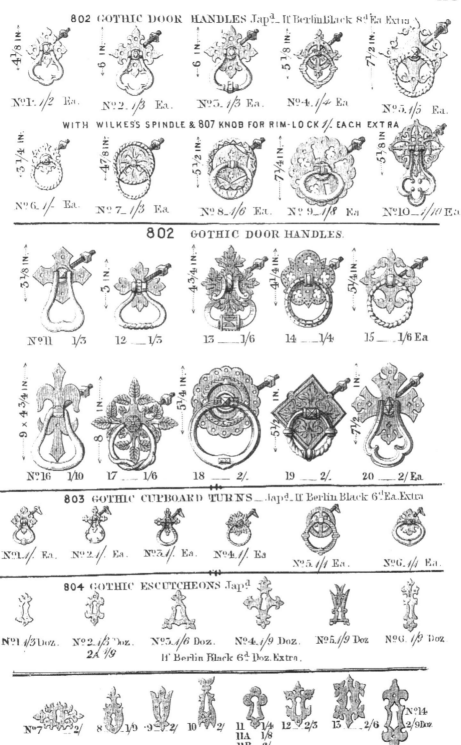

802 GOTHIC DOOR HANDLES Jap^d. If BerlinBlack 8^d Ea Extra

4⅛ IN. — N°1. 1/2 Ea.

6 IN. — N°2. 1/3 Ea.

6 IN. — N°3. 1/3 Ea.

5⅛ IN. — N°4. 1/4 Ea

7½ IN. — N°5. 1/5 Ea.

WITH WILKES'S SPINDLE & 807 KNOB FOR RIM-LOCK 1/. EACH EXTRA

3¼ IN. — N°6. 1/- Ea.

4⅞ IN. — N°7. 1/3 Ea.

5½ IN. — N°8. 1/6 Ea.

7¼ IN. — N°9. 1/8 Ea

5⅛ IN. — N°10. 1/10 Ea

802 GOTHIC DOOR HANDLES.

3⅛ IN. — N°11. 1/3

3 IN. — 12. 1/3

4¾ IN. — 13. 1/6

4¼ IN. — 14. 1/4

5¼ IN. — 15. 1/6 Ea

9 × 4¾ IN. — N°16. 1/10

8 IN. — 17. 1/6

5¼ IN. — 18. 2/.

5½ IN. — 19. 2/.

7½ IN. — 20. 2/ Ea.

803 GOTHIC CUPBOARD TURNS Jap^d. If Berlin Black 6^d Ea. Extra

N°1. 1/. Ea.

N°2. 1/. Ea.

N°3. 1/. Ea.

N°4. 1/. Ea

N°5. 1/1 Ea.

N°6. 1/1 Ea.

804 GOTHIC ESCUTCHEONS Jap^d

N°1. 1/3 Doz.

N°2. 1/3 Doz.
2A 1/9

N°3. 1/6 Doz.

N°4. 1/9 Doz.

N°5. 1/9 Doz

N°6. 1/9 Doz

If Berlin Black 6^d Doz. Extra.

N°7. 2/

8. 1/9

9. 2/

10. 2/

11. 1/4
11A 1/8
11B 2/

12. 2/3

13. 2/6

N°14. 2/9 Doz

804 GOTHIC ESCUTCHEONS JAP^d If Berlin Black 6^d Doz Extra

801 GOTHIC LATCHES Japan'd
If Berlin Black 1/. Ea. Extra

Nº 9. 1/9 Ea.   Nº 10. 2/- Ea.   Nº 11. 2/2 Ea.   Nº 12. 2/4 Ea.   Nº 13. 2/6 Ea.

9 In.

If 12 In. Latch 3ᵈ Ea Extra.

WITH WILKES'S SPINDLE & 807 GOTHIC KNOB FOR RIM LOCK SAME PRICE

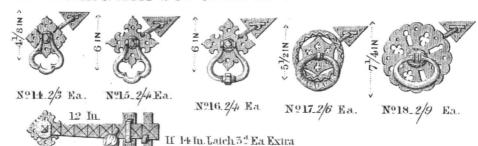

Nº 14. 2/3 Ea.   Nº 15. 2/4 Ea.   Nº 16. 2/4 Ea   Nº 17. 2/6 Ea.   Nº 18. 2/9 Ea.

12 In.

If 14 In. Latch 3ᵈ Ea Extra

801. GOTHIC LATCHES Japan'd
If Berlin Black 1/ Ea Extra

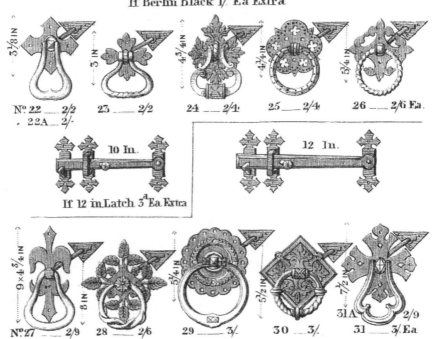

Nº 22 ___ 2/2   23 ___ 2/2   24 ___ 2/4   25 ___ 2/4   26 ___ 2/6 Ea.
22A. 2/-

10 In.   12 In.

If 12 in Latch 3ᵈ Ea Extra

Nº 27 ___ 2/9   28 ___ 2/6   29 ___ 3/.   30 ___ 3/.   31A ___ 2/9
                                                          31 ___ 3/. Ea

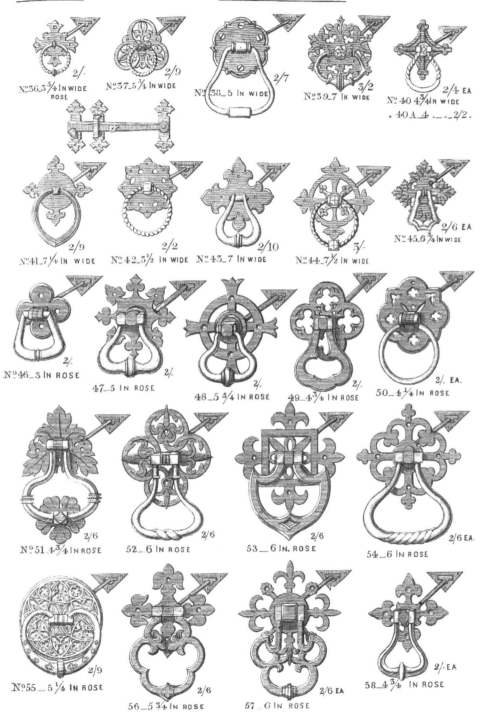

801 GOTHIC LATCHES JAP.ᴰ IF BERLIN 1/5 EACH EXTRA
DOOR HANDLES WITH WILKES'S SPINDLES ONLY. 9ᴰ TO 1/5 EACH LESS FOR RIM LOCKS

Nº36 3¾ IN WIDE ROSE — 2/.
Nº37 5¾ IN WIDE — 2/9
Nº38 5 IN WIDE — 2/7
Nº39 7 IN WIDE — 3/2
Nº40 4¾ IN WIDE — 2/4 EA .40A 4 — 2/2.

Nº41 7¼ IN WIDE — 2/9
Nº42 3½ IN WIDE — 2/2
Nº43 7 IN WIDE — 2/10
Nº44 7½ IN WIDE — 3/.
Nº45 6¾ IN WIDE — 2/6 EA

Nº46 3 IN ROSE — 2/.
47 5 IN ROSE — 2/.
48 5¾ IN ROSE — 2/.
49 4¾ IN ROSE — 2/.
50 4¾ IN ROSE — 2/. EA.

Nº51 4¾ IN ROSE — 2/6
52 6 IN ROSE — 2/6
53 6 IN. ROSE — 2/6
54 6 IN ROSE — 2/6 EA.

Nº55 5¼ IN ROSE — 2/9
56 5¾ IN ROSE — 2/6
57 6 IN ROSE — 2/6 EA
58 4¾ IN ROSE — 2/. EA

801. GOTHIC LATCHES &c JAP^D—BERLIN 6^d EXTRA.
COMPLETE

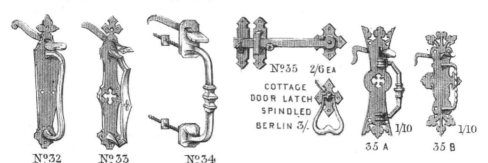

Nº35 2/6 EA

COTTAGE
DOOR LATCH
SPINDLED
BERLIN 3/.

1/10   1/10

35 A   35 B

Nº32   Nº33   Nº34
1/6 EA.   1/9 EA.   JAPᴰ 2/.
BERLIN 2/. BERLIN 2/3. BERLIN 2/6 EA.

---

431 MORTICE LOCK FURNITURE JAPᴰ
If Knobs are Bronzed or Berlin 3/. doz. extra.
Wilkes' Spindles Fitted 1/9 doz
Roses_____ 1/6 Japᵈ 2/6 Bronz'd. Doz.
Drop Escutcheons 2/. ___ 3/

KNOB Nº 30
1⅞ In.___4s 0d
2 .___5. 0.
2¼.___6. 6.

31
1⅞ In.___4s. 0d.
2⅛.___5. 0.

32
2 In.___5s. 0 d
2¼.___6. 0.

33
2 In.___5s. 0d Doz.
2¼.___6. 0.

KNOB Nº 34
1¾ In.___4s. 6d
2 .___5. 6.
2¼.___6. 6.

35
2 In.___5s. 0d. Doz.
2¼.___6. 0.
2⅝.___7. 0.

36
2¼ In.__6/-

37
2¼ In.__6/- Doz

802. GOTHIC DOOR HANDLES &c JAP^D IF BERLIN 6^d EXTRA

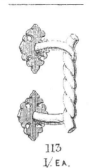

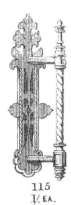

N° 111
1/. EA.

112
1/. EA.

113
1/. EA.

114
1/. EA.

115
1/. EA.

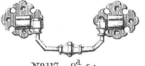

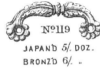

N^o116

N^o1   5/ DOZ. PAIR
. 2   6/.

N^o117   9^d. EA.

N^o118   1/. EA.

N^o119
JAPAN'D 5/. DOZ.
BRONZ'D 6/. "

807 GOTHIC KNOBS JAP^D

IF BERLIN 1/. DOZ. EXTRA

ROSES
2/. DOZ.
BERLIN
2/6

	FOR DOORS	LOCKS
1³/₄ IN.	4/6	4/ DOZ.
2 "	5/6	5/. "
2¼ "	7/.	6/6 .
2½ "	9/.	8/6 .
2³/₄ "	11/.	10/6 .

808 BEVIL HANDLE   LATCH HANDED

JAPAN'D   1/. EA.
BERLIN   1/6

814 GOTHIC DOOR CHAINS JAP^D

WITH BRASS PLATE
6 IN.	11^d	1/1 EA.
7 .	1/.	1/5 .
8 .	1/1	1/7 .
9 .	1/4	1/9 .

IF BERLIN 6^d EA EXTRA

810. GOTHIC BOLTS Jap'd

If Berlin Black 8ᵈ ea. Extra

Nº 3_4_5_6_HAVE STEEL SPRINGS

Nº 1 __ 8 in. __ 1/6 ea.

SMALLER IF REQUIRED

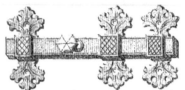

1/8 _ 1/9 _ 1/10_1/11 _ 2/_ 2/1 _ 2/2 ea.
Nº 2   6 _ 7 _ 8 _ 9 _ 10 _ 11 _ 12 in.

Nº 3 __ 9 in. __ 2/4 ea.

Nº 4 __ 8 in. __ 2/4 ea.

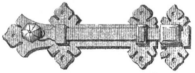

Nº 5 __ 9 in. __ 2/4 ea.

Nº 6 __ 9 in. __ 2/10 ea.

BOLTS MADE TO ANY LENGTH REQUIRED

813. GOTHIC LATCHES Jap'd

If Berlin Black 8ᵈ ea Extra

Nº 19 __ 5½ in. __ 2/7 ea.

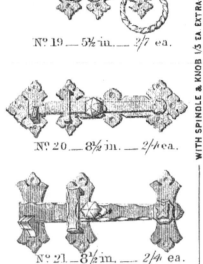

Nº 20 __ 8½ in. __ 2/4 ea.

Nº 21 __ 8½ in. __ 2/4 ea.

Nº 21A _____ 2/6 ea.

WITH SPINDLE & KNOB 1/3 EA. EXTRA

GOTHIC HANDLES SPINDLED, FOR LOCK, JAPᴰ

Nº 21B __ 1/-
BERLIN __ 1/6

Nº 21C __ 1/3 EA
__ 1/9

809 GOTHIC BELL PULLS JAPᴰ IF BERLIN 4ᵈ & 6ᵈ EA. EXTRA.

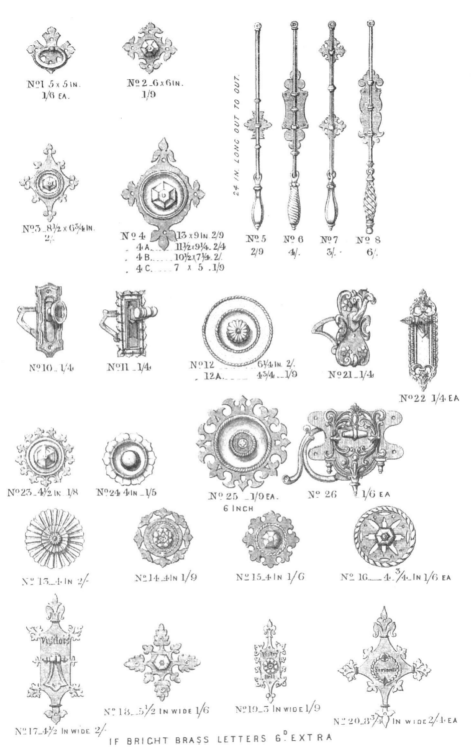

Nº1 5 x 5 IN.
1/6 EA.

Nº2 6 x 6 IN.
1/9

Nº3 8½ x 6¾ IN.
2/-

Nº 4   13 x 9 IN. 2/9
 4 A   11½ x 9¼. 2/4
 4 B   10½ x 7¼. 2/
 4 C   7 x 5 .1/9

24 IN. LONG OUT TO OUT.

Nº 5   Nº 6   Nº 7   Nº 8
2/9   4/.   3/.   6/.

Nº 10 1/4

Nº 11 1/4

Nº 12   6¼ IN. 2/.
 12 A   4¾ 1/9

Nº 21 1/4

Nº 22 1/4 EA

Nº 23 4½ IN. 1/8

Nº 24 4 IN. 1/5

Nº 25 1/9 EA.
6 INCH

Nº 26 1/6 EA

Nº 13 4 IN 2/-

Nº 14 4 IN 1/9

Nº 15 4 IN 1/6

Nº 16 4¾ IN 1/6 EA

Nº 17 4½ IN WIDE 2/-

Nº 18 5½ IN WIDE 1/6

Nº 19 5 IN WIDE 1/9

Nº 20 8¾ IN WIDE 2/4 EA

IF BRIGHT BRASS LETTERS 6ᴰ EXTRA

815. GOTHIC HINGES JAP? IF BERLIN 4ᵈ & 6ᵈ EXTRA

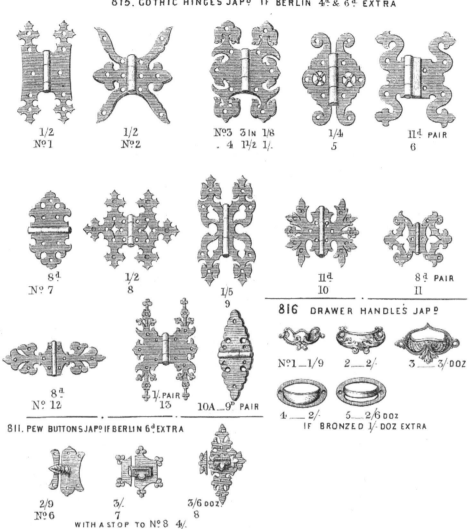

1/2
Nº1

1/2
Nº2

Nº3 3 IN 1/8
4 1½ 1/.

1/4
5

11ᵈ PAIR
6

8ᵈ
Nº 7

1/2
8

1/5
9

11ᵈ
10

8ᵈ PAIR
11

8ᵈ
Nº 12

1/. PAIR
13

10A — 9ᵈ PAIR

816 DRAWER HANDLES JAPᴰ

Nº1 — 1/9   2 — 2/.   3 — 3/. DOZ

4 — 2/.   5 — 2/6 DOZ

IF BRONZED 1/. DOZ EXTRA

811. PEW BUTTONS JAP? IF BERLIN 6ᵈ EXTRA

2/9
Nº6

3/.
7

3/6 DOZ.
8

WITH A STOP TO Nº 8 4/.

812 CABINET HINGE FRONTS If Berlin 2/. to 3/. Pr Doz Pair Extra
with Joints if required

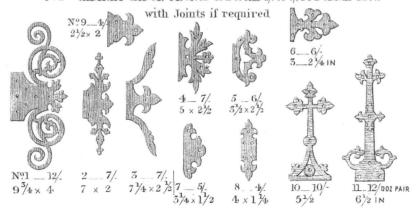

Nº9 — 4/.
2½ x 2

6 — 6/.
3 — 2¼ IN

4 — 7/.
5 x 2½

5 — 6/.
3½ x 2½

Nº1 — 12/.
9¾ x 4

2 — 7/.
7 x 2

3 — 7/.
7¼ x 2½

7 — 5/.
3¾ x 1½

8 — 4/.
4 x 1¼

10 — 10/-
5½

11 — 12/. DOZ PAIR
6½ IN

805. GOTHIC HINGE FRONTS, Per Pair.

No.	Japanned.	Berlin.	No.	Japanned.	Berlin.	No.	Japanned.	Berlin.
1	1/10	2/4	19	3/4	4/1	38	11/6	12/6
2	2/6	3/3	20	6/-	7/-	39	7/6	8/6
2A	3/6	4/3	20A	5/-	6/-	40	5/-	6/-
3	3/-	3/9	21	8/-	9/-	41	5/-	6/-
4	4/3	5/3	22	3/6	4/3	42	4/6	5/3
5	6/6	7/6	23	3/3	4/-	43	7/6	8/6
6	6/6	7/6	24	7/6	8/6	44	7/6	8/6
7	1/6	2/-	25	9/6	10/6	45	7/6	8/6
8	3/6	4/3	26	3/6	4/3	46	4/-	4/9
9	3/8	4/5	27	13/-	14/-	47	5/6	6/6
10	4/-	4/9	28	3/9	4/6	48	11/-	12/-
11	9/6	10/6	29	4/-	4/6	49	11/-	12/-
12	4/6	5/6	30	4/-	4/6	50 {	Top 2/6	3/6
13	5/-	6/-	31	4/6	5/3		Bottom 1/6	2/-
14	5/6	6/6	32	5/3	6/-	51 {	Top 2/-	2/9
15	13/-	14/-	33	4/-	4/9		Bottom 2/-	2/9
16	12/-	13/-	34	5/6	6/3	52	5/-	5/9
17	1/6	2/-	35	3/6	4/3	53	14/-	15/-
18	2/-	2/6	36	10/-	11/-			
18A	2/6	3/-	37	7/6	8/6			

805 GOTHIC HINGE FRONTS JAP^D PER PAIR.

If Berlin Black 6^d to 1/ Pr. Pair Extra.

GOTHIC HEAD SCREWS OF SUITABLE SIZES AS REQUIRED

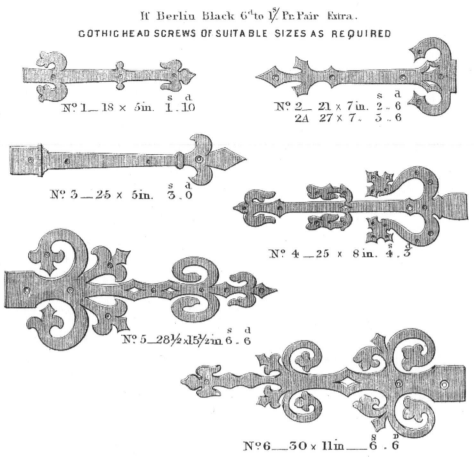

Nº 1 — 18 × 5in.   1.10 (s.d)

Nº 2 — 21 × 7in.   2.6 (s.d)
2A   27 × 7.   3.6

Nº 3 — 25 × 5in.   3.0 (s.d)

Nº 4 — 25 × 8in.   4.3 (s.d)

Nº 5 — 28½ × 15½in   6.6 (s.d)

Nº 6 — 30 × 11in — 6.6 (s.d)

805. GOTHIC HINGE FRONTS JAP.ᴰ PER PAIR.
If Berlin Black 6ᵈ to 1/ Per Pair Extra.

Nº 7 — 10½ in. 1/6

Nº 8 — 19½ x 10 in. — 3/6

Nº 9 — 21 x 11 in. — 3/8

Nº 10 — 21 x 13 in. — 4/.

Nº 11 — 23 x 32 in. — 9/6

Nº 12 — 24 x 17 4/6

Nº 13 — 29 x 16 in. — 5/

Nº 14 — 30 x 15 in. — 5/6

Nº 15 — 38 x 16 in. — 13/.

Nº 16 — 32 x 22 in. — 12/.

411

805 GOTHIC HINGE FRONTS JAPP PER PAIR.

If Berlin Black 6ᵈ to 1/ Pr. Pair Extra.

Nº 17 — 9½ in. — 1/6

Nº 18 — 12 in. — 2/-

Nº 19 — 25 × 5 in. — 3/4

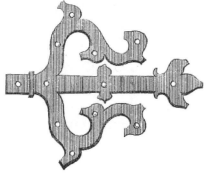

Nº 20 — 24½ × 24 in. 6/.
20A — 22 × 17 — 5/-

Nº 21 — 25 × 23 in. — 8/.

Nº 22 — 27½ × 4½ in — 3/6

Nº 23 — 21½ × 6 in. 3/3

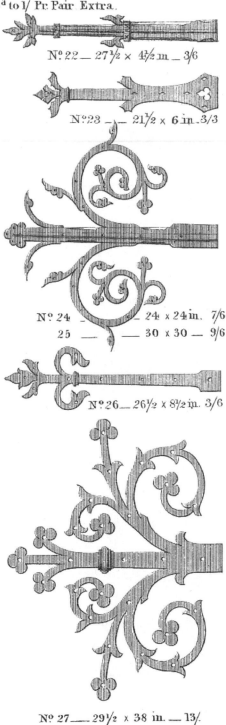

Nº 24 — 24 × 24 in. 7/6
25 — 30 × 30 — 9/6

Nº 26 — 26½ × 8½ in. 3/6

Nº 27 — 29½ × 38 in. — 13/.

805 GOTHIC HINGE FRONTS JAPᴰ PER PAIR
If Berlin Black 6ᵈ to 1/ Pr Pair Extra

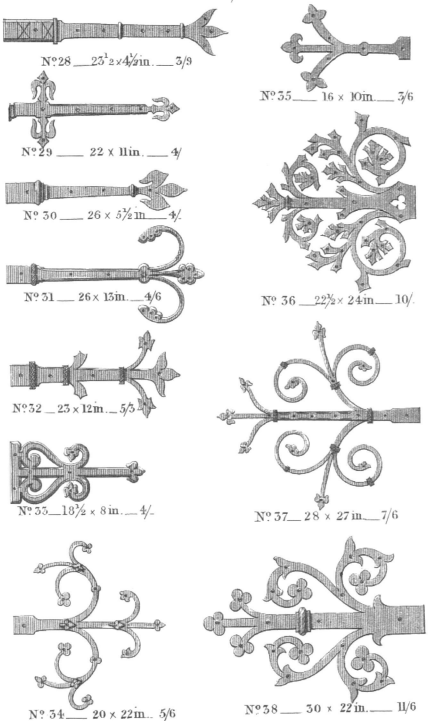

Nº 28 ____ 23½ × 4½ in. ____ 3/9

Nº 29 ____ 22 × 11 in. ____ 4/

Nº 30 ____ 26 × 5½ in ____ 4/.

Nº 31 ____ 26 × 13 in. ____ 4/6

Nº 32 ____ 23 × 12 in. ____ 5/3

Nº 33 ____ 18½ × 8 in. ____ 4/.

Nº 34 ____ 20 × 22 in. ____ 5/6

Nº 35 ____ 16 × 10 in. ____ 3/6

Nº 36 ____ 22½ × 24 in. ____ 10/.

Nº 37 ____ 28 × 27 in. ____ 7/6

Nº 38 ____ 30 × 22 in. ____ 11/6

805 GOTHIC HINGE FRONTS JAP.D PER PAIR
IF BERLIN 6.D TO 1/- PER PAIR EXTRA

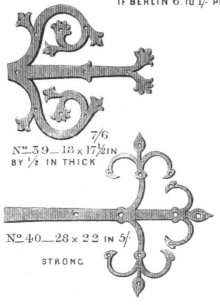

7/6

N.º 39 — 18 × 17½ IN
BY ½ IN THICK

N.º 44 — 24½ × 16 IN 7/6
STRONG

N.º 40 — 28 × 22 IN 5/-

STRONG

N.º 45 — 19½ × 14½ IN 7/6
BY ½ IN THICK

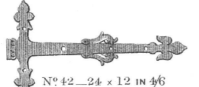

N.º 41 — 24 × 14½ IN 5/-

N.º 46 — 25 × 14 — IN 4/-

N.º 42 — 24 × 12 IN 4/6
STRONG

N.º 43 — 25 × 23 IN 7/6

N.º 47 — 24 × 20 IN 5/6

805 GOTHIC HINGE FRONTS JAP^D PER PAIR
IF BERLIN BLACK 1/- PER PAIR EXTRA

N° 48 — 33 × 28 In — 11/- — Pr

N° 49 — 28 × 26 In — 11/- Pr

805 GOTHIC HINGE FRONTS JAP.ᴰ PER PAIR BERLIN 1/-ˢ PAIR EXTRA

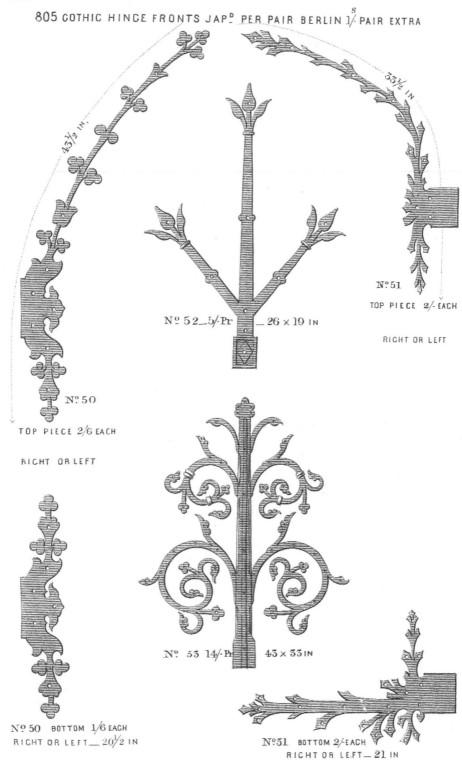

43½ IN.

33½ IN

N° 52_5/-Pr _ 26 × 19 IN

N° 51

TOP PIECE 2/- EACH

RIGHT OR LEFT

N° 50

TOP PIECE 2/6 EACH

RIGHT OR LEFT

N° 53 14/-Pr 43 × 33 IN

N° 50 BOTTOM 1/6 EACH
RIGHT OR LEFT_ 20½ IN

N°51 BOTTOM 2/-EACH
RIGHT OR LEFT— 21 IN

450. MOLE TRAPS.

	s.	d.	
No. 130	7	0	doz.
130A 3 tangs	9	6	
With plates, 1s. doz. extra.			

451. GARDEN RAKES.
WITH HOES.

	s.	d.	
5 teeth ...	4	0	doz.
6 ,, ...	4	6	
7 ,, ...	5	0	
8 ,, ...	5	6	
9 ,, ...	6	0	
10 ,, ...	7	0	
11 ,, ...	8	6	
12 ,, ...	10	0	

452. GARDEN RAKES.

	s.	d.	
5 teeth...	2	3	doz.
6 ,, ...	2	6	
7 ,, ...	3	0	
8 ,, ...	3	6	
9 ,, ...	4	0	
10 ,, ...	4	6	
11 ,, ...	5	0	
12 ,, ...	5	6	

If with sockets, 1s. doz. extra.

453. DIBBLE TIPS.

		s.	d.	
No. 0 ...4in.	1	6	doz.
1 ...5 ,,	2	0	
2 ...7 ,,	3	6	

454. POTATO SETTERS.
Large 7s. doz.

455. GRINDSTONE SPINDLES.
Turned centres, hard handles.

8s.	10s.	12s.	15s.	19s. doz.
No. 1	2	3	4	5

456. BRIDLE HOOKS.

	s.	d.	
No. 00	2	6	doz.
0	3	0	
1	6	0	
2	9	0	

457. HARNESS BRIDLE HOOKS.
1s. each.

459. PORTABLE JACK CRANE.
2s. each.

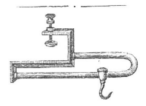

459A. PORTABLE JACK CRANE.
1s. 6d. each.

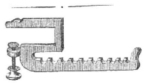

459B. PORTABLE JACK CRANE.
Japanned, 1s., bright, 1s. 6d. each.
460. JACK CRANE, WITH LOOSE HOOKS.
No. 20 ... . 1s. 6d. each.

461. JACK CRANES.

	Japanned.		Bright Racks.			Japanned.		Bright Racks.		
	s.	d.	s.	d.			s.	d.	s.	d.
4 inch	5	0	7	0	doz.	8 in.	6	0	8	6	doz.
5 ,,	5	3	7	3		9 ,,	6	6	9	0
6 ,,	5	6	7	6		10 ,,	7	0	9	6
7 ,,	5	9	7	9		12 ,,	8	0	10	6

462. HARNESS PEGS.

				s.	d.	
No. 0	.....	8 inch	....	1	0	each.
0x	......	9 ,,	....	1	3	
1	......10 ,,		....	1	6	
2	......12 ,,		....	1	10	

458. TOY CANNONS.

467.C. INK POT SLIDE—JAPAND 2/9 Doz.

MOUNTED.			BARRELS ONLY.					
	s.	d.		s.	d.		s.	d.
2 in.	0	10 each.	2 in.	0	3	6 in.	1	5 each.
2½ ,,	1	0	2½ ,,	0	4	7 ,,	1	8
3 ,,	1	2	3 ,,	0	5	8 ,,	2	2
3½ ,,	1	4	3½ ,,	0	7	9 ,,	2	8
4 ,,	1	6	4 ,,	0	9	10 ,,	3	4
4½ ,,	1	8	4½ ,,	0	11	11 ,,	4	0
5 ,,	1	10	5 ,,	1	1	12 ,,	5	0
5½ ,,	2	0	5½ ,,	1	3			
6 ,,	2	3						
7 ,,	2	7						
8 ,,	4	0						
8½ ,,	4	6	If bronzed barrels, 1d. each extra					

465. CORK SQUEEZERS.

		Japanned.		Bronzed.		
		s.	d.	s.	d.	
No. 10	....	0	9	1	3 each.
11	....	1	0	1	6
12	....	1	3	1	9
13	With Spring	1	9	2	2
14	Ditto	2	0	2	6

466A. NEW CORK SQUEEZER.

Japanned.		Bronzed.	
s.	d.	s.	d.
1	6	2	0 each.

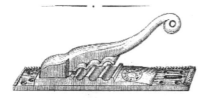

466B. FOOT CORK SQUEEZER.

WITH SPRING.

Japanned.		Bronzed.	
s.	d.	s.	d.
3	9	4	6 each.

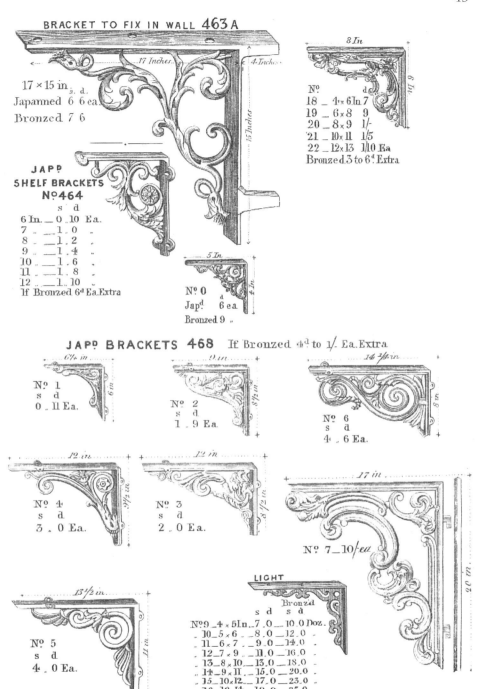

BRACKET TO FIX IN WALL 463A

17 Inches

4 Inches

15 Inches

17 × 15 in.
s. d.
Japanned 6 6 ea.
Bronzed 7 6

8 In

6 In

Nº		d
18	4×6 In.	7
19	6×8	9
20	8×9	1/-
21	10×11	1/5
22	12×13	1/10 Ea.

Bronzed 3 to 6ᵈ Extra

JAPᴰ SHELF BRACKETS Nº464

	s	d	
6 In.	0	10	Ea.
7	1	0	"
8	1	2	"
9	1	4	"
10	1	6	"
11	1	8	"
12	1	10	"

If Bronzed 6ᵈ Ea. Extra

5 In
4 In
Nº 0
d
Japᵈ 6 ea.
Bronzed 9 "

JAPᴰ BRACKETS 468 If Bronzed 4ᵈ to 1/ Ea. Extra

6½ in
6 in
Nº 1
s d
0 . 11 Ea.

9 in
8½ in
Nº 2
s d
1 . 9 Ea.

14 ½ in
8 in
Nº 6
s d
4 . 6 Ea.

12 in
9½ in
Nº 4
s d
3 . 0 Ea.

12 in
8½ in
Nº 3
s d
2 . 0 Ea.

17 in
20 in
Nº 7 — 10/ea

13½ in
11 in
Nº 5
s d
4 . 0 Ea.

LIGHT
Bronzᵈ

	s	d	s	d	
Nº 9	4×5 In.	7.0	10.0	Doz.
10	5×6	8.0	12.0	"
11	6×7	9.0	14.0	"
12	7×9	11.0	16.0	"
13	8×10	13.0	18.0	"
14	9×11	15.0	20.0	"
15	10×12	17.0	23.0	"
16	12×14	19.0	25.0	"

469

HALL   BRACKET

Japaned 2s 0d ea.   Bronzed 2s 6d ea.

SAILORS PALMS 470

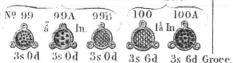

Nº 99	99A	99B	100	100A
⅞ In.			1¼ In.	
3s 0d	3s 0d	3s 0d	3s 6d	3s 6d Groce.

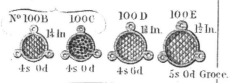

Nº 100B	100C	100 D	100 E
1¼ In		1⅜ In.	1½ In.
4s 0d	4s 0d	4s 6d	5s 0d Groce.

BAKERS LAMPS 471

Nº 1	2s 9d ea.
2	3 6

MEAT SCREEN HANDLES, 467
STRONG.
Plate 10 in by 3 in. 1s 3d ea.

Diamond.   Gothic.
ESCUTCHEONS. **472**
5/. 6/. 7/. 8/6 10/. Groce.
For 6 7 8 9 10 in. Lock.

1s. 6d. each.
BRACKET FOR PATENT SCALES **463**

STRING BOX, Japd **475**

	s. d.
¼ lb.	1 10 ea.
½ lb.	2 2
1 lb.	2 8
1½ lb.	3 2

Bronzed. 6d. extra.

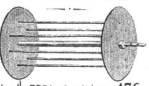

Japd. REEL, for String. **476**
9 in. by 7 in. 4s ea.
Ditto with wrought Plate to fix up to Ceiling 8s 0d

COUNTER REEL **477**

	Japan'd.	Bronzed.
Nº 1 Single	4s. 6d.	5s. 0d. ea.
Nº 2 Double	5 6	6 0

CLOCK BRACKET **478**
Japanned 8s. 0d. ea.
Bronzed with brass flowers 10s. 6d.

480. TOY ITALIAN IRONS.

	Iron barrel.		Brass barrel.		All brass.	
	s.	d.	s.	d.	s.	d.
No. 1	6	0	9	0	18	0 doz.
2	7	0	11	0	19	0
3	8	0	13	0	21	0
4	9	0	15	0	24	0

If loaded bottoms, 9d. per doz. extra.

481. ITALIAN IRONS.
LOW PRICED.

		Iron Barrels.		Solid Bottoms.		Brass Barrels.		Extra Heaters.	
		s.	d.	s.	d.	s.	d.	s.	d.
5	......	10	6 doz.	1	0 ea.	1	1 ea.	3	6 doz. pair
6	......	11	0	1	1	1	2	3	6 "
7	......	11	6	1	1	1	2	4	6 "
8	4½ in.	12	0	1	2	1	3	4	6 "
9	4½ "	12	6	1	3	1	5	4	6 "
10	4¾ "	14	6	1	4	1	7	4	6 "
11	5 "	15	0	1	5	1	9	5	0 "
12	5½ "	15	6	1	6	2	0	5	6 "
13	6 "	16	0	1	8	2	3	6	0 "
14	6½ "	16	6	1	10	2	6	6	6 "
15	6¾ "	17	6	2	0	2	9	7	0 "
16	7 "	20	6	2	4	3	3	8	0 "
17	7¼ "	23	6	2	9	3	6	9	0 "
18	7½ "	27	0	3	3	4	0	10	0 "

Thin Italian Irons, 7, 8, 9, 10, the same prices.

482. ITALIAN IRONS BEST BURNISHED.

	Iron barrel.		Brass barrel.	
	s.	d.	s.	d.
No. 00	2	0	2	9 each.
0	2	6	3	6
1	2	9	4	3
2	3	0	5	0
3	3	3	6	0

483. FRILL IRONS.
SOLID WROUGHT.
Takes out

		s.	d.
No. 0	....	1	4 each.
1	....	1	4
2	....	1	6
3	....	1	8
4	....	1	10
5	....	2	0

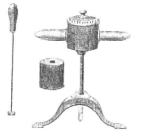

484. DOUBLE ITALIAN IRON.
BURNISHED.
3s. 9d. each.

485. FRENCH IRONS.
BURNISHED.

	Iron barrel.		Brass barrel.	
	s.	d.	s.	d.
A	1	6	2	6 each.
B	1	9	3	0
C	2	0	3	6
D	2	3	4	6

Extra large, 5s. each.

486. PUFFING IRONS.
BURNISHED.
With two wrought heaters.

		Iron barrel.		Brass barrel.	
		s.	d.	s.	d.
3	inch barrel	1	4	1	9 each.
3½	...... ,, ...	1	4	1	10
4	...... ,, ...	1	6	2	0
4½	...... ,, ...	1	8	2	3
5	...... ,, ...	1	10	2	6
5½	...... ,, ...	2	0	2	9
6	...... ,, ...	2	3	3	2
6½	...... ,, ...	2	6	3	6

487. EGG IRONS.

		s.	d.
No. 1	....	1	0 each.
2	....	1	0
3	....	1	0

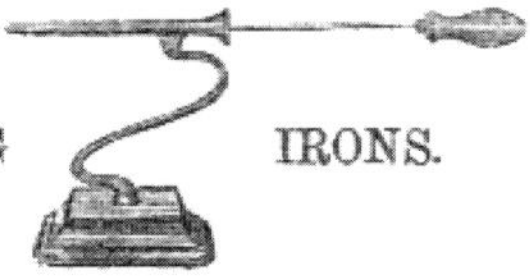

488. PIPING IRONS.

Burnished.	Iron barrel. s. d.	Brass barrel. s. d.
4 inch by $\frac{1}{4}$ inch	1 6	1 9 each.
$4\frac{1}{2}$,, by $\frac{1}{4}$	1 8	1 11
5 ,, by $\frac{5}{16}$,,	1 10	2 1

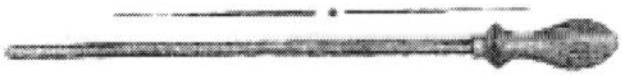

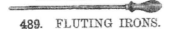

489. FLUTING IRONS.

		s. d.
No. 1	10 in. long by $\frac{1}{4}$ in. diameter	0 9 each.
2	10 ,, ,, by $\frac{5}{16}$,, ,,	0 10
3	10 ,, ,, by $\frac{3}{8}$,, ,,	0 11
4	10 ,, ,, by $\frac{7}{16}$,, ,,	1 0

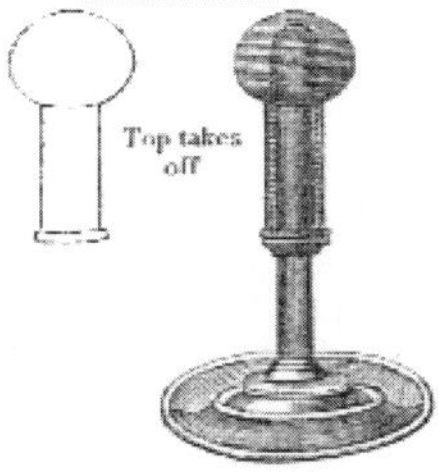

490. HOLLOW BALL IRON.

With two wrought heaters, 4s. each.

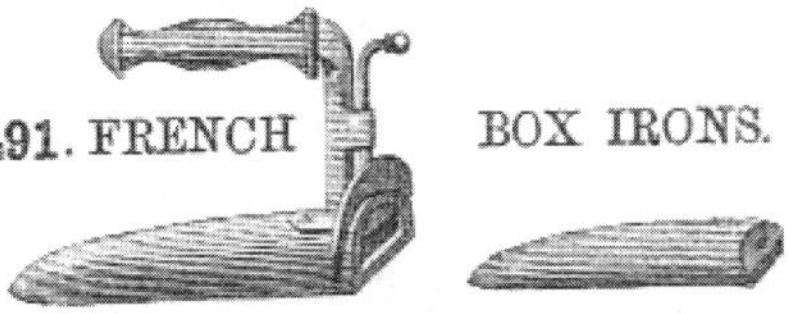

491. FRENCH BOX IRONS.

BURNISHED.		With two cast heaters. s. d.	With two wrought heaters. s. d.
No. 00	5 inch	2 0	2 4 each.
0	$5\frac{3}{4}$,,	2 3	2 8
1	$6\frac{1}{2}$,,	2 6	3 0
2	7 ,,	2 9	3 3
3	8 ,,	3 9	4 6
4	8 ,, by $3\frac{1}{2}$ in.	4 9	5 9

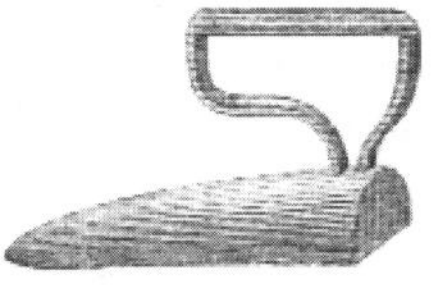

492. FLOUNCE IRONS, SOLID.

		s. d.
No. 1	6 inches	1 3 each.
2	$6\frac{1}{2}$,,	1 7
3	7 ,,	2 0

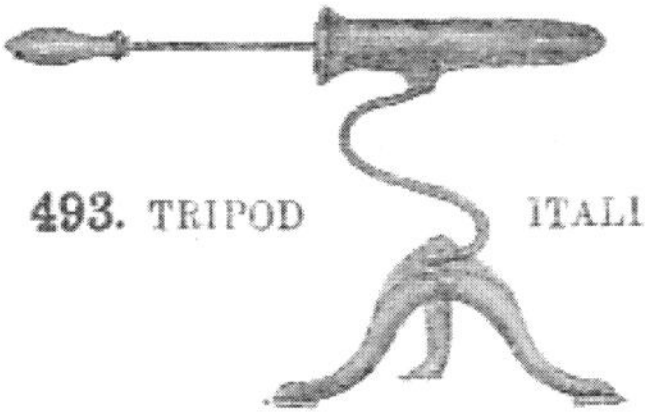

493. TRIPOD ITALIAN IRONS.

		Iron barrel. s. d.	Brass barrel. s. d.
No. 8	$4\frac{1}{4}$ inch	12 0 doz.	1 6 each.
9	$4\frac{1}{2}$,,	13 0	1 8
10	$4\frac{3}{4}$,,	15 0	1 10
11	5 ,,	16 0	2 0
12	$5\frac{1}{2}$,,	17 0	2 3
13	6 ,,	18 0	2 6
14	$6\frac{1}{4}$,,	19 6	2 9
15	$6\frac{3}{4}$,,	20 6	3 0
16	7 ,,	23 6	3 3
17	$7\frac{1}{4}$,,	26 6	3 9
18	$7\frac{1}{2}$,,	30 0	4 3

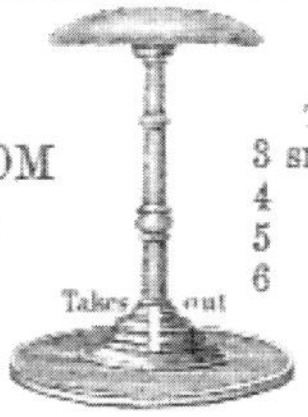

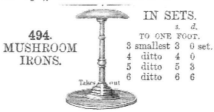

494. MUSHROOM IRONS.

IN SETS.

TO ONE FOOT.	s. d.
3 smallest	3 0 set.
4 ditto	4 0
5 ditto	5 3
6 ditto	6 6

s. d.	s. d.	s. d.	s. d.	s. d.	s. d.	s. d.
1.1	1.3	1.5	1.6	1.8	1.10	2.0 each.
$2\frac{1}{2}$	3	$3\frac{1}{4}$	$3\frac{1}{2}$	$3\frac{3}{4}$	4	$4\frac{1}{2}$ inch.

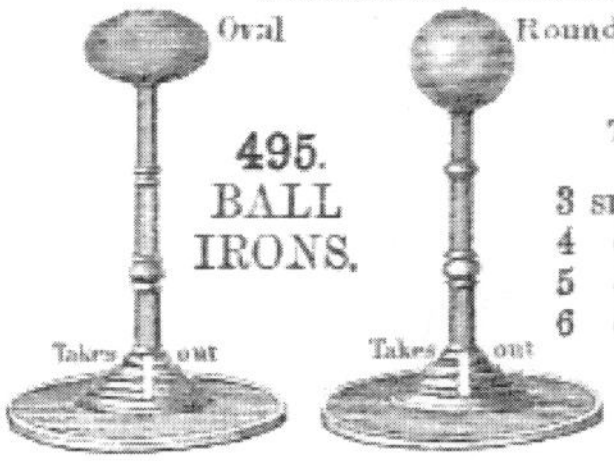

495. BALL IRONS.

IN SETS.

TO ONE FOOT.	s. d.
3 smallest	2 8 set.
4 ditto	3 6
5 ditto	4 0
6 ditto	4 6

	s. d.	s. d.	s. d.	s. d.	s. d.	s. d.	s. d.	s. d.	s. d.
	1.0	1.0	1.0	1.0	1.3	1.6	1.9	2.0	2.4 each.
No.	0000	000	00	0	1	2	3	4	5

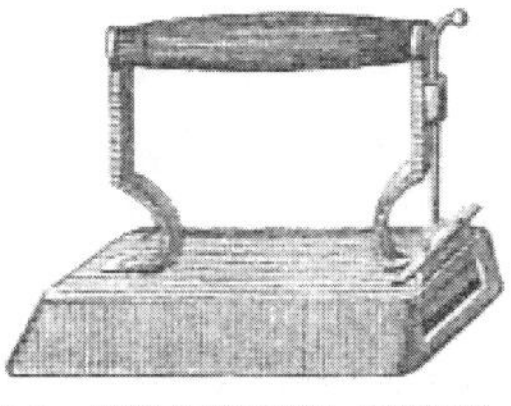

496. BILLIARD IRON.

With one heater.

$11\frac{1}{2}$ inches long, $5\frac{1}{2}$ inches wide, **11s. each.**

Solid, same price.

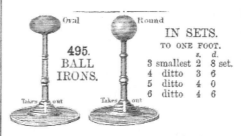

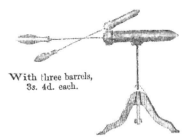

With three barrels,
3s. 4d. each.

497. DOUBLE TRIPOD ITALIAN IRONS.

		s.	d.
No. 0 with 4¼ and 5 inch barrel ...		1	9 each.
1 ,, 4½ ,, 5½ ,, ,, ...		1	10

498. SLEEVE IRONS.

		s.	d.
No. 1	....	1	0 each.
2	....	1	1
3	....	1	2

499. BONNET IRONS.

		s.	d.
4 inch	....	1	0 each.
4½ ,,	....	1	2
5 ,,	....	1	4

500. CONVEX IRONS.

		s.	d.
No. 0	....	0	11 each.
1	....	1	0
2	....	1	2
3	....	1	4

ℬ 524. IMPROVED BOX IRONS.

BEST BURNISHED.

		s.	d.
3 inch	....	2	2 each.
3½ ,,	....	2	2
4 ,,	....	2	2
4½ ,,	....	2	4
5 ,,	....	2	6
5½ ,,	....	2	9
6 ,,	....	3	0
6½ ,,	....	3	6

REGISTERED.

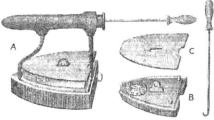

A Box Iron Complete.
B Heater for D?
C Plate as a Nonconducter of Heat.

503. OPEN BOX IRONS.

WITH ITALIAN IRON AND HEATERS.

		s.	d.
4 inches	......	1	9 each.
4½ ,,	......	2	0
5 ,,	......	2	3
5½ ,,	......	2	6
6 ,,	......	2	9

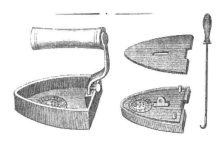

504. OPEN BOX IRONS.

WITH WOOD HANDLE.

		s.	d.
4 inches	......	1	8 each.
4½ ,,	......	1	11
5 ,,	......	2	2
5½ ,,	......	2	5
6 ,,	......	2	8

Covered Handle

505. GERMAN BOX IRONS.

WITH TWO HEATERS.

		Plain handle.		Covered handle.	
		s.	d.	s.	d.
4 inch	....	2	0	2	3 each.
4½ ,,	....	2	3	2	6
5 ,,	....	2	7	2	10
5½ ,,	....	3	0	3	3
6 ,,	... ...	3	8	3	11
6½ ,,	....	4	0	4	4
7 ,,	....	4	6	4	10
7½ ,,	... .	5	0	5	4

520. BEST BOX IRONS.

	Fine cast.	Common cast.	Fine brass bottoms.	Steel face.	Discount, per Cent. Fine real Wrought.
	s. d.	s. d.	s. d.	s. d.	s. d.
2 inch	2 4	1 11	3 5	3 2	3 6 each.
2¼ ,,	2 4	1 11	3 5	3 2	3 6
2½ ,,	2 4	1 11	3 5	3 2	3 6
2¾ ,,	2 4	1 11	3 5	3 2	3 6
3 ,,	2 7	2 2	3 10	3 7	3 8
3¼ ,,	2 7	2 2	3 10	3 7	3 8
3½ ,,	2 7	2 2	3 10	3 7	3 8
3¾ ,,	2 7	2 2	3 10	3 7	3 8
4 ,,	2 7	2 2	4 2	3 7	3 11
4¼ ,,	2 10	2 5	4 8	4 1	4 0
4½ ,,	2 10	2 5	4 11	4 3	4 1
4¾ ,,	2 10	2 5	5 3	4 5	4 3
5 ,,	3 0	2 7	5 6	4 6	4 6
5¼ ,,	3 0	2 7	5 6	4 6	4 9
5½ ,,	3 3	2 10	5 9	4 9	5 0
5¾ ,,	3 6	3 1	6 3	5 3	5 6
6 ,,	3 8	3 3	6 6	5 6	6 0
6¼ ,,	3 11	3 6	7 6	6 0	7 0
6½ ,,	4 5	4 0	8 6	7 0	8 0
6¾ ,,	4 11	4 6	9 6	8 0	9 0
7 ,,	5 5	5 0	10 6	9 0	10 0
7¼ ,,	5 11	5 6	11 6	10 0	11 0
7½ ,,	6 5	6 0	12 6	11 0	12 0
8 ,,	7 6	7 0	14 6	13 0	14 0
9 ,,	10 0				

CONVEX FACE BOX IRONS, or any other form or quality required.

521. INDIAN BOX IRONS.

	Wrought with brass face.	With brass face and copper sides.
	s. d.	s. d.
No. 1 ...	12 6	14 0 each.
2 ...	14 0	16 0
3 ...	16 0	18 6

522. OVAL BOX IRONS.

			s. d.
3½ inch, fine cast	...		2 7 each.
4 ,,	,,	..	2 7
4½ ,,	,,	...	2 10
5 ,,	,,	...	3 0
5½ ,,	,,	...	3 3
6 ,,	,,	...	3 8

523. DUTCH BOX IRONS.

	All wrought iron.	With brass face.
	s. d.	s. d.
No. 1 ...	5 6	7 0 each.
2 ...	6 6	8 6
3 ...	7 6	10 0

If Bronzed or Berlin, 4d. each extra.

No.	Jap'd. each.	No.	Jap'd. each.	No.	Jap'd. each.	No.	Jap'd. each.	No.	Jap'd. each.	No.	Jap'd. each.	No.	Jap'd. each.
0000	1/3	178B	1/6	247	1/8	291	1/9	336	1/-	382	1/2	428	1/-
000	1/8	179	3/-	248	1/8	292	1/6	337	1/3	383	1/2	429	1/1
00	2/-	179A	2/6	249	1/3	293	1/8	338	1/6	384	1/2	430	/11
0	2/3	180	1/-	250	1/6	294	1/-	339	1/2	385	1/8	431	1/1
1	2/6	210	1/3	251	1/2	295	1/9	340	1/-	386	1/3	432	1/-
2	2/9	211	1/6	252	1/3	296	/11	341	1/2	2319	1/8	433	1/4
3	3/-	212	2/4	253A	1/2	297	1/9	342	/11	2400	1/6	434	1/6
145	1/1	213	2/-	253	1/6	298	1/9	343	1/1	387	1/1	435	1/3
146	1/-	214	1/6	254	1/10	299	2/-	344	1/8	388	/11	436	1/2
147	1/3	215	1/1	255	1/3	300	1/-	345	1/-	389	1/2	437	1/2
148	1/1	215A	/11	256	1/8	301	1/-	346	1/4	390	1/1	438	1/2
149	1/-	216	1/6	257	2/-	302	1/-	347	1/6	391	1/3	439	1/1
150	1/1	217	1/1	258	1/4	303	1/4	348	1/10	392	1/2	440	1/6
151A	1/1	218	1/2	258X	1/3	303A	1/1	349	1/3	393	1/6	440A	1/3
151	1/2	218X	1/4	259	2/6	304	2/6	350	1/3	394	1/2	441	1/2
152	1/4	219	1/3	260	1/3	305	1/2	351	/11	395	1/2	442	1/6
153	1/8	220	1/2	261	1/3	306	3/6	352	1/3	396	1/6	443	/11
154	2/-	220X	1/4	262	1/6	306A	2/6	353	1/6	397	1/1	444	1/3
155	2/-	221	1/3	263	1/9	307	2/6	354	1/-	398	1/4	445	1/8
156	1/9	222	1/6	264	1/2	308	/11	355	1/2	399	1/2	446	1/3
157	1/3	223	1/9	265	1/3	309	1/3	356	1/6	400	1/3	447	1/1
157A	1/1	224	2/-	266	1/6	310A	1/-	357	1/2	401	1/1	448	1/2
157X	1/3	225	2/3	267	1/2	310	1/3	358	1/3	402	1/6	449	1/4
158	1/4	226	1/4	268	1/4	311	1/6	359	1/9	403	1/3	450	1/8
158A	1/1	227	1/5	269	1/8	312	1/9	360	1/2	404	1/2	451	1/2
159	1/6	228	1/4	270	1/4	313	1/3	361	/11	405	1/3	452	2/-
160	1/4	228A	1/6	271	1/8	314	1/4	362	1/1	406	1/-	453	1/4
161	1/3	229	2/-	272	2/-	315	1/6	363	/11	407	1/2	454	1/3
162	1/4	230	1/4	273	1/2	316	1/9	364	1/2	408	2/6	455	1/2
163	1/3	231	1/3	274	1/8	317	2/-	365	/11	409	1/3	456	1/3
164	1/2	232B	1/2	275	1/-	318	1/6	366	/11	410	1/4	457	1/3
165	1/4	232A	1/4	276	1/-	319	1/3	367	/11	411	1/6	458	1/9
166	1/8	232	1/6	277	4/6	320	2/-	368	1/4	412	1/3	459	1/6
167	1/2	233	1/6	278	1/3	321	/11	369	1/3	413	1/8	460	1/-
168	1/4	234	1/2	279	1/1	322	1/-	370	1/1	414	1/8	461	1/9
169	1/8	235	1/6	280	1/9	323	1/2	371	1/9	415	1/8	462	1/2
170	1/9	236	1/6	281	1/4	324	1/9	371A	1/-	416	1/-	463	1/8
170X	1/3	237	1/3	282	1/4	325	1/2	372	1/1	417	1/4	464	2/9
171	1/2	238	1/1	283	1/4	326	1/4	373	1/2	418	1/-	465	1/10
172	2/6	238A	1/-	284	1/2	327	1/4	374	1/2	419	2/-	465A	1/8
173	1/6	239	1/2	285	1/-	328	1/8	375	1/1	420	1/10	466	1/9
174A	1/-	240	2/8	286	1/2	329	1/9	376	1/1	421	2/-	467	3/-
174	1/2	241	1/-	287	1/1	330	1/9	376A	1/3	422	1/8	468	1/6
175	1/4	242	1/1	288	1/9	331	2/-	377	1/4	423	1/4	469	1/6
176	1/6	243	1/2	289	1/9	332	3/6	378	1/3	424	2/3	470	1/3
177	1/1	244	2/6	289B	2/3	333	2/3	379	1/3	425	/8	471	1/1
178	2/3	245	1/9	289A	3/3	334	1/9	380	1/2	426	/8	472	1/1
178A	1/9	246	1/8	290	1/3	335	1/6	381	1/-	427	/11	473	1/3

Door Knockers
550

IF WITH BRASS CENTRE	6ᴰ	EACH EXTRA	
IF WITH BRASS NAME PLATE	6ᴰ	DITTO	
IF BRONZED OR BERLIN BLACK	4ᴰ	DITTO	

Any of the following Knockers Brass if required.

WELLINGTON KNOCKER

With brass heads extra

Nº 000	3/8
Nº 00	4/-
Nº 0	4/4
Nº 1	4/8
Nº 2	5/-
Nº 3	5/-

| 1/3 | 1/8 | 2/- | 2/3 | 2/6 | 2/9 | 3/- | ea |
| Nº 0000 | 000 | 00 | 0 | 1 | 2 | 3 | |

Nº 145
1/1

Nº 146
4/- ea.

Nº 147
1/3

Nº 148
4/1

Nº 149
4/-

Nº 150
4/1

151A	4/1	ea
151	4/2	
152	4/4	
153	4/8	
154	2/-	

Nº 155
2/-

Nº 156
4/9

Nº 157 — 1/3
157A — 4/1

DOOR KNOCKERS CONTINUED. 550

If Bronzed or Berlin Black 4ᵈ ea. extra.

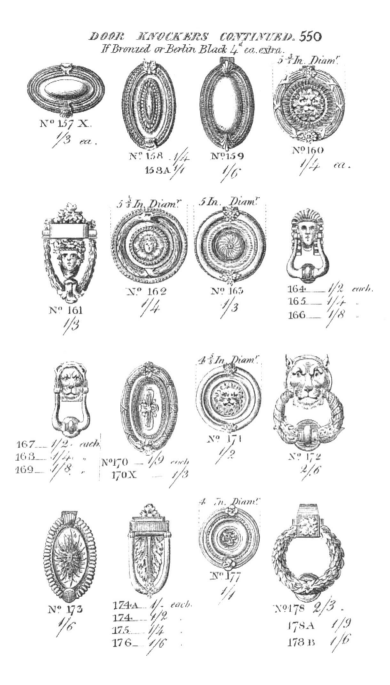

Nº 157 X.
1/3 ea.

5 ¼ In. Diamʳ.

Nº 158 1/4
158A 1/1

Nº 159
1/6

Nº 160
1/4 ea.

5 ⅜ In. Diamʳ.

5 In. Diamʳ.

Nº 161
1/3

Nº 162
1/4

Nº 163
1/3

164 — 1/2 each.
165 — 1/4 —
166 — 1/8 —

167 — 1/2 each.
168 — 1/4
169 — 1/8

Nº 170 — 1/9 each
170X — 1/3

4 ¾ In. Diamʳ.

Nº 171
1/2

Nº 172
2/6

Nº 173
1/6

174A 1/ each.
174 — 1/2
175 — 1/4 —
176 — 1/6

4 In. Diamʳ.

Nº 177
1/1

Nº 178 2/3 —
178A 1/9
178 B 1/6

If Bronzed or Berlin Black 4^d.ea.extra.

7 In. Diam.

Nº 179 3/
Nº 179A 2/6

Nº 180
1/-

Nº 210
1/3

Nº 211 1/6 ea.

6½ In. Diam.

Nº 212
2/4

Nº 213
2/-

Nº 214
1/6

Nº 215 1/1
215A 1/1

Nº 216
1/6

Nº 217
1/1

Nº218 1/3
218X 1/4

Nº 219 1/3

4¾ In. Diam.

Nº220 1/2
220X 1/4
5¼ In. Diam.

Nº221 1/3
222 1/6

Nº223.6In 1/9
224.7In. 2/
225.8In. 2/3

Nº 226
1/4

DOOR KNOCKERS CONTINUED. 550

H.Bronzed or Berlin Black 1/4 ea. extra.

Nº 227.
1/5 each.

Nº 228 — 1/4
228A — 1/6

Nº 229 2/-

Nº 230. 1/4 ea.

Nº 231.
1/3

Nº 232 B — 1/2
narrow
Nº 232 A — 1/4
Nº 232. — 1/6

Nº 233 1/6

Nº 234 1/2

5½ In. Diamʳ.
Nº 235.
1/6

Nº 236.
1/6

Nº 237.
1/3

Nº 238. 1/1
238A 1/-

Nº 239.
1/2

Nº 240.
2/8

4¼ In. Diamʳ.
Nº 241.
1/-

4⅜ In. Diamʳ.
Nº 242.
1/1

51

If Bronzed or Berlin Black 4ᵈ ea. extra.

4¾ In. Diamʳ.

Nº 243
1/2 ea.

Nº 244
2/6

Nº 245
1/9

Nº 246 1/8 ea.

Nº 247
1/8

Nº 248
1/8

249 _ 1/3
250 _ 1/6

Nº 251
1/2

Nº 252
1/3

253 A 1/2
253 _ 1/6
254 _ 1/10

255 _ 1/3
256 _ 1/8
257 _ 2/.

258 1/4
258 X Narrow 1/3

Nº 259
2/6

Nº 260
1/3 each.

Nº 261 — 1/3
Nº 262 — 1/6
Nº 263 — 1/9

Nº 264 1/2 ea.

Nº 265
1/3

1/6

Nº 266

Nº 267 1/2

Nº 268 1/4

Nº 269
1/8

Nº 270 — 1/4
Nº 271 — 1/8
Nº 272 — 2/-

Nº 273
1/2

Nº 274
1/8

Nº 275
1/-

N°.276
1/- ea.

N°.277 4/6

N°.278
1/3 ea.

N°.279
1/1

N°.280 1/9

N°.281
1/4

N°.282
1/4

N°.283 1/4

N°.284 1/2

N°.285
1/-

N°.286
1/2

N°.287
1/1

DOOR KNOCKERS CONTINUED. 550
If Bronzed or Berlin Black 4ᵈ ea. extra.

Nº 288 1/9

Nº 289 — 1/9
Nº 289 B — 2/3
289 A — 3/3

Nº 290 1/3 ea.

Nº 291
1/9

Nº 292
1/6

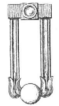

Nº 293
1/8

Nº 294
1/-

Nº 295
1/9

Nº 296
/11.

Nº 297
1/9

Nº 298
1/9

Nº 299 — 2/-

55

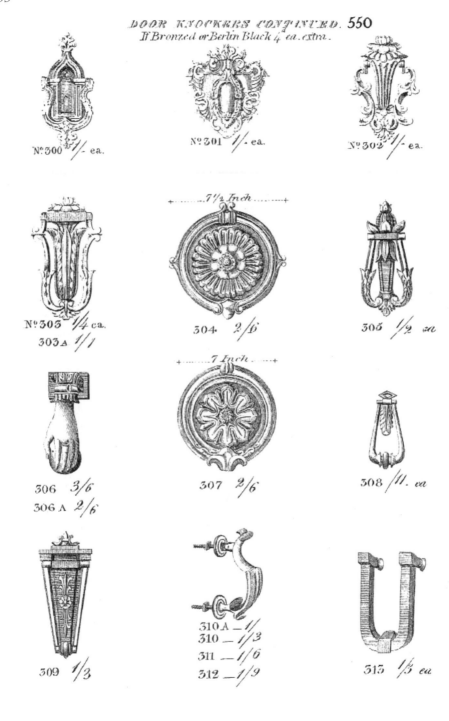

Nº 300   /- ea.

Nº 301   /- ea.

Nº 302   /- ea.

Nº 303   1/4 ea.
303 A 1/1

7½ Inch

304   2/6

305   1/2 ea

306   3/6
306 A 2/6

7 Inch

307   2/6

308   /11. ea

309   1/3

310 A — 1/
310 — 1/3
311 — 1/6
312 — 1/9

313   1/3 ea

DOOR KNOCKERS CONTINUED. **550**

H Bronzed or Berlin Black 4ᵈ ea. extra.

Nᵒ 314 — 1/4

315 — 1/6
316 — 1/9
317 — 2/-

318 — 1/6 ea.

319 — 1/3

320 — 2/-

321 — 1/1
322 — 1/-
323 — 1/2 ea

324 — 1/9

325 — 1/2
326 — 1/4

327 — 1/4 ea

328 — 1/8

329 — 1/9

330 — 1/9 ea

DOOR KNOCKERS CONTINUED. **550**
If Bronzed or Berlin Black 4ᵈ ea. extra.
·········8 In Diamᵗ·········

331 _2/-

332 _ 3/6

333 _ 2/3 ea

334 _ 1/9

335 _ 1/6

336 _1/-

337 _ 1/3

338 _ 1/6

339 _ 1/2

340 _1/-

341 _1/2

342 _/11

DOOR KNOCKERS CONTINUED. **550**
If Bronzed or Berlin Black 4ᵈ ea. extra.

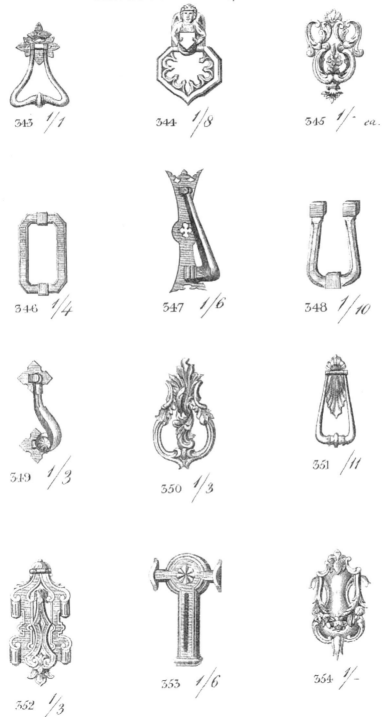

343 1/1

344 1/8

345 1/- ea.

346 1/4

347 1/6

348 1/10

349 1/3

350 1/3

351 /11

352 1/3

353 1/6

354 1/-

59

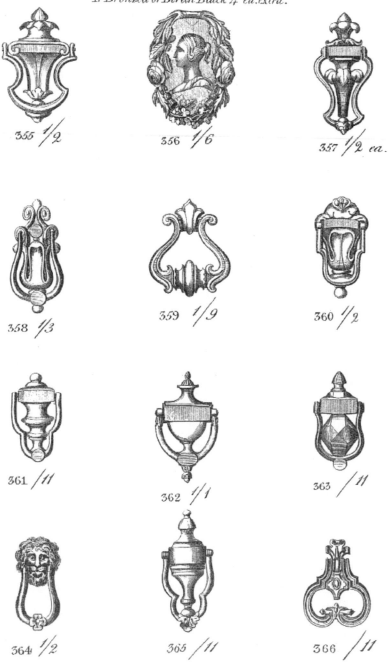

355 1/2

356 1/6

357 1/2 ea.

358 1/3

359 1/9

360 1/2

361 /11

362 1/1

363 /11

364 1/2

365 /11

366 /11

DOOR KNOCKERS CONTINUED. 550
If Bronzed or Berlin Black 1ᵈ ea. extra.

367 /11

368 1/4

369 1/3 ea

370 1/1

371 1/9
371 A 1/.

372 1/1

373 1/2

374 1/2

375 1/1

376 1/1
376 A 1/3

377 1/4

378 1/3

DOOR KNOCKERS. 550

Berlin Black or Bronzed 4ᵈ each extra.

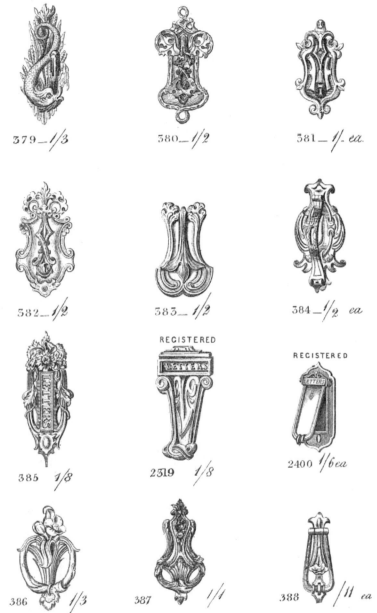

379 — 1/3

380 — 1/2

381 — 1/- ea.

382 — 1/2

383 — 1/2

384 — 1/2 ea

385   1/8

REGISTERED

2319   1/8

REGISTERED

2400 1/6 ea

386   1/3

387   1/1

388   /11 ea

LETTER BOX PLATES · 549

Nº 3 — 7 × 1½ in opening 1/6

Nº 0
Japanned ____ /10ᵈ
Bronzed or Berlin 1/-

REGISTERED

without Springs

Nº 2
Japanned ____ 1/3
Bronzed or Berlin 1/5

REGISTERED

Nº 1
Japanned ____ 1/- ea.
Bronzed or Berlin 1/2

DOOR KNOCKERS CONTINUED. **550**
If Bronzed or Berlin Black 4ᵈ ea. extra.

389 1/2

390 1/1

391 1/3 ea.

392 1/2

393 1/6

394 1/2

395 1/2

396 1/6

397 1/1

398 1/4

399 1/2

400 1/3

DOOR KNOCKERS CONTINUED 550
If Bronzed or Berlin Black $\frac{d}{4}$ ea. extra

Nº 401　1/1 　　　402　1/6 　　　403　1/3 each

404　1/2 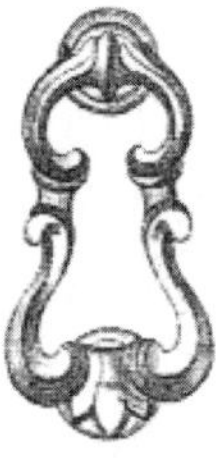　　　405　1/3 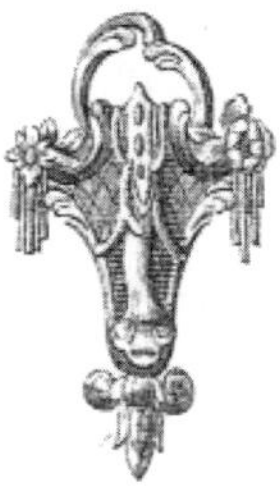　　　406　1/-

407　1/2 　　　408　2/6 　　　409　1/3

410　1/4 　　　411　1/6 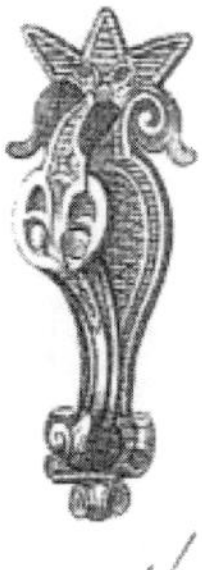　　　412　1/3

DOOR KNOCKERS CONTINUED. 550
If Bronzed or Berlin Black 4ᵈ ea. extra

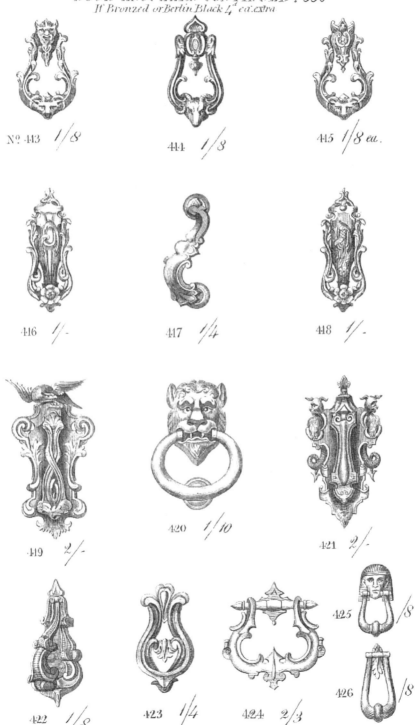

Nº 443 1/8

444 1/8

445 1/8 ea.

416 1/-

417 1/4

418 1/-

419 2/-

420 1/10

421 2/-

422 1/8

423 1/4

424 2/3

425 /8

426 /8

DOOR KNOCKERS CONTINUED, 550
If Bronzed or Berlin Black 4ᵈ ea. extra.

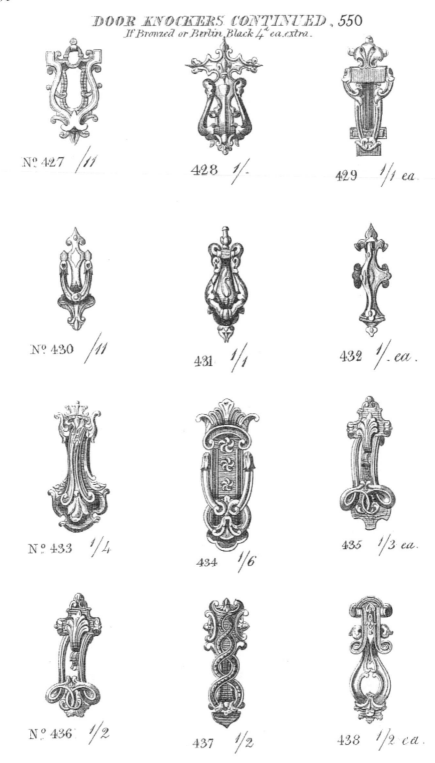

Nº 427 /11

428 1/-

429 1/1 ea

Nº 430 /11

431 1/1

432 1/. ea.

Nº 433 1/4

434 1/6

435 1/3 ea.

Nº 436 1/2

437 1/2

438 1/2 ea.

DOOR KNOCKERS CONTINUED. 550

If Bronzed or Berlin Black 4ᵈ ea. extra.

No. 439 *1/1*

440 *1/6*
440 A *1/3*

441 *1/2 ea.*

No. 442 *1/6*

443 *11ᴰ*

444 *1/3*

No. 445 *1/8*

No. 446 *1/3*

No. 447 *1/1*

No. 448 *1/2*

449 *1/4*

450 *1/8*

DOOR KNOCKERS CONTINUED. 550.
If Bronzed or Berlin Black 4ᵈ ea. extra.

N? 451 1/2

452 2/-

453 1/4 EACH

454 1/3

455 1/2

456 1/3

457 1/3

458 1/9

459 1/6

460 1/-

461 1/9

462 1/2

DOOR KNOCKERS CONTINUED. 550.
If Bronzed or Berlin Black 4ᵈ ea. extra

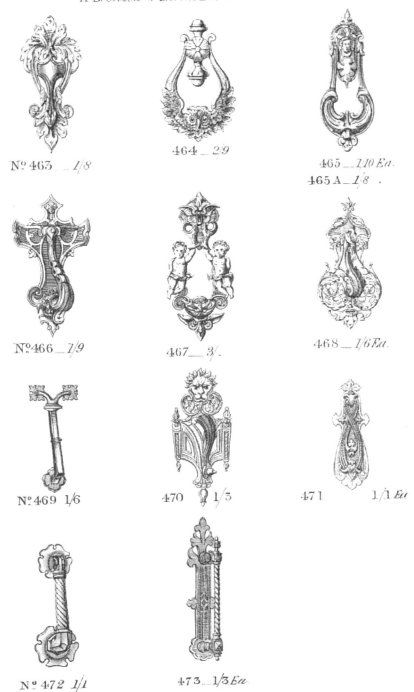

Nº 463 __ 1/8

464 __ 2/9

465 __ 1/10 Ea.
465 A __ 1/8 .

Nº 466 __ 1/9

467 __ 3/.

468 __ 1/6 Ea.

Nº 469 1/6

470   1/3

471   1/1 Ea

Nº 472 1/1

473 __ 1/3 Ea

DOOR PORTERS—551 LONG.

No.	Jap'd. each.	Bronzed or Berlin. each.	No.	Jap'd. each.	Bronzed or Berlin. each.	No.	Jap'd. each.	Bronzed or Berlin. each.
0	2/-	2/6	28	1/6	2/-	102	3/9	4/3
1	2/-	2/6	29	2/8	3/2	103	2/3	2/9
2	1/9	2/3	30	3/3	3/9	104	3/3	3/9
3	2/9	3/3	31	2/3	2/9	105	2/9	3/3
4	2/3	2/9	32	2/3	2/9	106	3/6	4/-
5	2/6	3/-	33	3/-	3/6	107	2/6	3/-
6	2/-	2/6	34	2/6	3/-	108	2/6	3/-
7	2/-	2/6	83	2/6	3/-	109	2/8	3/2
8	2/9	3/3	84	2/9	3/3	110	2/10	3/4
9	3/6	4/-	85	2/6	3/-	111	3/.	3/6
9 ×	6/-	6/6	86	2/6	3/-	112	3/-	3/6
10	3/-	3/6	87	4/-	4/6	113	2/4	2/10
11	2/9	3/3	88	2/3	2/9	114	4/-	4/6
12	2/4	2/10	89	2/-	2/6	115	2/3	2/9
13	3/3	3/9	90	2/6	3/-	115 Short	2/-	2/6
14	2/9	3/3	91	2/6	3/-	116	2/6	3/-
15	2/3	2/9	92	2/6	3/-	117	2/6	3/-
16	2/6	3/-	92 Short	2/3	2/9	118	2/6	3/-
17	1/6	2/-	93	3/-	3/6	119	2/6	3/-
18	1/8	2/2	94	2/4	2/10	119 Short	2/3	2/9
19	3/-	3/6	95	2/-	2/6	120	3/-	3/6
20	2/3	2/9	95 Short	1/9	2/3	121	3/3	3/9
21	3/3	3/9	96	2/6	3/-	121 Short	3/-	3/6
22	2/3	2/9	97	2/3	2/9	122	5/-	5/6
23	2/9	3/3	98	2/-	2/6	123	2/6	3/-
24	2/-	2/6	99	2/9	3/3	124	4/6	5/-
25	2/3	2/9	100	2/3	2/9	125	2/9	3/3
26	2/6	3/-	101	2/6	3/-	126	2/3	2/9
27	3/-	3/6						

DOOR PORTERS—551 SHORT.

No.	Jap'd. each.	Bronzed or Berlin. each.	No.	Jap'd. each.	Bronzed or Berlin. each.	No.	Jap'd. each.	Bronzed or Berlin. each.
35	2/6	3/-	47	2/6	3/-	59	1/6	2/-
36	2/3	2/9	48	1/9	2/3	60	2/3	2/9
37	2/-	2/6	49	2/-	2/6	61	2/3	2/9
38	2/9	3/3	50	2/9	3/3	62	2/-	2/6
39	2/6	3/-	51	2/6	3/-	63	2/-	2/6
40	2/6	3/-	52	2/-	2/6	64	2/6	3/-
41	2/6	3/-	53	2/6	3/-	65	1/6	2/.
42	1/10	2/4	54	2/6	3/-	66	2/3	2/9
43	2/3	2/9	55	2/3	2/9	67	1/6	2/-
44	2/9	3/3	56	2/4	2/10	68	2/3	2/9
45	2/-	2/6	57	2/9	3/3	69	1/6	2/.
46	2/6	3/-	58	1/6	2/-	70	1/10	2/4

DOOR PORTERS JAPANNED. 551

If Bronzed or Berlin 6ᵈ each extra.

No. 0
2/- ea.

No. 1
2/- ea.

No. 2
1/9 ea.

1/- Extra

No. 3
2/9 ea.

2/- Extra

No. 4
2/3 ea.

1/9 Extra

No. 5
2/6 ea.

2/- Extra

No. 6 2/- ea.

2/- Extra

No. 7
2/- ea.

No. 8
2/9 ea.

No. 9
3/6

No. 9X
If 20 ʰˢ 6/

If with Brass handle as marked + extra.

DOOR PORTERS JAPANNED. 551
If Bronzed 6 d ea. extra — If with Brass handle as marked + extra.

Nº 10 3/. ea.

Nº 11 2/9 ea.

Nº 12 2/4 ea.

2/6 Extra

Nº 13 3/3

1/9 Extra

Nº 14 2/9

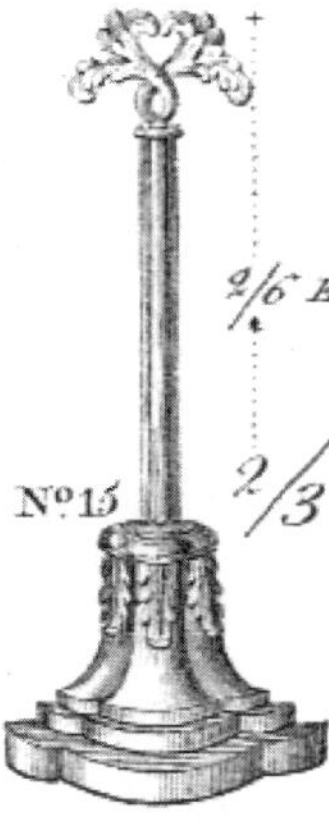

2/3 Extra

Nº 15 2/3

2/6 Extra

Nº 16 2/6

2/3 Extra

Nº 17 1/6

1/9 Extra

Nº 18 1/8

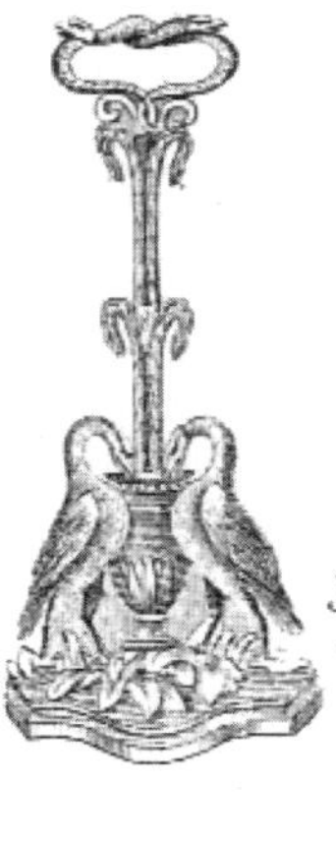

1/9 Extra

Nº 19 3/.

DOOR PORTERS, JAPANNED. 551

If Bronzed 6 d. each extra.

Nº 20 . 2/3 ea.

Nº 21 . 3/3 ea.

Nº 22 . 2/3 ea.

Nº 23 . 2/9 ea.

Nº 24 . 2/- ea.

Nº 25 . 2/3 ea.

Nº 26 . 2/6 ea.

Nº 27 . 3/- ea.

Nº 28 . 1/6 ea.

DOOR PORTERS, JAPANNED. 551

If Bronzed 6 d. each extra.

Nº 29   2/8   30   3/3   31   2/3 ea

Nº 32   2/3   33   3/-   34   2/6 ea

83   2/6   84   2/9   85   2/6

64

DOOR PORTERS, JAPANNED. 551

If Bronzed 6d. each extra.

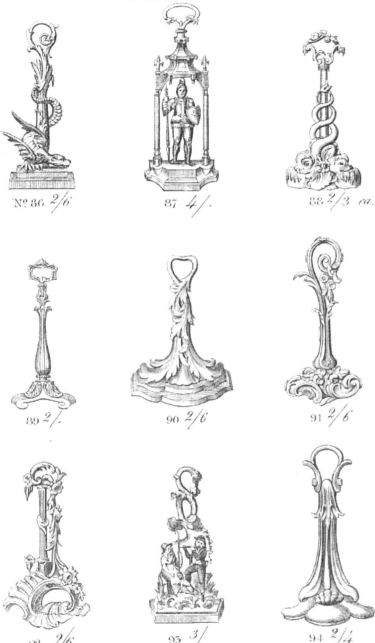

Nº 86 2/6   87 4/.   88 2/3 ea.

89 2/.   90 2/6   91 2/6

92 2/6   93 3/   94 2/4
SHORT 2/3

DOOR PORTERS JAPANNED. 551
If Bronzed 6d. each extra

Nº 95 2/   96 2/6   97 2/3 *ea*
SHORT 1/9

98 2/.   99 2/9   100 2/3

101 2/6   102 3/9   103 2/3

DOOR PORTERS. JAPANNED. 551

If Bronzed 6 d. each extra.

Nº 104   3/3

105   2/9

106   3/6 *ea.*

107   2/6

108   2/6

109   2/8

110   2/10

111   3/-

112   3/-

DOOR PORTERS, JAPANNED. 551

If Bronzed 6 d. each extra.

No 115   2/4

114   4/- ea.

115   2/3 each
SHORT 2/-

No 116   2/6

117   2/6

118   2/6 ea

119   2/6
SHORT 2/3

120   3/-

121   3/3 ea
SHORT 3/

551 DOOR PORTERS JAP^D

IF BRONZED 6^D EACH EXTRA

Nº 122 — 5/-

Nº 123 — 2/6

Nº 124 — 4/6 EACH

Nº 125 — 2/9

Nº 126 — 2/3 EACH

65

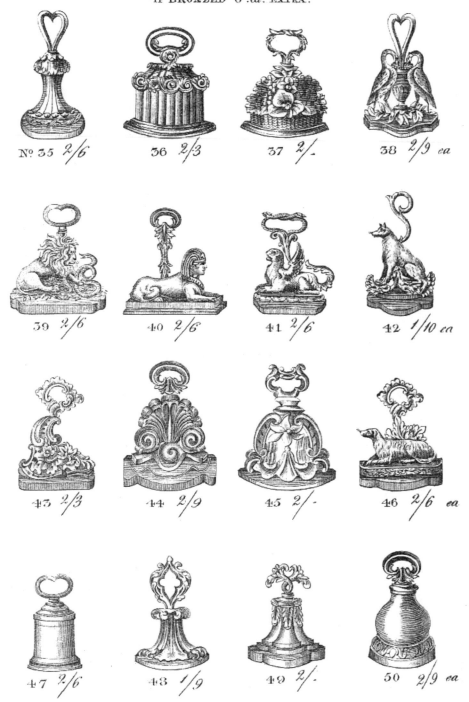

Nᵒ 35 2/6 36 2/3 37 2/- 38 2/9 ea

39 2/6 40 2/6 41 2/6 42 1/10 ea

43 2/3 44 2/9 45 2/- 46 2/6 ea

47 2/6 48 1/9 49 2/- 50 2/9 ea

SHORT DOOR PORTERS, JAPANNED. 551

IF BRONZED 6 d. ea. EXTRA.

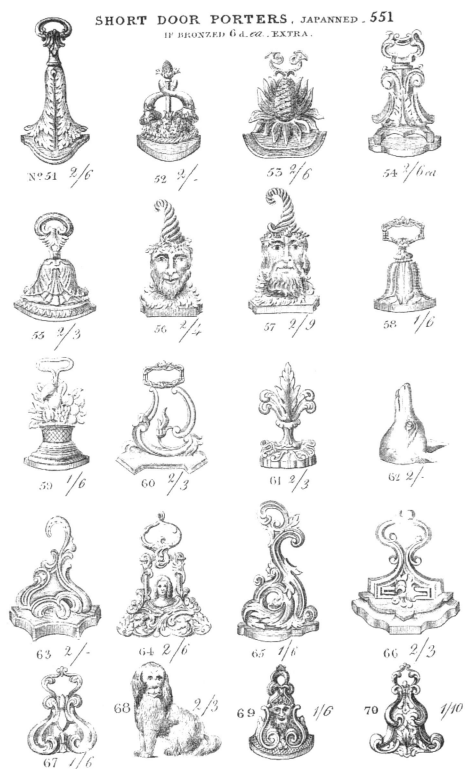

Nº 51 2/6

52 2/-

53 2/6

54 2/6 ea

55 2/3

56 2/4

57 2/9

58 1/6

59 1/6

60 2/3

61 2/3

62 2/-

63 2/-

64 2/6

65 1/6

66 2/3

67 1/6

68 2/3

69 1/6

70 1/10

552. SUPERIOR SHOE TIPS.

PER GROSS PAIRS.

No.	No.			s.	d.
C323	1	$1\frac{5}{8}$	inch	10	0
C 54	2	$1\frac{3}{4}$	,,	10	0
C331	3	$1\frac{7}{8}$	,,	10	0
C 6	4	2	,,	10	0
C 7	5	$2\frac{1}{8}$	,,	11	0
C 8	6	$2\frac{1}{4}$	,,	12	0
C 9	7	$2\frac{3}{8}$	,,	13	0
C 48	$7\frac{1}{2}$	$2\frac{1}{2}$	,,	14	0
C 49	8	$2\frac{5}{8}$	,,	15	0
C 50	$8\frac{1}{2}$	$2\frac{3}{4}$	,,	16	0
C 51	9	$2\frac{7}{8}$	,,	17	0
C386	10	3	,,	18	0

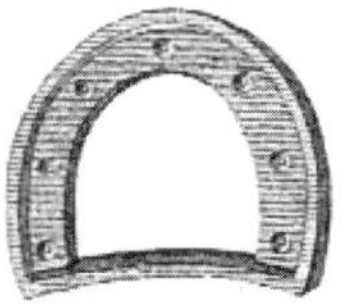

No.	No.			s.	d.
C62	13	$1\frac{3}{4}$	inch	10	0
C $40\frac{1}{2}$	14	2	,,	10	0
C40	15	$2\frac{1}{8}$	,,	11	0
C59	16	$2\frac{1}{4}$	,,	12	0
C64	17	$2\frac{3}{8}$	,,	13	0
C63	18	$2\frac{1}{2}$	,,	14	0
C65	19	$2\frac{5}{8}$	,,	15	0
C66	20	$2\frac{3}{4}$	,,	16	0
C67	21	$2\frac{7}{8}$	,,	17	0
C68	22	3	,,	18	0

No.	No.			s.	d.
C353	23	2	inch	10	0
C337	24	$2\frac{1}{8}$	,,	11	0
C298	25	$2\frac{1}{4}$	,,	12	0
C338	26	$2\frac{3}{8}$	,,	13	0
C316	27	$2\frac{1}{2}$	,,	14	0
C299	28	$2\frac{5}{8}$	,,	15	0
C354	29	$2\frac{3}{4}$	,,	16	0
C355	30	$2\frac{7}{8}$	,,	17	0
C356	31	3	,,	18	0

No.	No.			s.	d.
C417	32	$2\frac{1}{8}$	inch	11	0
C418	33	$2\frac{1}{4}$	,,	12	0
C224	34	$2\frac{3}{8}$	,,	13	0
C225	35	$2\frac{1}{2}$	,,	14	0
C219	36	$2\frac{5}{8}$	,,	15	0
C220	36A	$2\frac{3}{4}$	,,	16	0
C221	36B	$2\frac{7}{8}$	,,	17	0
C222	36C	3	,,	18	0

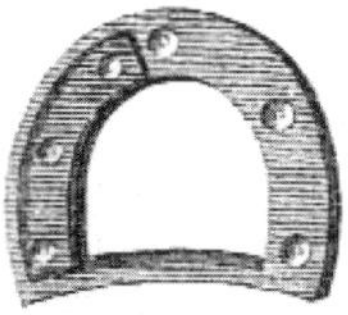

No.	No.			s.	d.
C $42\frac{1}{2}$	37	2	inch	10	0
C 42	38	$2\frac{1}{8}$	,,	11	0
C 41	39	$2\frac{1}{4}$	,,	12	0
C341	40	$2\frac{3}{8}$	,,	13	0
C260	41	$2\frac{1}{2}$	,,	14	0
C261	41A	$2\frac{5}{8}$	,,	15	0
C262	42	$2\frac{3}{4}$	,,	16	0
C263	42A	$2\frac{7}{8}$	,,	17	0
C264	42B	3	,,	18	0

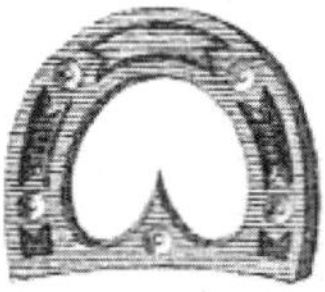

No.	No.			s.	d.
C110	43	2	inch	10	0
C111	44	$2\frac{1}{8}$	,,	11	0
C112	45	$2\frac{1}{4}$	,,	12	0
C113	46	$2\frac{3}{8}$	,,	13	0
C114	47	$2\frac{1}{2}$	,,	14	0
C115	48	$2\frac{5}{8}$	,,	15	0
C116	48A	$2\frac{3}{4}$	,,	16	0
C117	48B	$2\frac{7}{8}$	,,	17	0
C118	48C	3	,,	18	0

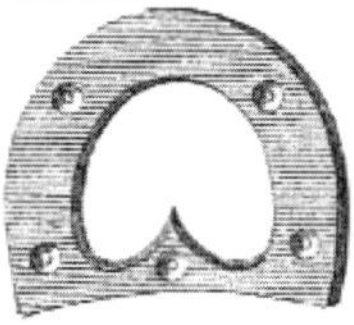

No.	No.			s	d.
	49	$1\frac{7}{8}$	inch	10	0
C147	50	$2\frac{1}{8}$	,,	11	0
C148	51	$2\frac{1}{4}$	,,	12	0
C149	52	$3\frac{3}{8}$	,,	13	0
C156	53	$2\frac{1}{2}$	,,	14	0
C150	54	$2\frac{5}{8}$	,,	15	0
C151	55	$2\frac{3}{4}$	,,	16	0
C152	56	$2\frac{7}{8}$	,,	17	0
C153	56A	3	,,	18	0
C154	56B	$3\frac{1}{8}$	,,	49	0
C155	56C	$3\frac{1}{4}$	,,	20	0

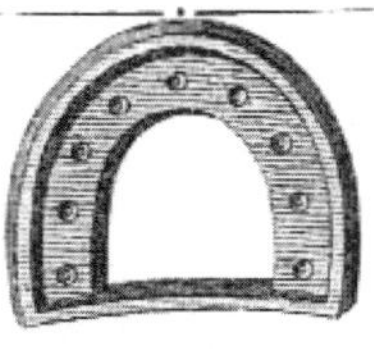

No.			s.	d.
57	$2\frac{1}{8}$	inch	11	0
58	$2\frac{1}{4}$	,,	12	0
59	$2\frac{3}{8}$	,,	13	0
60	$2\frac{1}{2}$	,,	14	0
61	$2\frac{5}{8}$	,,	15	0
62	$2\frac{3}{4}$	,,	16	0
63	$2\frac{7}{8}$	,,	17	0
64	3	,,	18	0

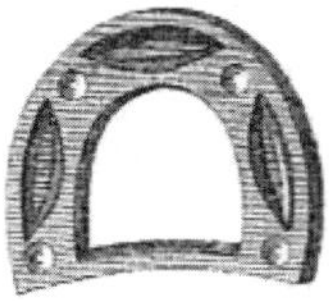

	No.				
C $32\frac{1}{2}$	65	2	inch	10	0
C 32	66	$2\frac{1}{8}$	,,	11	0
C 31	67	$2\frac{1}{4}$	,,	12	0
C $31\frac{1}{2}$	68	$2\frac{3}{8}$	,,	13	0
C236	69	$2\frac{1}{2}$	,,	14	0
C237	70	$2\frac{5}{8}$	,,	15	0
C238	71	$2\frac{3}{4}$	,,	16	0
C239	72	$2\frac{7}{8}$	,,	17	0
C514	73	3	,,	18	0

N.B.—The figures in red ink are *Messrs. Crowley and Co.'s* numbers.

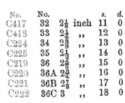

552. SUPERIOR SHOE TIPS.

PER GROSS PAIRS.

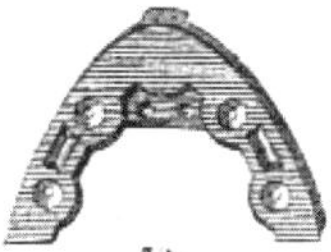

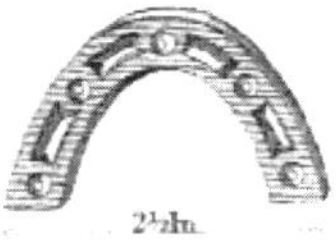

No. 92 3 inch	s. d. 11 0	No. 93 3 inch	s. d. 11 0	No. 94 2⅝ inch	s. d. 11 0	No. 95 2½ inch	s. d. 10 0

No.	No.		s.	d.		No.		s.	d.		No.	No.		s.	d.
C52	74	2¼ inch	10	0		81	2 inch	10	0		C180	85	2¼ inch	10	0
C52A	75	2⅜ ,,	10	0		82	2¼ ,,	10	0		C181	86	2¼ ,,	10	0
C52B	76	2½ ,,	10	0		83	2½ ,,	10	0		C182	87	2⅜ ,,	10	0
C319	77	2⅝ ,,	11	0		84	2⅝ ,,	11	0		C183	88	2½ ,,	10	0
C320	78	2¾ ,,	11	0							C184	89	2⅝ ,,	11	0
C321	79	2⅞ ,,	11	0							C185	90	2¾ ,,	11	0
C322	80	3 ,,	11	0							C186	91	2⅞ ,,	11	0

No.		s.	d.		No.	No.		s.	d.		No.		s.	d.
103	1⅞ inch	10	0		C427	118	2 inch	10	0		127	2⅜ inch	18	0
104	2 ,,	10	0		C428	119	2⅛ ,,	11	0		128	2½ ,,	19	0
105	2⅛ ,,	10	0		C429	120	2¼ ,,	12	0		129	2⅝ ,,	20	0
106	2¼ ,,	10	0		C243	121	2⅜ ,,	13	0		130	2¾ ,,	21	0
107	2⅜ ,,	10	0		C244	122	2½ ,,	14	0					
108	2½ ,,	10	0		C245	123	2⅝ ,,	15	0					
109	2⅝ ,,	11	0		C246	124	2¾ ,,	16	0					
110	2¾ ,,	11	0		C447	125	2⅞ ,,	17	0					
111	2⅞ ,,	11	0		C248	126	3 ,,	18	0					
112	3 ,,	11	0											

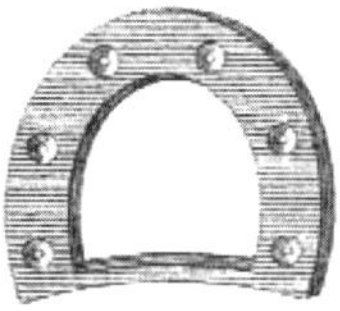

No.	No.		s.	d.		No.		s.	d.		No.		s.	d.
C266	133	2¼ inch	12	0		140	2 inch	10	0		149	2 inch	10	0
C267	134	2⅜ ,,	13	0		141	2⅛ ,,	10	0		150	2⅛ ,,	10	0
C268	135	2½ ,,	14	0		142	2¼ ,,	10	0		151	2¼ ,,	10	0
C269	136	2⅝ ,,	15	0		143	2⅜ ,,	10	0		152	2⅜ ,,	10	0
C270	137	2¾ ,,	16	0		144	2½ ,,	10	0		153	2½ ,,	10	0
C348	138	2⅞ ,,	17	0		145	2⅝ ,,	11	0		154	2⅝ ,,	11	0
C389	139	3 ,,	18	0		146	2¾ ,,	11	0		155	2¾ ,,	11	0
						147	2⅞ ,,	11	0		156	2⅞ ,,	11	0
						148	3 ,,	11	0		157	3 ,,	11	0

N.B.—The figures in red ink are *Messrs. Crowley and Co.'s* numbers.

552. SUPERIOR SHOE TIPS.

PER GROSS PAIRS.

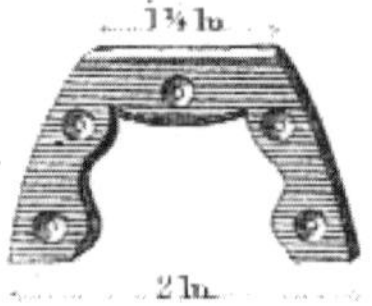

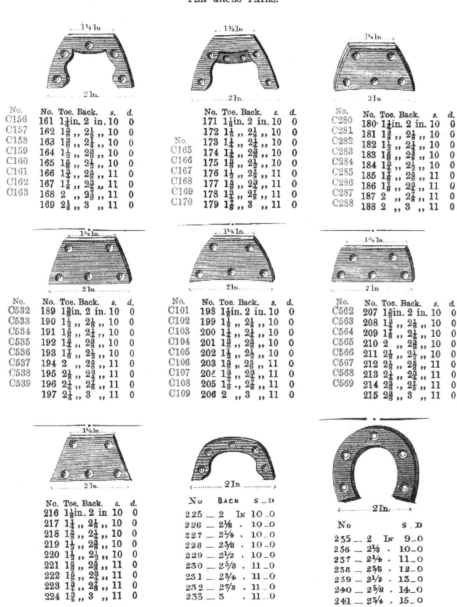

No.	No.	Toe.	Back.	s.	d.
C156	161	1¼in.	2 in.	10	0
C157	162	1⅜ ,,	2⅛ ,,	10	0
C158	163	1⅜ ,,	2¼ ,,	10	0
C159	164	1½ ,,	2⅜ ,,	10	0
C160	165	1⅝ ,,	2½ ,,	10	0
C161	166	1¾ ,,	2⅝ ,,	11	0
C162	167	1⅞ ,,	2¾ ,,	11	0
C163	168	2 ,,	2⅞ ,,	11	0
	169	2⅛ ,,	3 ,,	11	0

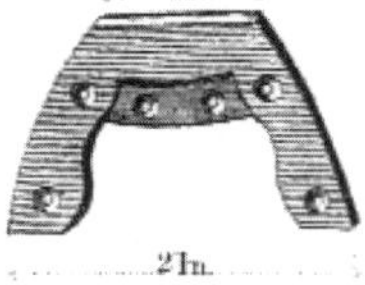

No.	No.	Toe.	Back.	s.	d.
	171	1⅛in.	2 in.	10	0
	172	1⅛ ,,	2⅛ ,,	10	0
	173	1¼ ,,	2¼ ,,	10	0
C165	174	1¼ ,,	2⅜ ,,	10	0
C166	175	1⅜ ,,	2½ ,,	10	0
C167	176	1½ ,,	2⅝ ,,	11	0
C168	177	1⅝ ,,	2¾ ,,	11	0
C169	178	1¾ ,,	2⅞ ,,	11	0
C170	179	1⅞ ,,	3 ,,	11	0

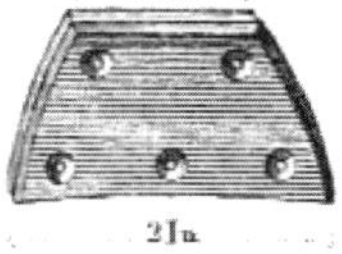

No.	No.	Toe.	Back.	s.	d.
C280	180	1¼in.	2 in.	10	0
C281	181	1⅜ ,,	2⅛ ,,	10	0
C282	182	1½ ,,	2¼ ,,	10	0
C283	183	1⅝ ,,	2⅜ ,,	10	0
C284	184	1¾ ,,	2½ ,,	10	0
C285	185	1⅞ ,,	2⅝ ,,	11	0
C286	186	1⅞ ,,	2¾ ,,	11	0
C287	187	2 ,,	2⅞ ,,	11	0
C288	188	2 ,,	3 ,,	11	0

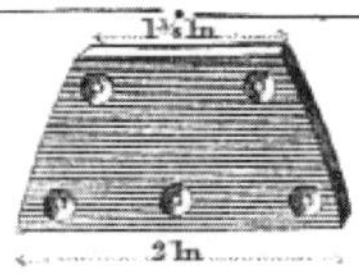

No.	No.	Toe.	Back.	s.	d.
C532	189	1⅜in.	2 in.	10	0
C533	190	1½ ,,	2⅛ ,,	10	0
C534	191	1⅝ ,,	2¼ ,,	10	0
C535	192	1¾ ,,	2⅜ ,,	10	0
C536	193	1⅞ ,,	2½ ,,	10	0
C537	194	2 ,,	2⅝ ,,	11	0
C538	195	2⅛ ,,	2¾ ,,	11	0
C539	196	2¼ ,,	2⅞ ,,	11	0
	197	2¼ ,,	3 ,,	11	0

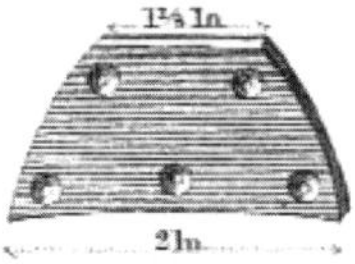

No.	No.	Toe.	Back.	s.	d.
C101	198	1⅛in.	2 in.	10	0
C102	199	1⅛ ,,	2⅛ ,,	10	0
C103	200	1¼ ,,	2¼ ,,	10	0
C104	201	1⅜ ,,	2⅜ ,,	10	0
C105	202	1½ ,,	2½ ,,	10	0
C106	203	1⅝ ,,	2⅝ ,,	11	0
C107	204	1¾ ,,	2¾ ,,	11	0
C108	205	1⅞ ,,	2⅞ ,,	11	0
C109	206	2 ,,	3 ,,	11	0

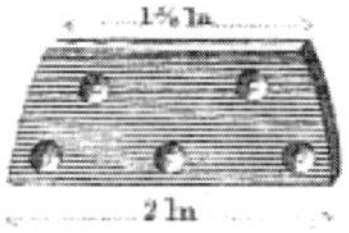

No.	No.	Toe.	Back.	s.	d.
C562	207	1⅝in.	2 in.	10	0
C563	208	1¾ ,,	2⅛ ,,	10	0
C564	209	1⅞ ,,	2¼ ,,	10	0
C565	210	2 ,,	2⅜ ,,	10	0
C566	211	2⅛ ,,	2½ ,,	10	0
C567	212	2⅛ ,,	2⅝ ,,	11	0
C568	213	2¼ ,,	2¾ ,,	11	0
C569	214	2⅜ ,,	2½ ,,	11	0
	215	2⅜ ,,	3 ,,	11	0

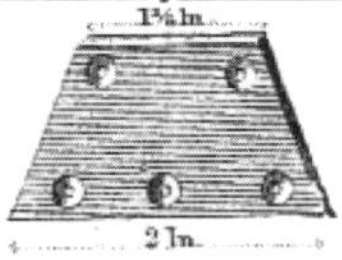

No.	Toe.	Back.	s.	d.
216	1⅛in.	2 in	10	0
217	1¼ ,,	2⅛ ,,	10	0
218	1⅜ ,,	2¼ ,,	10	0
219	1½ ,,	2⅜ ,,	10	0
220	1½ ,,	2½ ,,	10	0
221	1⅝ ,,	2⅝ ,,	11	0
222	1⅝ ,,	2¾ ,,	11	0
223	1¾ ,,	2⅞ ,,	11	0
224	1¾ ,,	3 ,,	11	0

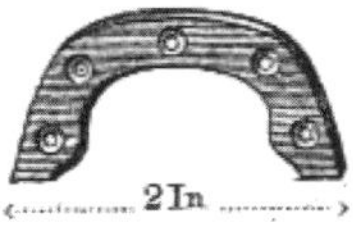

No	Back	s _ d
225	2 In	10 _ 0
226	2⅛ .	10 _ 0
227	2¼ .	10 _ 0
228	2⅜ .	10 _ 0
229	2½ .	10 _ 0
230	2⅝ .	11 _ 0
231	2¾ .	11 _ 0
232	2⅞ .	11 _ 0
233	3 .	11 _ 0

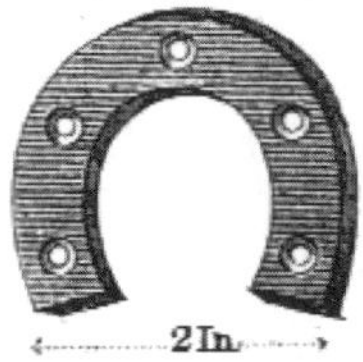

No		s . d
235	2 In	9 _ 0
236	2⅛ .	10 _ 0
237	2¼ .	11 _ 0
238	2⅜ .	12 _ 0
239	2½ .	13 _ 0
240	2⅝ .	14 _ 0
241	2¾ .	15 _ 0
242	2⅞ .	16 _ 0
243	3 .	17 _ 0

N. B —The figures in red ink are *Messrs Crowley and Co.'s* numbers.

PATENT SAD IRON HEATERS. 553

FRONT VIEW.

FRONT VIEW.

Nº 2. To hold two Irons $2 - 6$ ea.   Nº 3. To hold three Irons $3 - 0$ ea.

Nº 1 _ Do. Light $2 - 0$

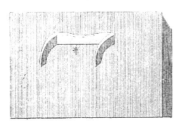

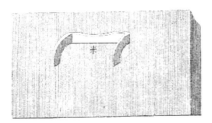

BACK VIEW.

BACK VIEW.

* Hooks to hang it on the Bars of the Grate.

REGISTERED.

SAD and ITALIAN IRONS. 554
WITH HEATERS.

Size of 00	Sad Iron	s. 10	d. 0 doz.
_ 0	_	10	6
_ 1	_	11	0
_ 2	_	11	6
_ 3	_	12	6
_ 4	_	13	6
_ 5	_	15	0
_ 6	_	16	6
_ 7	_	18	0
_ 8	_	19	6

SAD IRON WARMERS. 555

			s.	d.
A takes 0 and 1 Sad Iron			4	6 doz.
B _ 2 _ 3		_	5	0
C _ 4 _ 5		_	5	6
D _ 6 _ 7		_	6	6
E _ 8 _ 9		_	7	6

REGISTERED

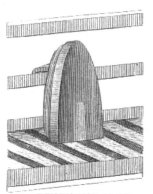

REVOLVING IRON,
on the Bar of the Grate.

REVOLVING IRON,
with Handle detached.

REVOLVING IRON.
Complete for Use.

564. REVOLVING SAD IRONS.

	11s. 6d.	12s.	13s.	14s.	15s.	16s. 6d.	18s. 6d.	20s. 6d.	26s. doz.
Nos.	0.	1.	2.	3.	4.	5.	6.	7.	8.

When in use.

When in the fire.

Face, 8¾ by 2 inches.

565. REVOLVING TAILORS' IRON.

12 lb., 3s. 6d. each.

Darwin oval   Round or Sharp Points.

570. BEST SAD IRONS.

s.   d.

Nos. 0000...000...00...0   per cwt. nett.
Nos. 1 to 10...............   ,,   ,,
Weight per pair.

No. 0000... 3lb.   No. 1 ... 4¾lb.   No. 6... 10lb.
   000... 3¼   2 ... 5¼   7... 11¼
    00... 3¾   3 ... 6¼   8... 13
     0... 4   4 ... 7¼   9... 15
               5 ... 9   10... 18

PATTERN A

PATTERN B

571. BEST TAILORS' IRONS.

s.   d.

5 and 5½ inch ....   per cwt. nett.
No. 0000 and 000.. ...   ,,   ,,
No. 00 and 0 ....   ,,   ,,
No. 1 up to 9 ....   ,,   ,,
From 2¾ to 20lb. each Iron.
The A pattern is the lightest.

572. BEST HATTERS' IRONS.

per cwt. nett.

No. 0 ... 7¾lb. each   No. 4 ... 17lb. each
     1 ... 10   5 ... 22¼
     2 ... 11½   6 .. 24
     3 ... 15½

573. BEST M. IRONS.   per cwt. nett.

Round or Sharp points.

     4¼   4½   4¾   5¾   6¼   7¾lb. per pair.
Nos. 1   2   3   4   5   6   7

574. SPANISH IRONS.   per cwt. nett.

Lighter than M. irons.
Round or sharp points.

No. 1......2.. ..3.. ...4.....5.....6......7.....

Round or Sharp Points.   Darwin 576   Oval 578

575. TOY IRONS.   577. HEAVY OVAL CAP IRONS.

No.	s.	d.	No.		s.	d.
0	3	3 doz.	0		4	6
1	3	6	1		4	9
2	4	0	2		5	0
3	4	6	3		5	6
4	5	0	4		6	0
5	5	6	5		7	0
6	6	0	6		8	0
7	6	6	7		9	0
8	7	0	8		10	6
9	7	6	9		11	6

576. DARWIN TOY IRONS.
579. OVAL TOY IRONS.
Same Sizes and Prices as Toy Irons, 575.

Nº 1.

Nº 2.

Nº 3.

579. SAD IRON STANDS.   BRIGHT

	Nos. 1	2	3
	s. d.	s. d.	s. d.
Iron handle...	4 9	6 0	7 3 doz.
Wood handle	5 9	7 0	8 3

4½ ... 5 in.

5½ in.

580. ROUND STANDS, BRIGHT.

4½ inch 6s. doz. | 5 inch 7s. doz. | 5½ inch 8s. doz.

BRASS SAD IRON STANDS, BRIGHT.

No. 10 ... 11s. | No. 11 .. 13s. doz. nett.

581. FANCY CAP IRONS.

9s. 6d.	11s. 3d.	13s.	14s. doz.
Nos. 1	2	3	4

582. IRON FLAT WEIGHTS.

WARRANTED CORRECT.

Plugged with Copper and Stamped.

¼ oz. and ½ oz. weights are brass.

			Solid Brass.		
	s.	d.	s.	d.	
4 lb. to ¼ oz.	2	4 ...	8	6	per set
2 lb. to ¼ oz.	1	7 ...	4	6	
1 lb. to ¼ oz.	1	1 ..	2	6	
¼ oz.	2	3 ...	0	10	per doz.
½ oz.	2	6 ...	1	0	
1 oz.	1	8 ...	1	3	
2 oz.	1	10 ...	2	3	
4 oz.	2	2 ...	4	0	
8 oz.	2	9 ...	7	3	
1 lb.	3	9 ...	15	0	
2 lb.	6	0 ...	27	0	
4 lb.	10	0 ...	51	0	

IRON WEIGHTS,

COPPER PLUGGED AND STAMPED.

ROUND. **583.** SQUARE. **584.** BELL. **585.**

If Japanned, 1d. and 2d. each extra.
If ditto and Gilt Figures, 2d. and 3d. each extra.

	s.	d.	
¼ lb.......	2	9	doz.
½ ,, ...	3	0	
1 ,, ...	4	0	
2 ,, ...	6	0	
4 ,, ...	9	0	
7 ,, ...	13	0	
14 ,, ...	23	0	
28 ,, ...	43	0	
56 ,, ...	81	0	

WEIGHTS OF ALL NATIONS.

619. SPIKING FOR WOOD FENCES.

24 inches long, 6d. each.

587. BAR WEIGHTS.

Plugged with Copper and Stamped.

	s.	d.	
¼ lb.......	2	9	doz.
½ ,, ...	3	0	
1 ,, ...	4	0	
2 ,, ...	6	0	
4 ,, ...	9	0	
7 ,, ...	13	0	
14 ,, ...	23	0	
28 ,, ...	43	0	
56 ,, ...	81	0	

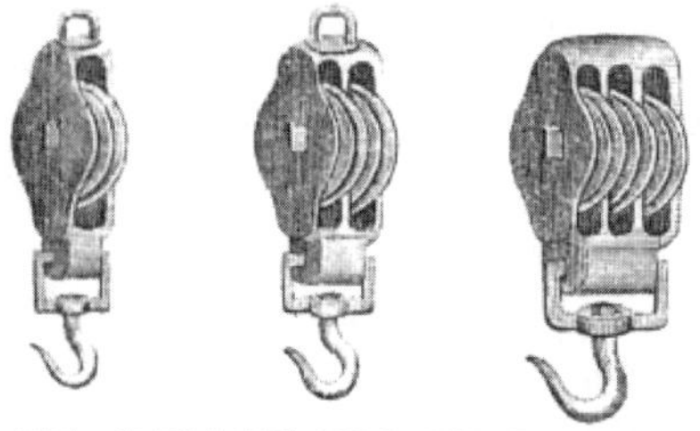

588. PULLEY BLOCKS, JAPANNED.

Inch.	Takes a Rape	1-wheel s.	d.	2-wheel s.	d.	3-wheel s.	d.	
2	... ½ inch	4	0	5	6	7	0	each
2½	... ½ ,, full	5	0	6	6	8	0	
3	... ⅝ ,, ...	6	0	7	6	9	0	
3½	... ⅝ ,, full	7	0	8	6	10	0	
4	... ¾ ,, ...	8	0	9	6	11	0	
4½	... ⅞ ,, ...	9	9	11	6	14	0	
5	...1⅛ ,, ..	11	9	14	0	17	6	

With solid Brass Wheels, if required.

PAPER WEIGHTS with Brass Knobs. **589**

Square Round

No.		s.	d.	No.		s.	d.
0	... 4 by 3 inch	8	0 doz.	3	in. diameter	7	0 doz.
1	... 4½ ,, 3 ,,	9	6	3½	... ,, ...	8	0
2	... 5 ,, 3¼ ,,	11	6	4	... ,, ...	9	0
3	... 5½ ,, 3½ ,,	14	0	4½	... ,, ...	11	0
4	... 6 ,, 3¾ ,,	16	0	5	... ,, ...	13	0
4x	... 8 ,, 4 ,,	17	6				
5	... 5 ,, 4½ ,,	18	6				
6	... 3½ ,, 2 1 in. thick	13	0				

If bronzed, 2d. each extra.

Octagon Hand

No.		s.	d.	No.		s.	d.
7	... 2¾in.	11	0 doz.	9	Hand only......	6	6 doz.
8	... 3½in.	14	0	10	Hand on plate	8	6

If Bronzed, 2d. each extra.

591. ROUND SINK TRAPS.
JAPD.

s. d.		s. d.
2 inches 3 9	6½ inches	13 6 doz.
2½ ,,.. 3 9	7 ,,...	15 0
3 ,,... 4 6	7½ ,,...	16 6
3½ ,,... 5 6	8 ,,...	18 0
4 ,,.. 6 6	9 ,,...	21 0
4½ ,,... 7 6	10 ,,...	25 6
5 ,,... 9 6	11 ,,...	32 0
5½ ,,..11 0	12 ,,...	39 0
6 ,,..12 0		

If tinned to solder pipe, 4d. each
extra.

592. SQUARE SINK TRAPS, JAPD.
With bars.

s. d.
3 inches ... 7 0 doz.
4 ,, ... 9 0
5 ,, ...11 0
6 ,, ...14 0
7 ,, ...18 0
8 ,, ...23 0
9 ,, ...28 0
10 ,, ...33 0
11 ,, ...44 0
12 ,, ...54 0

593. SQUARE SINK TRAPS, JAPD.
With round holes.

s. d.
3 inches ... 7 0 doz.
4 ,, ... 9 0
5 ,, ...11 0
6 ,, ...14 0
7 ,, ...18 0
8 ,, ... 23 0
9 ,, ...28 0
10 ,, ...33 0
11 ,, ...44 0
12 ,, ... 54 0

594. PATENT SINK TRAPS, JAPD.

			s. d.
No. 0 ... 8½ inches by 6½ inches	1 9 each
1 ... 9¾ ,, ... 8½ ,,	3 6
2 ... 13 ,, ... 11 ,,	5 3
3 ... 14½ ,, ... 13 ,,	6 9
Patent round 10 inch	4 0

595. IMPROVED SINK TRAPS.
JAPD. SQUARE OR ROUND.

s. d.		s. d.
4 inches 8 6 doz.	9 inches	27 0 doz.
5 ,, 10 6	10 ,, ...	36 0
6 ,, 14 0	11 ,, ...	48 0
7 ,, 18 0	12 ,, ...	56 0
8 ,, 23 0		

With hinge covers, 4d. each extra.
To dip from 3 inches to 6 inches, if required.

596. STABLE DRAINS, JAPD.

s. d.
4 inches square 0 8 each.
6 ...... ,, ... 0 10
8 ...... ,, ... 1 6
10 ...... ,, ... 2 3
12 ...... ,, ... 3 3
13 ...... ,, ... 3 9

597. STRONG STABLE DRAINS.
JAPD.
With holes. With bars.

	s. d.	s. d.
10 inch...	4 6 ...	4 6 each.
12 ,, ...	6 6 ...	7 0

598. STRONG GRATE AND FRAME.
JAPD., FOR GRAVEL WALKS.
6 inches square at top, 3s. each

599. SOUGH GRATES.

	JAPD.	With Frames
	s. d.	s. d.
4 inches square	2 0 ...	5 3 doz.
5 ...... ,, ...	3 0 ...	6 6
6 ...... ,, ...	4 6 ...	9 0
7 ...... ,, ...	6 6 ...12 0
8 ...... ,, ...	8 6 ...15 0
9 ...... ,, ...	12 0 ...19 6
10 ...... ,, ...	15 0 ...23 6

600. STRONG SOUGH GRATES.
WITH BARS, JAPD.
With Frames.

	s. d.	s. d.
4 inches square	3 0 ...	6 6 doz.
5 ...... ,, ...	4 0 ...	7 6
6 ...... ,, ...	5 6 ...10 0
7 ...... ,, ...	7 6 ...13 0
8 ...... ,, ...	9 6 . 16 0
9 ...... ,, ...	13 0 ...20 6
10 ...... ,, ...	16 0 ...24 6

AIR BRICKS. 586

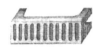

Nº 00. 9In. 2/9 Doz.

Nº 5 __ 14 × 6In __ 15/. Doz.
With Slide

Nº 0 __ 9In __ 3/6 _____ 2/6 Doz.
1 __ 9 __ 4/6 _____ 3/.

Nº 9 __ 9In. 4/ Doz.

Nº 2 __ 9In __ 5/6 _____ 4/ Doz.
3 _____ 7/6 _____ 4/9

Nº 10 __ 9In. 4/ _____ 3/. Doz.

Nº 6 __ 9 × 6In __ 8/. Doz.

Nº 11 __ 14 × 6In __ 12/ Doz.
. 12 __ 9 × 6 . __ 10/ .
. 13 __ 14 × 9 . __ 13/ .

Nº 7 __ 9 × 6In. 8/6 Doz.

Nº 14 __ 9In. 4.0 Doz.

Nº 8. 14 × 6In. __ 12/ Doz.

Nº 15 __ 9In __ 4/ Doz

Nº 4 9In. With Slide 8/6 Doz.
4x __ No Slide 7/. __

Nº 16. 9In. 4/ Doz

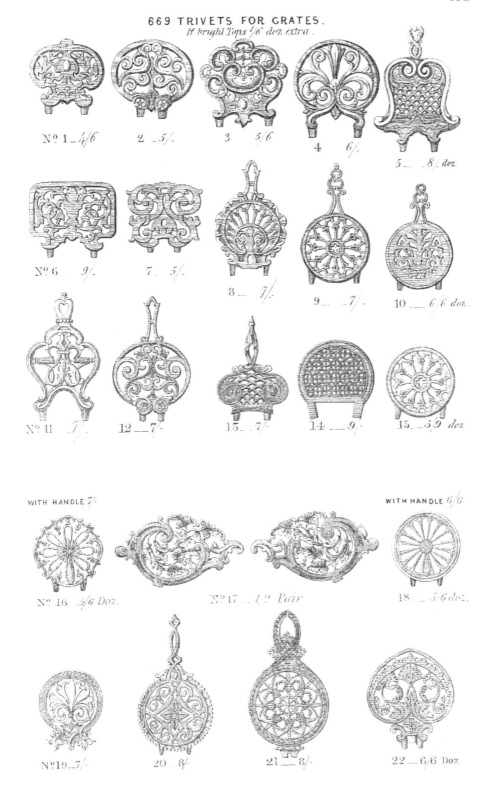

669 TRIVETS FOR GRATES.

If bright Tops 1/6 dez. extra.

Nº 1 _ 4/6   2 _ 5/   3 _ 5/6   4 _ 6/   5 _ 8/ dez.

Nº 6 _ 9/   7 _ 5/   8 _ 7/   9 _ 7/   10 _ 6/6 doz.

Nº 11 _ 7/   12 _ 7/   13 _ 7/   14 _ 9/   15 _ 5/9 dez

WITH HANDLE 7/

WITH HANDLE 6/6

Nº 16 _ 5/6 Doz.   Nº 17 _ 12 Pair   18 _ 5/6 dez.

Nº 19 _ 7/   20 _ 8/   21 _ 8/   22 _ 6/6 Doz

601. RINGS AND LOOPS, JAPD.

		s.	d.	
1½ inch diameter		0	10	doz.
1¾ ,,	,,	1	0	
2 ,,	,,	1	2	
2½ ,,	,,	1	6	
3 ,,	,,	1	9	

602. SHOE ANVILS, JAPD.

		s.	d.	
4 inch	....	4	6	doz.
5 ,,	....	5	3	
6 ,,	... .	6	0	
7 ,,	....	8	0	
8 ,,	....	9	0	
9 ,,	....	10	0	
10 ,,	.. ..	12	6	

Jap.ᵈ PUMP   SPOUTS. **603**

Straight *s. d.*   Bent *s. d.*
No. 1 ... 1 6 each   No. 0 ... 1 3 each.
             · 1 ... 1 6

604. DUMB BELLS, JAPD.
From 2lb. to 30lb. per pair.

per cwt. nett.

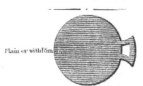

Plain or with Tom Tit.

605. BAKE PLATES.

per cwt. nett.

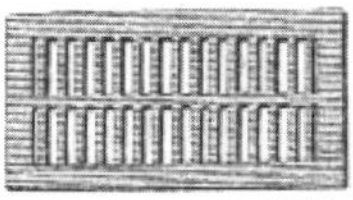

606. ASH GRATES.

Black   per cwt. nett
Bright   ,,   ,,

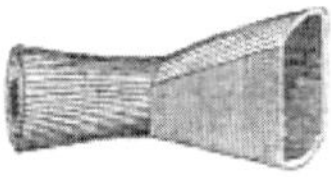

607.
TUE IRONS, FOR SMITHS' HEARTHS.
¼, ½, ¾, ⅞, 1⅛ inch hole, 1s. each.

608
STRONG   SHEAVES
DRILLED OUT   OF THE SOLID.

Under 2 inch......... 36/- to 28/- per cwt. nett.
2 to 2½ inch ....
2½ to 3½ in. inclusive
Above 3½ inch ......
    Of any thickness or hole required.

If hole is cast in ...   per cwt. less.

609. URN HEATERS.   per cwt. nett.
4......4½......5......5½......6 inches long.
by 1½, 1¾, and 2 inch diameter.

610. BOX IRON HEATERS.

per cwt. nett.

Triangle    Round

611. COGS, FOR BLOCK PULLEYS.

per cwt. nett.

No.	Barrel.	Hole.	No.	Barrel.	Hole.
A1	½ inch	⅜ inch	E2	1 inch	¾ inch.
A2	½ ,,	½ ,,	E3	1 ,,	⅞ ,,
B1	⅝ ,,	⅜ ,,	F1	1⅛ ,,	⅝ ,,
B2	⅝ ,,	½ ,,	F2	1⅛ ,,	¾ ,,
B3	⅝ ,,	⅝ ,,	F3	1⅛ ,,	⅞ ,,
C1	¾ ,,	½ ,,	F4	1⅛ ,,	1 ,,
C2	¾ ,,	⅝ ,,	G1	1¼ ,,	¾ ,,
C3	¾ ,,	¾ ,,	G2	1¼ ,,	⅞ ,,
D1	⅞ ,,	½ ,,	G3	1¼ ,,	1 ,,
D2	⅞ ,,	⅝ ,,	H1	1⅜ ,,	¾ ,,
D3	⅞ ,,	¾ ,,	H2	1⅜ ,,	⅞ ,,
E1	1 ,,	⅝ ,,	H3	1⅜ ,,	1 ,,

612.
KETTLE STAND HEATERS.
OVAL AND ROUND.

s. d.
per cwt. nett.

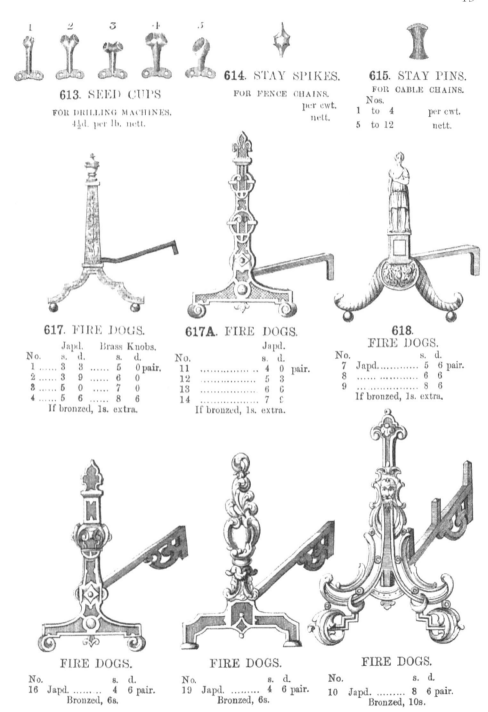

613. SEED CUPS

FOR DRILLING MACHINES.
4½d. per lb. nett.

614. STAY SPIKES.

FOR FENCE CHAINS.
per cwt.
nett.

615. STAY PINS.

FOR CABLE CHAINS.
Nos.
1 to 4 per cwt.
5 to 12 nett.

617. FIRE DOGS.

No.	Japd.		Brass Knobs.	
	s.	d.	s.	d.
1	3	3	5	0 pair.
2	3	9	6	0
3	5	0	7	0
4	5	6	8	6

If bronzed, 1s. extra.

617A. FIRE DOGS.

Japd.

No.	s.	d.
11	4	0 pair.
12	5	3
13	6	6
14	7	6

If bronzed, 1s. extra.

618.
FIRE DOGS.

No.		s.	d.
7	Japd.	5	6 pair.
8		6	6
9		8	6

If bronzed, 1s. extra.

FIRE DOGS.

No.		s.	d.
16	Japd.	4	6 pair.

Bronzed, 6s.

FIRE DOGS.

No.		s.	d.
19	Japd.	4	6 pair.

Bronzed, 6s.

FIRE DOGS.

No.		s.	d.
10	Japd.	8	6 pair.

Bronzed, 10s.

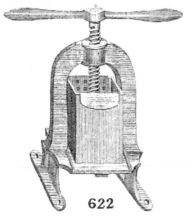

PORTABLE TINCTURE PRESS
Wrought Tined Cylinder
6¾ + 5½ in. 6/6 ea.

622

SQUARE TINCTURE PRESS.
s d.
14 6 each.

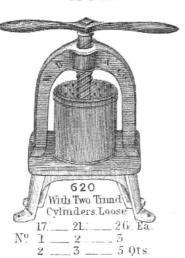

620
With Two Tinnd
Cylinders. Loose

N?.	17/.	21/.	26/. Ea.
	1	2	3
	2	3	5 Qts.

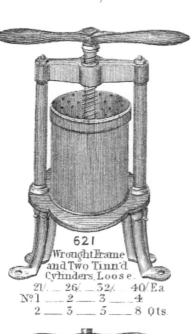

621
Wrought Frame
and Two Tinn'd
Cylinders. Loose.

N?.	21/.	26/.	32/.	40/. Ea
	1	2	3	4
	2	3	5	8 Qts.

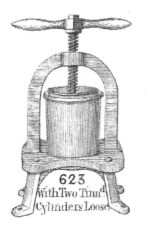

623.
With Two Tinn'd
Cylinders. Loose

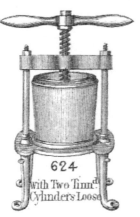

624
With Two Tinn'd
Cylinders. Loose

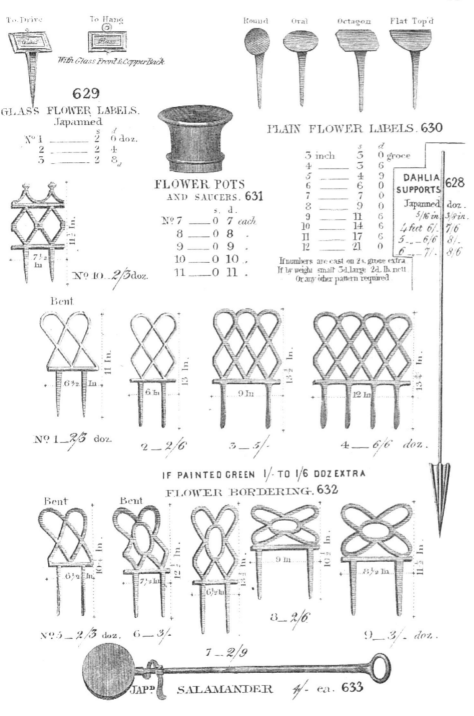

To Drive   To Hang
Glass   *Glass*
With Glass Front & Copper Back.

629

GLASS FLOWER LABELS.
Japanned

	s	d	
Nº 1	2	6	doz.
2	2	4	
3	2	8	d

Round   Oral   Octagon   Flat Top'd

PLAIN FLOWER LABELS. 630

	s	d	
3 inch	3	0	groce
4	3	6	
5	4	9	
6	6	0	
7	7	0	
8	9	0	
9	11	6	
10	14	6	
11	17	6	
12	21	0	

If numbers are cast on 2s. groce extra
If by weight small 3d. large 2d. lb. nett
Or any other pattern required

DAHLIA SUPPORTS 628
Japanned doz.

	5/16 in.	3/8 in.
4 feet	6/.	7/6
5	6/6	8/.
6	7/.	8/6

FLOWER POTS
AND SAUCERS. 631

	s.	d.	
Nº 7	0	7	each
8	0	8	
9	0	9	
10	0	10	
11	0	11	

11½ In   7½ In   Nº 10. 2/3 doz.

Bent

Nº 1 _ 2/3 doz.   6½ In   11 In
2 — 2/6   6 In   13 In
3 — 5/-   9 In   13½ In
4 — 6/6 doz.   12 In   13¾ In

IF PAINTED GREEN 1/- TO 1/6 DOZ EXTRA

FLOWER BORDERING. 632

Bent   Bent

Nº 5 _ 2/3 doz.   6½ In   10½ In
6 — 3/-   7½ In   12 In
7 — 2/9   6½ In
8 — 2/6   9 In   10½ In
9 — 3/- doz.   8½ In   11½ In

JAP.ᵈ   SALAMANDER   4/- ea. 633

634.
SQUARE HAND GLASS FRAMES.

	s.	d.
18 inch	4	0 each.
20 ,,	4	6
22 ,,	5	6

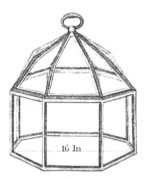

635.
OCTAGON HAND GLASS FRAMES.

	s.	d.
12 inch	3	0 each.
16 ,,	4	6
20 ,,	5	6
24 ,,	8	0

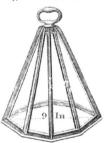

636. HAND GLASS FRAMES. .

	s.	d.
9 inch	1	2 each.
12 ,,	1	6

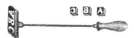

637. CAST BURN MARKS.

Letters and Figures full ⅜ inch. Full ⅝ inch.   Full ¾ inch.

	s.	d.	s.	d.		s.	d.
To hold 2 letters	3	0	... 4	0 doz.	...	1	0 each.
3 ,,	... 3	6	... 4	9	,, ...	1	1
4 ,,	... 4	6	... 6	0	,, ...	1	2
5 ,,	... 7	0	... 8	0	,, ...	1	4
6 ,,	... 9	6	...10	6	,, ...	1	6
7 ,,	...12	0	...13	0	,,		
8 ,,	...14	6	...15	6	,,		
9 ,,	...16	6	...17	6	,,		
10 ,,	...20	0	...21	0	,,		

638. CAST LETTERS & FIGURES FOR DITTO

Full ⅜ in. 7d. doz.
Full ⅝ in. 1s. 2d.
Full ¾ in. 2s.

639.	**640.**
TEA POT HANDLES.	TEA POT HANDLES.
NEW PATTERN.	Japd. with wires cast in.
Japd. with wires cast in.	

No.	s.	d.	No.	s.	d.
13	 2	0 doz.	1	 1	1 doz.
14	 2	4	2	 1	3
15	 2	9	3	 1	6
If tinned wires,			4	 1	9
5d. doz. extra.			5	 2	0
			6	 2	3

641. PLANT PROTECTOR, JAPD.

	s.	d.
8 inch	6	9 doz.
9 ,,	8	3
10 ,,	10	0

642. EARS FOR COPPER POTS.

No.	s.	d.
0	2	6 doz.
1	3	9
2	4	4
3	5	6
4	7	0
5	9	0

643 FIRE LICHTERS JAPᴰ

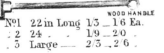

WOOD HANDLE

Nº1	22 in Long	1/3 _ 1/6 Ea.
,, 2	24 ,, ,,	1/9 _ 2/0 ,,
,, 3	Large	2/3 _ 2/6 ,,

FLOWER STAND 644

43 Inches high. 37½ Inches wide

Nº 2 Japanned 17. 0 ea
  3 Green 18. 0
  4 Bronzed 19. 0

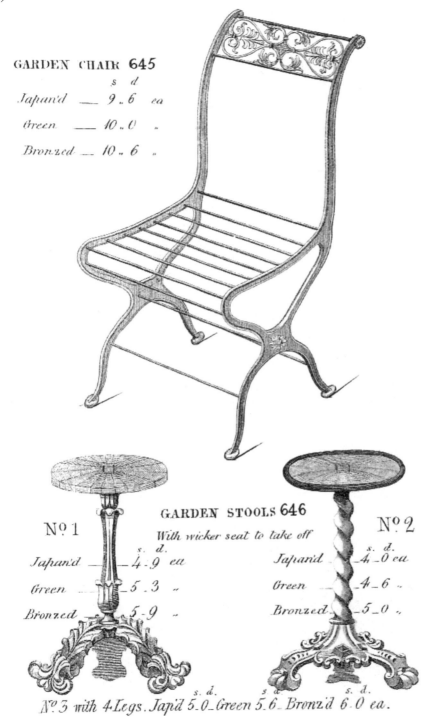

GARDEN CHAIR 645

	s	d	
Japan'd	— 9	6	ea
Green	— 10	0	„
Bronzed	— 10	6	„

GARDEN STOOLS 646

With wicker seat to take off

Nº 1

	s	d	
Japan'd	4	9	ea
Green	5	3	„
Bronzed	5	9	„

Nº 2

	s	d	
Japan'd	4	0	ea
Green	4	6	„
Bronzed	5	0	„

Nº 3 with 4 Legs. Jap'd 5.0. Green 5.6. Bronz'd 6.0 ea.

647 GARDEN SEATS JAP.D
IF PAINTED GREEN OR BRONZED 9.D EACH EXTRA
WOOD BACKS & SEATS

N.O 1 __ 4 FT _ 6 IN 30/- EA

N.O 2 __ 4 FT _ 6 IN __ 16/6 EA

N.O 3 _ 4 FT _ 6 IN 35/- EA

MADE ANY LENGTH REQUIRED

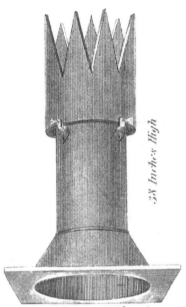

38 Inches High

13 Inch by 9 Inch Diameter
Jap.d CHIMNEY CAP **650**
Nº 1 *11/* each.

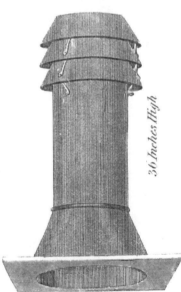

36 Inches High

13 Inch by 9 Inch Diameter
Jap.d CHIMNEY CAP **650**
Nº 2 *11/* each.

with feet

651. DUTCH STOVES, JAPD.

	Trivit.				Trivit.	
	s.	d.	d.		s.	d.	d.
7 inch	2	5	... 1½ each.	12½ inch	4	9	... 4 each.
7½ ,,	2	7	... 1½	13 ,,	5	0	... 5
8 ,,	2	9	... 2	13½ ,.	5	3	... 5
8½ ,,	3	0	... 2	14 ,,	5	6	... 5
9 ,,	3	2	... 3	14½ ,,	6	0	... 5
9½ ,,	3	5	... 3	15 ,,	6	6	... 7
10 ,,	3	7	... 3	16 ,,	7	6	... 7
10½ ,,	3	10	... 3	17 ,,	8	6	... 7
11 ,,	4	0	... 4	18 ,,	9	6	... 7
11½ ,,	4	3	.. 4	22 ,,	12	6	... 9
12 ,,	4	6	... 4	24 ,,	14	0	... 9

With ring handles and three feet, same sizes and prices.

If by weight   s.   d.   per cwt. nett.

652. DUTCH STOVES.
WITH BRAZIER TOP, JAPD.
12 inch diameter, 7s. | 14 inch diameter, 9s. each.

653. WATER CLOSET CASTINGS.
s.   d.
In sets about 46lb. weight,   per cwt. nett.

COOKING STOVES

654
ROUND

WITH EARS	Q. lb		WITH FLANCH	Q. lb
Weight per set	2 12		Weight per set	1 25
6 in. diameter 3½ in deep			7 in. diameter 2½ in. deep	
6½	3½		8	3
7	4		9	3¼
7¾	4		10	3¼
8¼	4		11	3½
8¾	4			
9¼	4			

per Cwt. nett.

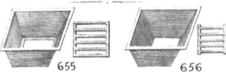

655   **656**

SQUARE COOKING STOVES

WITH FLANCH TO SUPPORT GRATE			PLAIN	
Weight per set 2 Q. 2 lb.			Weight per set 1 Q 14 lb.	
7 in. diameter 3¾			5 in. diameter 3¾	
8	3¾	inch deep inside	6	3¾
9	3¾	from the	7	4
10	3½	Top to	8	4¾
11	3½	the Grate	9	4¾
			10	5½

inches deep as 655

per Cwt. nett.

657 BOTTLEING MACHINE

	s	d
Japanned	6	0 ea
Green	6	3
Bronzed	6	6

IRON FOOTMEN,   **658**

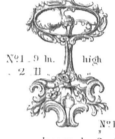

Nº 1 . 9 in.   high
. 2 . 11

	Nº 1		Nº 2	
	s	d	s	d
Japanned	2	0	2	3
Bronzed	2	6	2	9 ea.

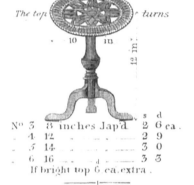

The top . . . turns

10 in
12 in

			s	d
Nº 3	8 inches	Jap'd	2	6 ea.
. 4	12		2	9
. 5	14		3	0
. 6	16	d	3	3

If bright top 6 ea. extra.

659 SOOT DOOR

Inside Measure

		s	d
Nº 1	5½ × 4¾ in.	1	6 ea
. 2			
. 3			

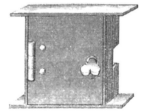

Inside Measure

		s	d
Nº 4	7¾ × 7 in.	2	0 ea.

684

685

680 CAMP OVEN or BAKE PAN

	s	d
		per Cwt NETT

From 6 to 20 in. diameter.
Covers for do 2/Cwt extra.

THREE LEG'D POT per cwt.		NEGRO POT with rim at bottom
	s d	NO LEGS s d per cwt
Under 2 gal.	NETT	Under 2 gal. NETT
2 gal & above.		2 gal & above.

THREE LEG'D POTS and NEGRO POTS.
WITH BAILS. NETT.

		s	d			s	d
2 pints	0	5½		2 gallons	1	2 each
3	__	0	6	2¼	__	1	4
4	__	0	7	2½	__	1	6
3 quarts	0	8	3	__	1	8
4	__	0	9	3½	__	1	10
5	__	0	10½	4	__	2	1
6	__	1	0	4½	__	2	4
7	__	1	1	5	__	2	7

MARMONT or FRENCH POT 681

	s	d
Under 2 Gallon __		per Cwt NETT
2 Gals & above __		

RICE BOWL 682

	s	d
No.1 to No.10		
9 to 16 in. diam.		per Cwt NETT

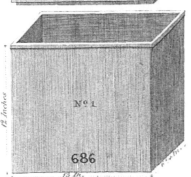

Cast Cover

No.1

686

DANISH POT
683

	s	d
Under 2 Gallon __		
2 Gals & above __		per Cwt NETT

SUPPLY CISTERN

	Tined	Untined
No.1. 13 x 6¼ In. & 12 In. deep __ 12/.		6/6 ea.
2. 12 x 6 In. & 9 In. deep taper __ 10/.		4/6
3. 12 x 6 In. & 12 In deep taper __ 11/.		5/9

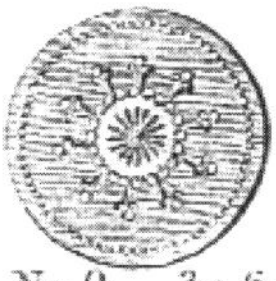

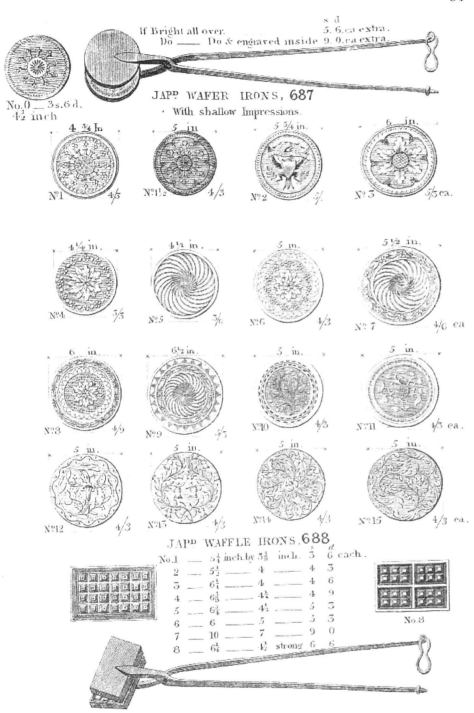

No. 0 __ 3s. 6d.
$4\frac{1}{2}$ inch

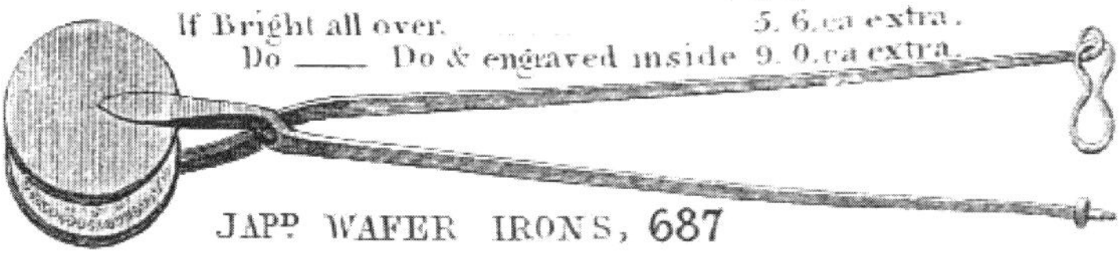

	s	d
If Bright all over	5. 6.	ea extra.
Do ____ Do & engraved inside	9. 0.	ea extra.

JAPD WAFER IRONS, 687

With shallow Impressions.

4 3/4 In

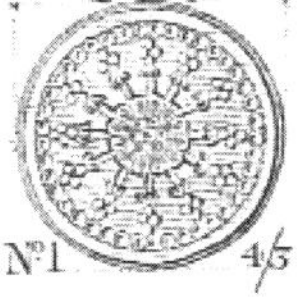

No 1 4/3

5 in

No $1\frac{1}{2}$ 4/3

5 3/4 in.

No 2 5/

6 in.

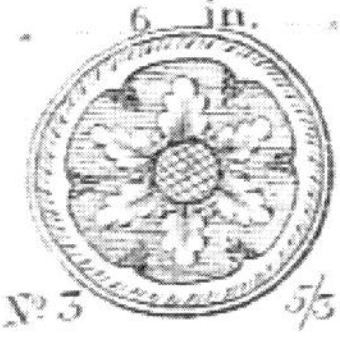

No 3 5/3 ea.

$4\frac{1}{4}$ in.

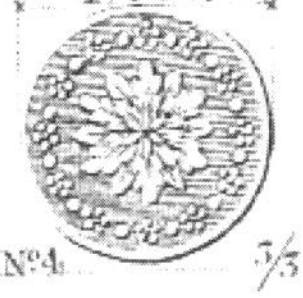

No 4 3/3

$4\frac{1}{2}$ in.

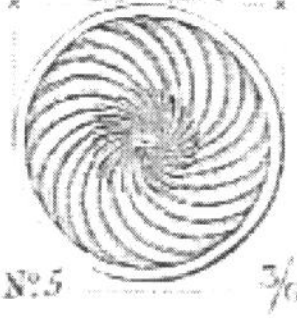

No 5 3/6

5 in.

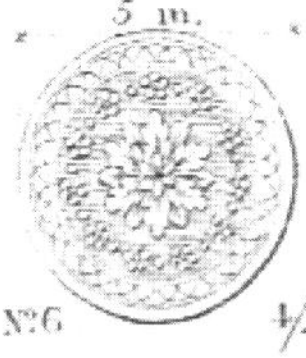

No 6 4/3

$5\frac{1}{2}$ in.

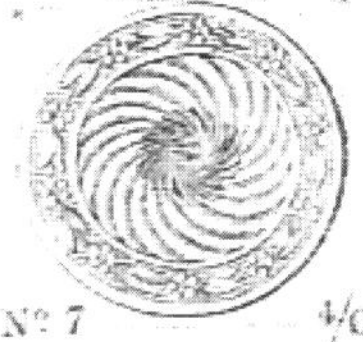

No 7 4/6 ea

6 in.

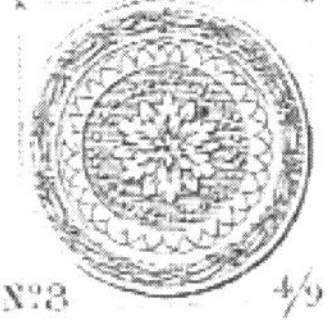

No 8 4/9

$6\frac{1}{2}$ in.

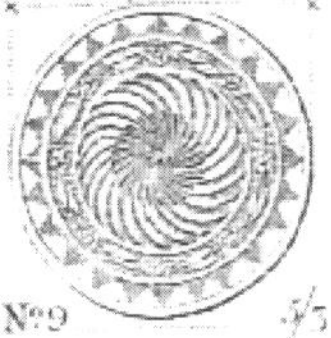

No 9 5/3

5 in.

No 10 4/3

5 in.

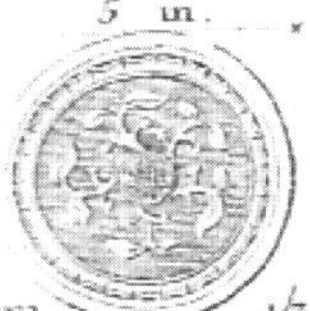

No 11 4/3 ea.

5 in.

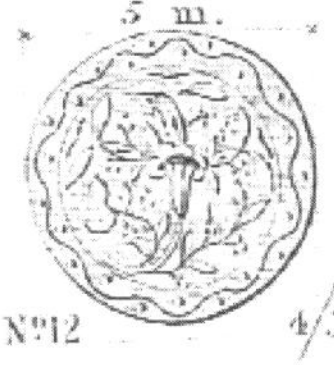

No 12 4/3

5 in.

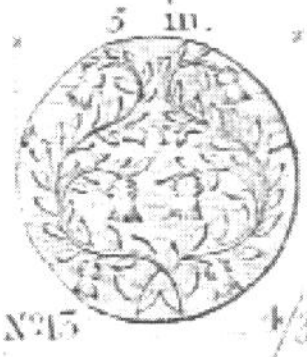

No 13 4/3

5 in.

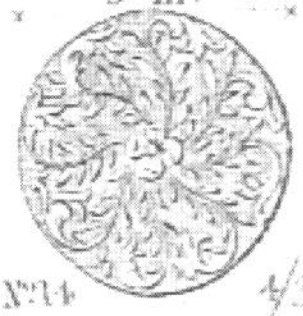

No 14 4/3

5 in.

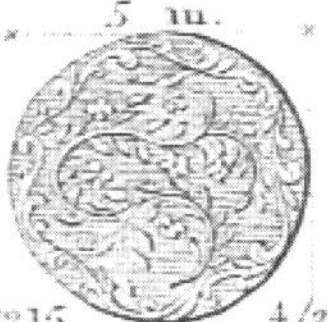

No 15 4/3 ea.

JAPD WAFFLE IRONS, 688

No.			s	d
No. 1	$5\frac{1}{4}$ inch by	$3\frac{1}{8}$ inch	3	6 each.
2	$5\frac{1}{2}$	4	4	3
3	$6\frac{1}{4}$	4	4	6
4	$6\frac{3}{8}$	$4\frac{1}{4}$	4	9
5	$6\frac{3}{4}$	$4\frac{1}{4}$	5	3
6	6	5	5	3
7	10	7	9	0
8	$6\frac{1}{4}$	$4\frac{1}{2}$ strong	6	6

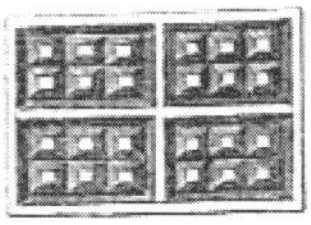

No. 8

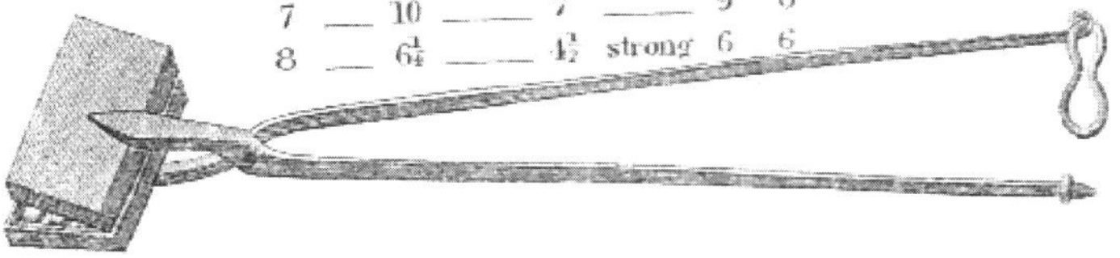

JAPANNED SCRAPERS FOR STONE WORK, 689.

If Bronzed or Berlin, 9d. each extra.

No.	Each.	No.	Each.	No.	Each.
0	-/9	107	1/2	151	2/-
1	-/10	108	2/-	152	1/3
2	1/-	109	2/8	153	2/9
2A	1/2	110	1/9	154	1/-
3	1/9	111	1/-	155	2/6
4	2/6	112	1/-	156	1/3
5	3/6	113	1/9	157	1/9
6	4/9	114	2/-	158	3/-
6A	3/6	115	1/2	159	2/-
7	3/-	116	2/-	160	1/4
8	5/3	116A	5/6	161	1/4
9	5/-	117	2/3	162	1/3
10	4/4	117A	4/-	163	-/9
11	5/3	118	2/3	164	1/4
12	1/5	119	3/-	165	1/-
13	2/7	120	1/5	166	-/9
14	2/7	121	3/-	167	-/10
15	3/6	122	4/-	168	1/-
16	2/-	123	4/-	169	1/1
17	2/-	124	2/8	170	1/-
18	3/6	124A	6/-	171	2/9
19	1/2	125	3/-	172	4/6
31A	1/6	126	2/6	172A	3/3
31B	-/10	127	-/8	173	1/2
54	1/4	128	1/6	174	1/6
55	1/6	129	1/-	175	2/6
60	1/5	130	1/-	176	2/-
60A	1/2	131	1/6	177	2/3
60B	1/6	132	1/6	178	-/10
61	-/10	133	4/4	179	3/6
62	-/6	134	3/3	180	1/6
63	-/6	135	3/-	181	7/-
64	6/6	136	2/2	182	2/6
64A	4/8	137	2/4	183	2/6
65	1/2	138	2/9	184	1/4
66	1/-	139	-/10	185	5/6
67	-/5	140	2/9	186	1/2
68	-/7	141	-/10		
69	1/4	142	-/8	GARDEN.	
70	-/6	143	3/-		
100	-/6	144	1/-	29	-/8
101	-/10	145	1/6	30	1/-
102	-/10	146	1/2	31	1/5
103	-/7	147	1/6	32	1/5
104	-/10	148	1/-	49	1/5
105	1/2	149	2/-	49A	1/7
106	1/6	150	1/-		

JAPANNED **SCRAPERS**, FOR STONE WORK 689

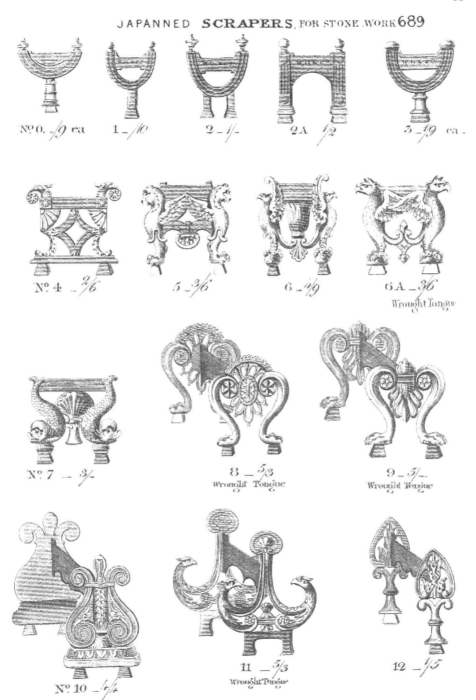

N°. 0. _/9 ea   1 _ /10   2 _ 1/-   2A /2   3 _/9 ea.

N°. 4 _ 2/6   5 _ 3/6   6 _ 4/9   6A _ 3/6
Wrought Tongue

N°. 7 _ 3/-   8 _ 5/3
Wrought Tongue   9 _ 5/-
Wrought Tongue

N°. 10 _ 4/4   11 _ 5/3
Wrought Tongue   12 _ 1/5

JAPANNED **SCRAPERS** FOR STONE WORK 689

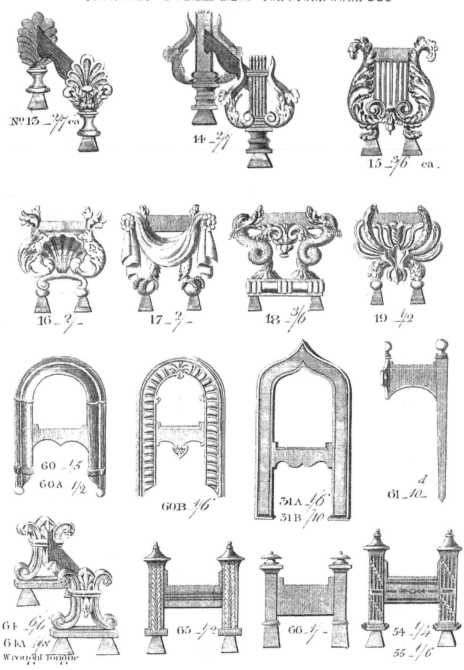

Nº 13 _ 2/7 ea

14 _ 2/7

15 _ 2/6 ea .

16 _ 2/-

17 _ 2/-

18 _ 3/6

19 _ 4/2

60 _ 4/5
60 A 4/2

60 B _ 4/6

31 A _ 4/6
31 B _ 7/10

d
61 _ 10 _

64 _ 9/6
6 1 A _ 9/8
Wrought Tongue

65 _ 4/2

66 _ 4/-

54 _ 4/4
55 _ 4/6

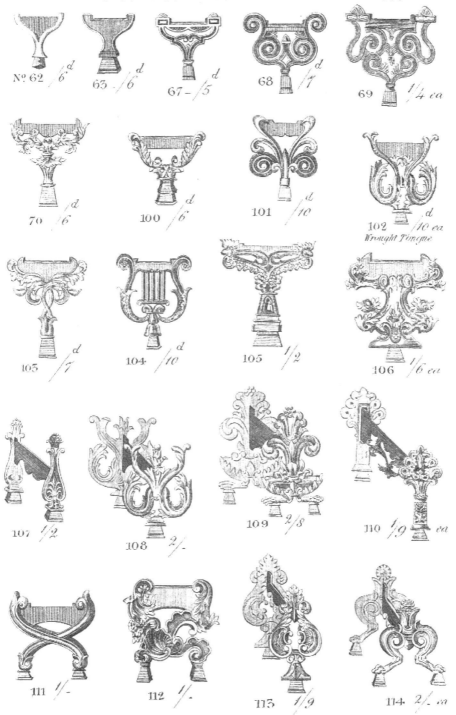

Nº 62 /6 d   63 /6 d   67 – /5 d   68 /7 d   69 1/4 ea

70 /6 d   100 /6 d   101 /10 d   102 /10 ea
Wrought Tongue

103 /7 d   104 /10 d   105 1/2   106 1/6 ea

107 1/2   108 2/-   109 2/8   110 1/9 ea

111 1/-   112 1/-   113 1/9   114 2/- ea

88

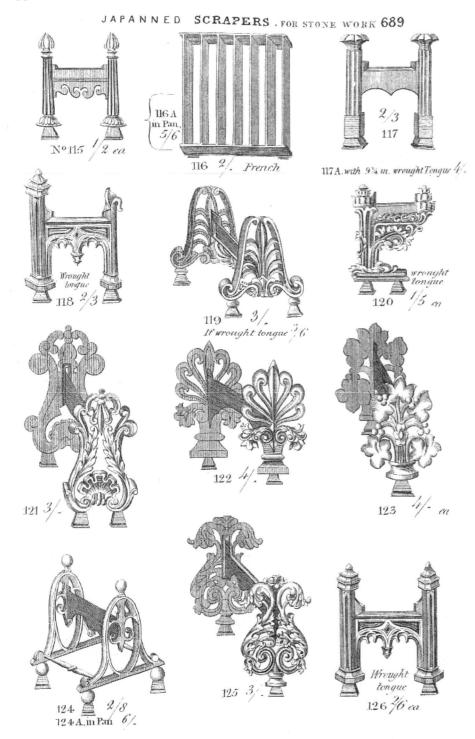

Nº 115 *1/2 ea*

116 A in Pan. 5/6

116 *2/. French*

2/3 117

117 A. with 9¾ in. wrought Tongue 4/.

Wrought tongue 118 *2/3*

119 *3/.*
If wrought tongue 3/6

wrought tongue 120 *1/5 ea*

121 *3/-*

122 *4/.*

123 *4/- ea*

124 *2/8*
124 A. in Pan *6/.*

125 *3/.*

Wrought tongue 126 *2/6 ea*

JAPANNED SCRAPERS, FOR STONE WORK 689

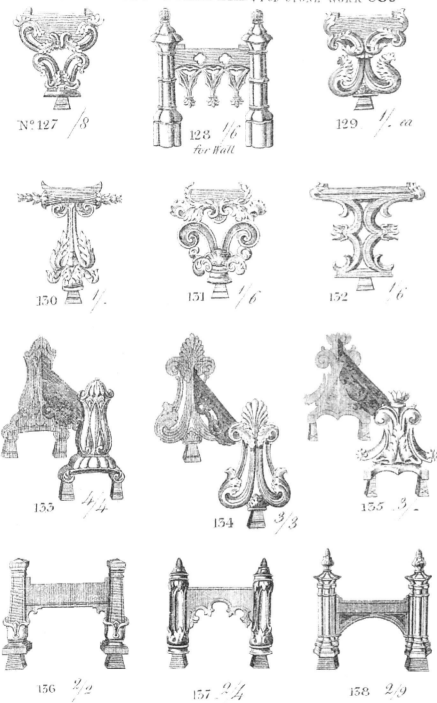

Nº 127 /8

128 1/6
for Wall

129 1/- ea

130 1/-

131 1/6

132 1/6

133 4/4

134 3/3

135 3/-

136 2/2

137 2/4

138 2/9

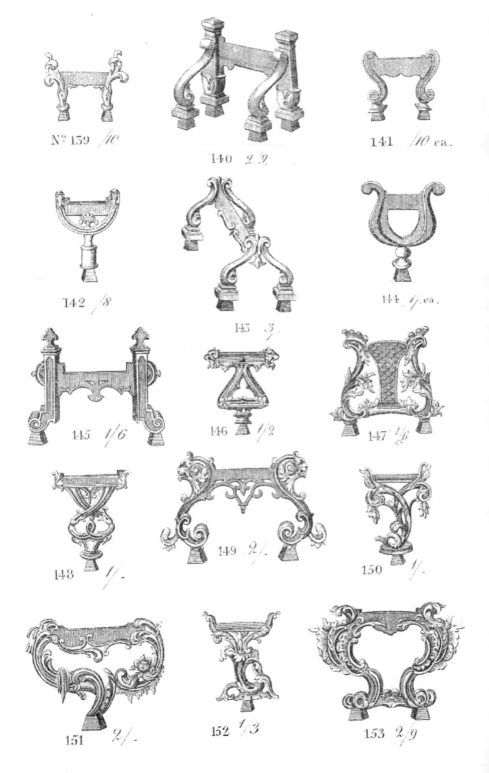

Nº 139 /10

140 2/2

141 /10 ea.

142 /8

145 3/

144 1/ ea.

145 1/6

146 1/2

147 1/6

148 1/-

149 2/.

150 1/.

151 2/-

152 1/3

153 2/9

JAPANNED SCRAPERS, FOR STONE WORK 689

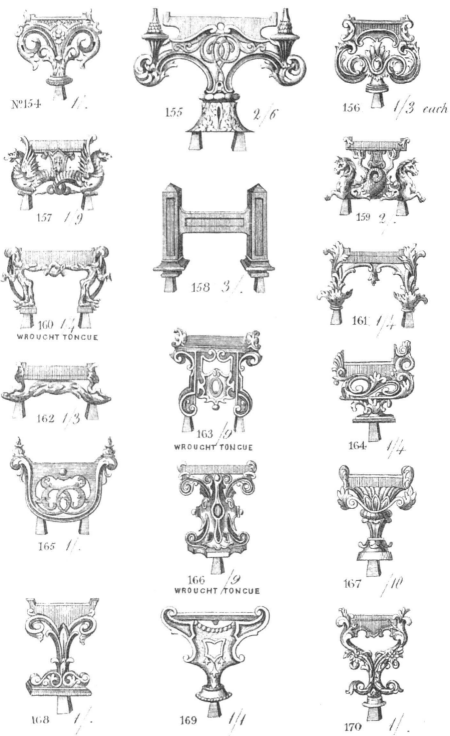

Nº154   1/.

155   2/6

156   1/3 each

157   1/9

159   2/.

158   3/.

160   1/.
WROUGHT TONGUE

161   1/4

162   1/3

163   1/9
WROUGHT TONGUE

164   1/4

165   1/.

166   1/9
WROUGHT TONGUE

167   1/10

168   1/.

169   1/.

170   1/.

689 JAP.D SCRAPERS FOR STONE WORK
IF GREEN 9.D TO 1/- EACH EXTRA

Nº 171 __ 2/9

Nº 172 __ 4/6 EACH

172 A __ 3/3 .

Nº 173 __ 1/2

Nº 174 __ 1/6 EACH

Nº 175 __ 2/6

Nº 176 __ 2/-

Nº 177 __ 2/3 EACH

Nº 178 __ 10.D

WROUGHT IRON

Nº 179 __ 3/6

Nº 180 __ 1/6 EACH

689 JAP.ᴰ SCRAPERS FOR STONE WORK

Nº 181 ___ FOR OUT OF DOORS 30 × 21 IN ___ 7/- EACH

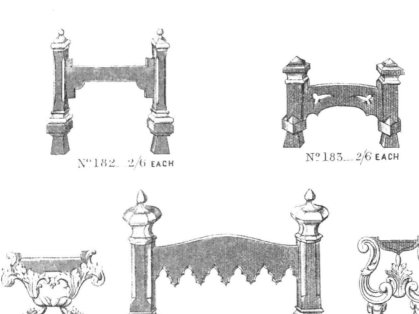

Nº 182 __ 2/6 EACH

Nº 183 ___ 2/6 EACH

Nº 184 __ 1/4 EACH

Nº 185 ___ 5/6 EACH

Nº 186 __ 1/2 EACH

No.	Jap'd. each.	Green. each.	Bronz'd each.	No.	Jap'd. each.	Green. each.	Bronz'd each.	No.	Jap'd. each.	Green. each.	Bronz'd each.
20B	-/9	1/-	1/6	77	2/-	2/3	3/-	226	5/-	5/3	6/3
20A	1/-	1/3	1/9	78	4/-	4/3	5/6	227	3/6	3/9	4/6
20	1/3	1/6	2/-	79	1/2	1/5	1/11	228	2/-	2/3	3/-
21A	1/3	1/6	2/-	80	2/6	2/9	3/6	229	5/3	5/6	6/6
21	1/9	2/-	2/6	81	2/-	2/3	3/-	230	6/-	6/3	7/6
21B	2/-	2/3	2/9	82	2/-	2/3	2/9	231	7/-	7/3	8/6
22A	1/3	1/6	2/-	83	2/-	2/3	2/9	232	6/6	6/9	8/-
22	1/9	2/-	2/6	84	1/9	2/-	2/10	233	4/3	4/6	5/6
22B	2/-	2/3	2/9	85	3/-	3/3	4/3	234	2/6	2/9	3/6
23A	2/6	2/9	3/6	86	4/-	4/3	5/3	235	2/3	2/6	3/3
23	3/-	3/3	4/-	87	4/-	4/3	5/6	236	2/6	2/9	3/6
24	5/3	5/6	6/3	88	4/8	4/11	6/2	237	2/3	2/6	3/3
25	8/-	8/3	9/-	89	4/3	4/6	5/9	238	4/4	4/7	5/10
26	5/6	5/9	6/6	90	3/3	3/6	4/6	239	2/3	2/6	3/3
27	7/7	7/10	8/7	91	3/6	3/9	5/-	240	2/3	2/6	3/3
28A	5/-	5/3	6/-	92	5/-	5/3	6/6	241	2/3	2/6	3/3
28	6/-	6/3	7/-	93	8/-	8/3	9/6	242	3/3	3/6	4/3
33	3/-	3/3	4/-	94	10/-	10/3	11/6	243	3/3	3/6	4/3
34	7/6	7/9	8/9	200	2/-	2/3	3/-	244	3/-	3/3	4/-
35	4/4	4/7	5/7	201	2/6	2/9	3/6	245	3/6	3/9	4/6
36	4/4	4/7	5/7	202	2/6	2/9	3/6	246	5/6	5/9	7/-
37	7/6	7/9	8/9	203	2/2	2/5	3/4	247	9/-	9/3	10/-
38	8/6	8/9	9/9	204	1/9	2/-	2/9	247A	5/-	5/3	6/6
39	7/6	7/9	9/-	205	3/6	3/9	4/9	248	3/3	3/6	4/3
40A	7/-	7/3	8/-	206	2/3	2/6	3/3	249	2/6	2/9	3/6
40	9/-	9/3	10/6	207	3/3	3/6	4/3	250	2/9	3/-	3/9
41	7/-	7/3	8/-	208	3/2	3/5	4/3	251	3/-	3/3	4/-
42	4/4	4/7	5/7	209	2/3	2/6	3/3	252	2/-	2/3	3/-
43	1/2	1/5	1/11	210	4/4	4/7	5/10	253	3/6	3/9	4/6
44	1/9	2/-	2/6	211	4/2	4/5	5/8	254	2/6	2/9	3/6
45	2/4	2/7	3/7	212	5/6	5/9	7/-	255	6/-	6/3	7/-
46	3/2	3/5	4/7	213	3/9	4/-	5/-	256	8/-	8/3	9/6
47	4/8	4/11	6/-	214	5/3	5/6	6/9	257	2/9	3/-	3/9
48	1/2	1/5	1/11	215	3/9	4/-	5/-	258	2/6	2/9	3/9
50	8/3	8/6	9/6	216	2/3	2/6	3/3	259	1/8	1/11	2/8
51	9/6	9/9	11/-	217	5/9	6/-	7/-	260	2/9	3/-	3/9
52	8/3	8/6	9/6	218	2/6	2/9	3/6	261	2/3	2/6	3/3
53	9/6	9/9	11/-	219	2/8	2/11	3/8	262	5/3	5/6	6/3
71	2/6	2/9	3/3	220	4/6	4/9	5/6	263	4/6	4/9	5/6
72	1/9	2/-	2/6	221	3/-	3/3	4/-	264	2/9	3/-	3/9
73	2/-	2/3	2/9	222	4/9	5/-	6/-	264A	1/6	1/9	2/3
74	2/3	2/6	3/3	223	2/8	2/11	3/8	265	7/-	7/3	8/6
75	3/2	3/5	4/6	224	3/-	3/3	4/-	266	3/-	3/3	4/-
76	3/2	3/5	4/6	225	4/9	5/-	6/-				

PAN SCRAPERS JAPANNED. 690

If Bronzed from /9 to /6 ea. extra.

Nº 20B _/9
20A /_
20 /3 ea
Oval Pan

Nº 25 _8/_ea

Nº 21A /3
21 /9
21B 2/_
With Oval Square or Octagon Pan.

26 _5/6

Nº 22A _/3
22 /9
22B 2/_
With Oval Square or Octagon Pan.

27 _7/7 *Wrought tongue*

Nº 23A 2/6
23 3/_
With Oval Square or Octagon Pan.

Nº 24 5/3 ea
Green 5/6

28A 5/_
Wrought tongue

No 49 — 1/5 ca.
49 A — 1/7

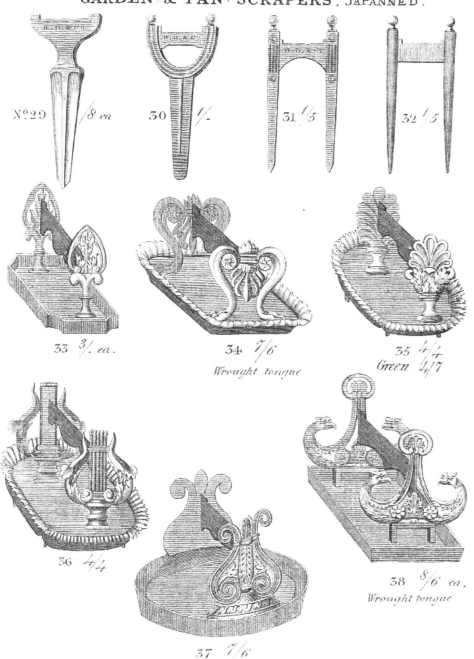

Nᵒ 29   /8 ea.

30   1/.

31 1/5

32 4/5

33 3/. ea.

34 7/6
Wrought tongue

35 4/4
Green 4/7

36 4/4

37 7/6

38 8/6 ea.
Wrought tongue

PAN SCRAPERS, JAPANNED. 690

If Bronzed from 9 to 1/6 ea. extra.

If Circular Brushes 1. ea. extra.

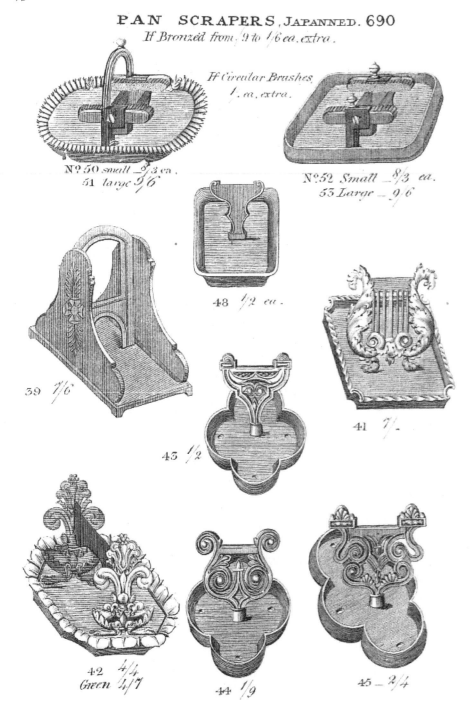

Nº 50 small — 8/3 ea.
51 large 9/6

Nº 52 Small — 8/3 ea.
53 Large — 9/6

48 1/2 ea.

39 7/6

41 7/.

43 1/2

42 4/4
Green 4/7

44 1/9

45 — 2/4

PAN SCRAPERS. JAPANNED. 690

If Bronzed from 9 to 16 ea. extra.

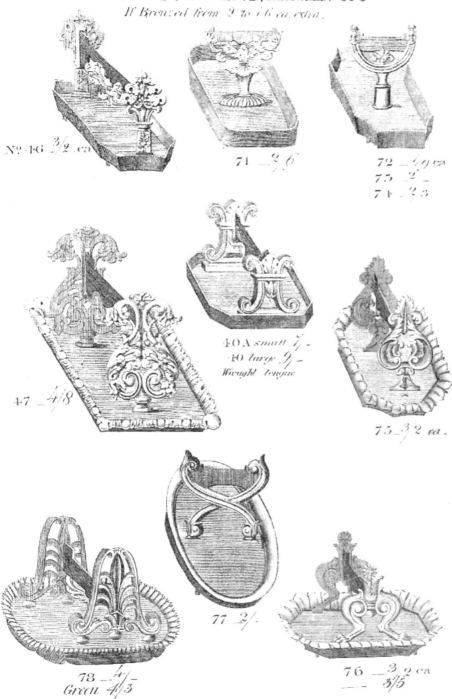

Nº 46 *3/2 ea.*

71 — *2/6*

72 — *1/9 ea*
75 — *2/-*
74 — *2/3*

47 — *4/8*

40 A *small 7/-*
40 *large 9/-*
Wrought tongue

75 — *3/2 ea.*

77 *2/-*

78 — *4/-*
Green *4/3*

76 — *3/0 ea*
—— *3/5*

PAN SCRAPERS, JAPANNED. 690

If Bronzed from 9 to 6 each extra.

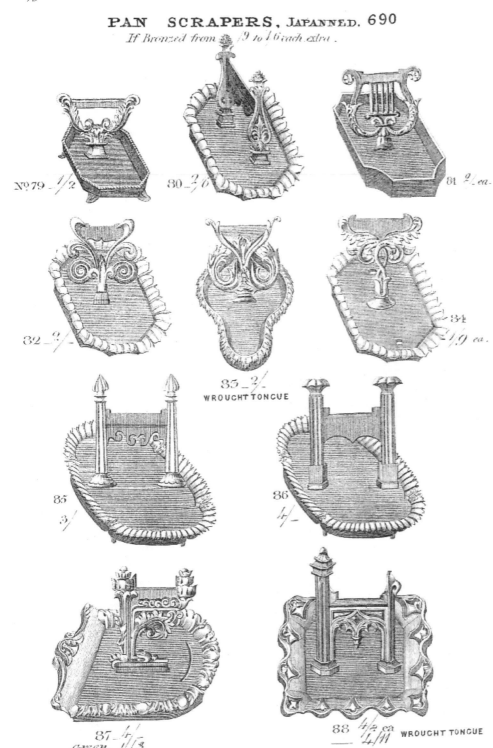

N.º 79 — 1/2

80 — 2/6

81 — 2/ ea.

82 — 2/-

85 — 2/
WROUGHT TONGUE

84 — 1/9 ea.

85
3/

86
4/-

87 — 4/
Green 4/3

88 — 4/2 ea
4/11 WROUGHT TONGUE

PAN SCRAPERS JAPANNED. 690

If Bronzed 1/6. each extra.

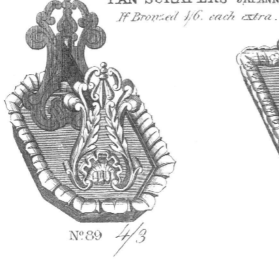

№ 89 *4/3*

90 *3/3 ea*

91 *3/6*
Green *3/9*

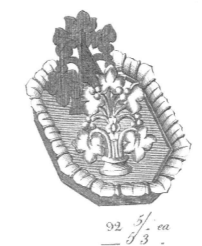

92 *5/. ea*
    5/3 .

93, with Brushes *8/. ea.*
without Brushes *6/. .*

94, with Brushes *10/. ea.*
without Brushes *7/6 .*

PAN SCRAPERS JAPANNED. 690

If Bronzed from 9/6 | 6ea extra.

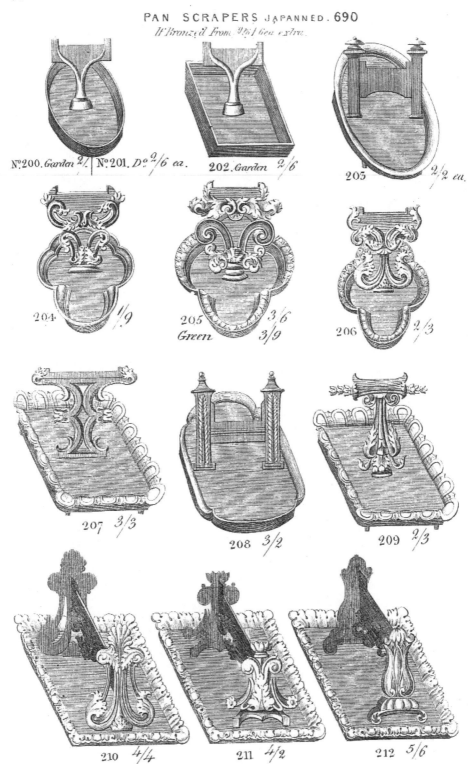

Nº 200. *Garden* 2/ | Nº 201. Dº 2/6 *ea.*

202. *Garden* 2/6

203 2/2 *ea.*

204 1/9

205 3/6
Green 3/9

206 2/3

207 3/3

208 3/2

209 2/3

210 4/4

211 4/2

212 5/6

PAN SCRAPERS, JAPANNED. 690

If Bronzed from /9 to /6 ea. extra.

Nº 213 3/9

214 5/3
WROUGHT TONGUE

215 3/9 ea.

216 2/3

217 5/9
Green 6/-

218 2/6 ea.

219 2/8

220 4/6

221 3/. ea.

222 4/9

223 2/8

224 3/. ea.

PAN SCRAPERS JAPANNED. 690

If Bronzed from /9 to 1/6 ea. extra.

Nº 225   4/9

226   5/-
Green 5/3

227   3/6

228   2/-

229   5/3

230   6/-

231   7/-

232   6/6

233   4/3

PAN SCRAPERS JAPANNED. 690

If Bronzed from /9 to/6 ea extra.

No 254 2/6   255 2/3   256 2/6 each
                          WROUGHT TONGUE

257 2/3   258 4/4   259 2/3

240 2/3   241 2/3   242 3/3
Green 2/6   ——— 2/6   ——— 3/6
WROUGHT TONGUE   WROUGHT TONGUE   WROUGHT TONGUE

243 3/3   244 3/-   245 3/6

PAN SCRAPERS, JAPANNED. 690

If Bronzed from 1/9 to 4/6 ea. extra.

Nº 246   5/6

247A Small 5/- ea.
247 Large 9/-

248   3/3
Green   3/6

249   2/6
  2/9

WROUGHT TONGUE
250   2/9
3/-

251   3/-

252   2/-

253   3/6

254   2/6

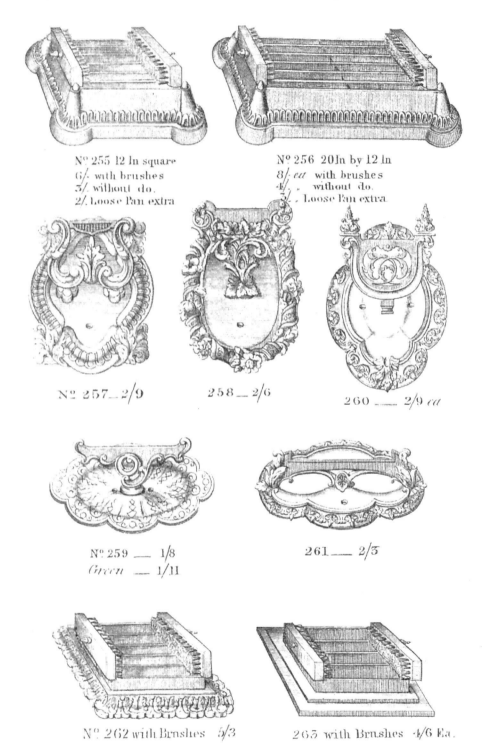

690 PAN SCRAPERS JAP? BRONZED 9? TO 2/- EACH EXTRA

Nᵒ 255 12 In square
6/- with brushes
3/- without do.
2/- Loose Pan extra

Nᵒ 256 20In by 12 In
8/- ea with brushes
4/- „ without do.
3/- „ Loose Pan extra

Nᵒ 257 _ 2/9

258 _ 2/6

260 _ 2/9 ea

Nᵒ 259 _ 1/8
Green _ 1/11

261 _ 2/3

Nᵒ 262 with Brushes 5/3

263 with Brushes 4/6 Ea.

690 PAN SCRAPERS JAP.ᴰ
IF BRONZED 9ᴰ TO 1/6 __ EACH EXTRA

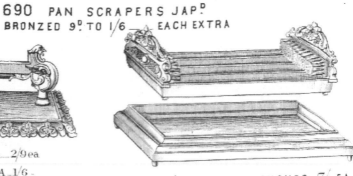

Nº 264 __ 2/9 ea

FOR STONE __ 264A 1/6.

Nº 265 WITH BRUSHES 7/- EA

Nº 266 __ 3/- each

Best Cast Iron Nails.

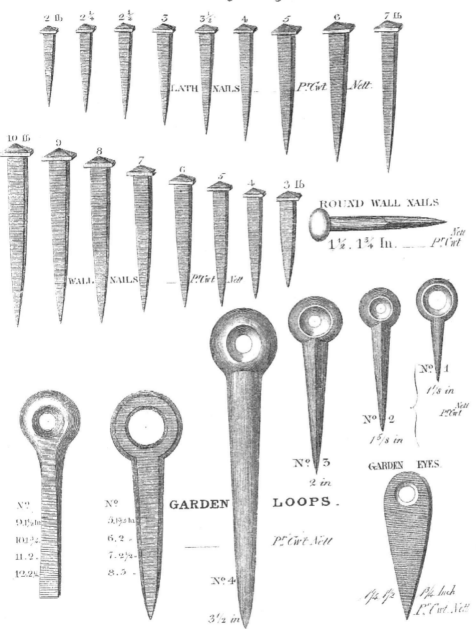

2 ℔ 2¼ 2½ 3 3½ 4 5 6 7 ℔

LATH NAILS P.ʳ Cwt Nett.

10 ℔ 9 8 7 6 5 4 3 ℔

WALL NAILS P.ʳ Cwt Nett

ROUND WALL NAILS
1½ . 1¾ In. .... Nett
P.ʳ Cwt

Nᵒ 1
1⅛ in
Nett
P.ʳ Cwt

Nᵒ 2
1⅝ in

Nᵒ 3
2 in

GARDEN LOOPS.

P.ʳ Cwt Nett

Nᵒ
9. 1½ in
10. 1¾
11. 2
12. 2½

Nᵒ
5. 1¾ in
6. 2
7. 2½
8. 5

Nᵒ 4
3½ in

GARDEN EYES.

1¼ 1½ 1¾ Inch
P.ʳ Cwt Nett.

BEST HEADED BILLS.

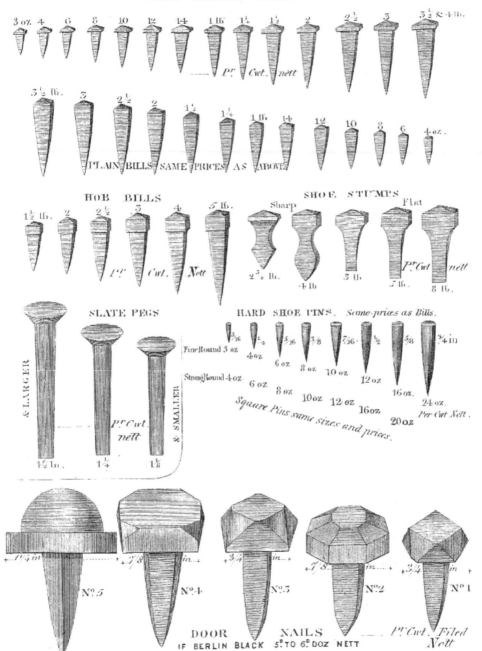

Pr. Cwt. nett

PLAIN BILLS SAME PRICES AS ABOVE

HOB BILLS   SHOE STUMPS

Sharp   Flat

Pr. Cwt. Nett   Pr. Cwt. nett

SLATE PEGS   HARD SHOE PINS. Same prices as Bills.

Fine Round 3 oz

Strong Round 4 oz

Square Pins same sizes and prices.

Per Cwt Nett.

& LARGER   & SMALLER

Pr. Cwt. nett

DOOR NAILS
IF BERLIN BLACK 5ᵈ TO 6ᵈ DOZ NETT

Pr. Cwt. Filed Nett

DOOR NAILS

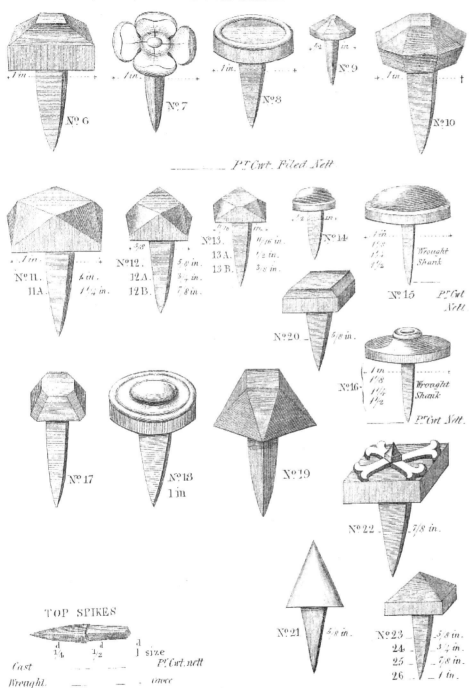

Nº 6

Nº 7 . 1 in.

Nº 8 . 1 in.

Nº 9

Nº 10 . 1 in.

Pᵗ Cwt. Filed Nett.

Nº 11 . 1 in.
11 A . 1¼ in.

Nº 12 . 5/8 in.
12 A . 3/4 in.
12 B . 7/8 in.

Nº 13
13 A . 1/2 in.
13 B . 3/8 in.

Nº 14

Nº 15 . 1 in. 1/8 1¼ 1½ Wrought Shank . Pᵗ Cwt Nett

Nº 20 . 5/8 in.

Nº 16 . 1 in. 1/8 1¼ 1½ Wrought Shank . Pᵗ Cwt. Nett.

Nº 17

Nº 18 1 in

Nº 19

Nº 22 . 7/8 in.

Nº 21 . 5/8 in.

Nº 23 . 5/8 in.
24 . 3/4 in.
25 . 7/8 in.
26 . 1 in.

TOP SPIKES

d 1/4   d 1/2   d 1 size

Cast ———— Pᵗ Cwt. nett
Wrought ———— once
If Brass ——— If Filed ——— Pᵗ lb. nett

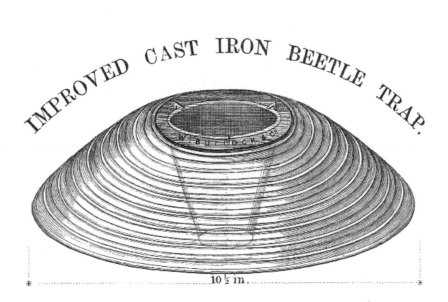

IMPROVED CAST IRON BEETLE TRAP.

10½ in.

THIS Trap will be found much superior to all others. The construction is such that Beetles are readily caught, and cannot possibly escape; but the principal advantage is, that they can be destroyed instantly, without ANY INJURY TO THE TRAP, which is of Cast Iron, ENAMELLED INSIDE, and may be cleaned with very little trouble.

DIRECTIONS FOR USE.

Bait the Trap with crumbs of bread, *or beer is preferable*, and place it where the Beetles resort; they will soon enter it in search of food, and will be unable to get out again; then pour boiling water into the Trap; which kills the Beetles; empty the Trap, and *when* wiped clean, bait it again for use.

696. BEETLE TRAP, painted white and enamelled inside, with Glass, 2*s*. 9*d*. each.

Extra Glass for ditto......... 4*d*. each.

INDEX.

A.

PAGE

73A Air Bricks
12 Arnott Shovels
74 Ash Grates
29 AXLE PULLEYS (and 25)
30 Axle Rollers
28A Angle Screw Pulleys

B.

26 Back Flaps
74 Bake Plates
83 Bake Pans
3 Bakers' Pots
43A Bakers' Lamps
45 Ball Irons
72 Bar Weights
10 BASINS
33A Basket Castors
29 Bedstead Joints
102 Beetle Traps
36 Bell Cranks
34 Bell Pulls (and 41F)
72 Bell Weights
45 Billiard Irons
100 Bills, headed and plain
41E Bolts
24G Boot Jacks
24G Boot and Shoe Racks
45A Bonnet Irons
82 Bottling Machines
29 Bowls and Pins
14 BOW-HANDLE POTS
46 BOX IRONS (45A and 25)
74 Box Iron Heaters
43 Brackets (and 43A)
40 Brackets, Hat and Coat
29 Brass Frame Pulleys (and 25)
72 Brass Weights
42 Bridle Hooks
28 Broad Butts
77 Burn Marks
25 BUTTS (and 26, 27, and 28)
39 Buttons (and 25 and 41FX)

C.

37 Cabin Hooks
41FX Cabinet Hinges and Hinge Fronts
16 Camp Coffee Mills
83 Camp Ovens

PAGE

41A Candle Hooks
42A Cannons, Toy
71 Cap Irons
29A Casement Stays
77 Cast Letters and Figures
99 Cast Nails, &c.
31 CASTORS (and to 33A and 25)
30 Centre Hinges
36 Chain Bolts
25 CHEAP ARTICLES, various
81 Chimney Caps
41A Chimney Hook
13 Chocolate Pots
43A Clock Brackets
12 Cinder Sifters
12 Coal-box Shovels
40 Coat Hooks and Pins (and 41A)
17 COFFEE MILLS (16 and 25)
13 COFFEE POTS
74 Cogs, for Block Pulleys
37 Combs
45A Convex Irons
82 Cooking Stoves
12 Copper-hole Shovels
42A Cork Squeezers
28 Cottage Hinges
43A Counter Reel, for String
39 Cow Knobs
39 Cupboard Buttons (and 25)
35 Cupboard Knobs
35 Cupboard Turns (and 41D)

D.

76 Dahlia Supports
83 Danish Pots
71 Darwin Irons
14 Deep Round Pots
42 Dipple Tips
41FX Drawer Handles
5 DIGESTERS (and 13A)
9 Dinner Plates
30 Door Centres
36 Door Chains (and 41E)
35 Door Handles (and 41C, 41D, 41E)
47 Door Knockers (and to 59J)
35 Door Knobs (and 34, 41A, 41E)
100 Door Nails (and 101)
60 Door Porters (and to 66)
85 Door Scrapers (and to 98E)

PAGE

38 Door Springs
44 Double Italian Irons (and 45A)
4 Drinking Cups
74 Dumb Bells
12 Dust Pans
46 Dutch Box Irons
81 Dutch Stoves

E.

77 Ears, for Copper Pots
27 Egg Hinges
44 Egg Irons
40 Escutcheons (and 41D)

F.

71 Fancy Cap Irons
75 Fire Dogs
24F Fire Irons Stand
77 Fire Lighters
7 FISH KETTLES
17 Flanch Mills (and 25)
72 Flat Weights
45 Flounce Irons
76 Flower Bordering
76 Flower Labels
76 Flower Pots
78 Flower Stands
34 Flush Bell Pulls (and 41F, 41G)
36 Flush Latches
37 Flush Plate and Rings
38 Flush Shutter Lifts
45 Fluting Irons
31 Four Wheel Castors
82 Footmen, to turn round
44 French Irons
45 French Box Irons
31 French Castors (and 25)
30 French Curtain Rod Ends
83 French Pots
6 FRENCH STEWPANS
44 Frill Irons
8 FRYING PANS

G.

79 Garden Chairs
29 Garden Eyes and Loops
42 Garden Rakes
79 Garden Stools
80 Garden Seats
36 Gate Latches
45A German Box Irons
76 Glass Flower Labels
9 GLUE POTS
41E Gothic Bolts
41F ,, Bell Pulls

PAGE

41E Gothic Bevil Handle Latches
41D ,, Cup'd Turns
41FX ,, Cabinet Hinges
41FX ,, ,, Hinge Fronts
41C ,, Door Handles (& 41D, 41E, 41EX)
41E ,, Door Chains
41D ,, Escutcheons
41FX ,, Hinges
41FX ,, Hinge Fronts (and to 41N)
41B ,, Latches (and 41C, 41DX, 41DXX, 41E, 41EX)
29A ,, Staples
73 Grate and Frame, for Walks
9 Grid Irons
42 Grindstone Spindles
17 Grocers' Mills
14 Grog Pots
30 Guarded Screw Pulleys
36 Gun Hooks

H.

43A Hall Brackets
39 Halter Balls
77 Hand Glass Frames
35 Handles, various (38, 41D, 41E, 41EX, 43A, and 41FX)
100 Hard Shoe Pins
42 Harness Bridle Hooks
42 Harness Pegs
4 Harvest Cup
18A Hat and Coat Stands (and 18B, 19 and 20)
40 Hat and Coat Pins (41 and 25)
40 Hat Hooks, Pins and Brackets (and 41)
41A Hat Holders
71 HATTERS' IRONS
100 HEADED BILLS and PINS
74 Heaters for Urns, Kettles, and Box Irons
40 Hinge Escutcheons
41FX Hinge Fronts (and to 41N)
38 Hot Bed Fastenings
29A Hot House Pulleys
22A Hot House Latches
29A Hot House Rack Rollers

I.

42 Jack Cranes
3A Imperial Hd'le Kettle
25 Improved Box Irons (and 45A)
46 Indian Box Irons
42A Ink Pot Slides
38 Inside Shutter Lifts

PAGE

29 IRON FRAME PULLEYS (and 25)
44 ITALIAN IRONS (45 and 25)

K.

74 Kettle Stand Heaters
27 Knee'd Butts
34 Knobs, for Doors, Locks, &c. (and 35, 41A, and 41G)
47 KNOCKERS (and to 59J)

L.

36 Latches (and 37, 41B, C, and 41DX, 41DXX, 41E, 41EX)
99 LATH NAILS
29A Lazy Pulleys
77 Letters and Figures, for Burn Marks
35 LIFTING HANDLES
25 Light Butts Light French
   ,, Pulleys   Castors
   ,, Axle Pulleys ,, Italian Irons
   ,, Skew Butts ,, Impr'd. Box
   ,, Surplice Pins   Irons
   ,, Hat and Coat ,, Square Mills
      Pins   ,, Flanch Mills
   ,, Three-wheel ,, Cheap Sad
      Castors   Irons, &c.
   ,, Buttons
35 Lock Knobs (41A and 41G)
40 Lock Staples
27 Loose Butts
33 Low Castors, for Pianofortes

M.

71 M Irons (and 25)
18 Man Traps
39 Mane Combs
39 Manger Rings and Rollers
10 Maslin Kettles
43A Meat Screen Handles
9 Milk Pans (and 12)
16 MILLS (and 17 and 25)
42 Mole Traps
11 MORTARS AND PESTLES
41A Mortice Lock Furniture
45 Mushroom Irons

N.

99 Nails—Lath, Wall, and Door
41A Napkin Hooks
83 Negro Pots
36 Night Bolts
36 NORFOLK LATCHES (and 37)

O.

PAGE

45A Open Box Irons
46 Oval Box Irons
2 OVAL POTS (and 3)
8 Oval Saucepans
8 Oval Stewpans
4 Oval Tea Kettles
39 Ox Knobs

P.

72 Paper Weights
26 Parliament Hinges (and 27)
33 Patent Castors (and 33A)
43A Patent Scale Bracket
73 Patent Sink Traps
26 Pew Butts (and Hinges 27)
39 Pew Buttons (and 41FX)
37 Pew Door Latches (and Fastenings 41A)
33 Pianoforte Castors
9 Pikelet Pans
45 Piping Irons
31 Pivot Castors (and 32 and 33)
77 Plant Protectors
14 Porringers
16 Portable Coffee Mills
42 Portable Jack Cranes
42 Potato Setter
3 Potato Steamer
2 POTS, Round and Oval (and 3, 13A, and 14)
10 Preserving Pans
100 Prison Door Nails (and 101)
44 Puffing Irons
72 PULLEY BLOCKS
29 Pulley Wheels
29 PULLEYS, Iron and Brass Framed (and 25)
74 Pump Spouts

R.

43A Reel, for String
70B Revolving Sad Irons
70B Revolving Tailors' Irons
83 Rice Bowls
14 Rice Pans
72 Ring Weights
74 Rings and Loops
30 ROLLERS, for partitions (and for Sashes 39)
30 Roller Blind Ends
12 Round Back Sifters
5 RUMFORD POTS
2 ROUND POTS (and 14 & 13A)

S.

PAGE
71 SAD IRONS (25, 70, and 70B)
70 Sad and Italian Irons
70 Sad Iron Heaters and Warmers
71 Sad Iron Stands
43A Sailors' Palms
76 Salamander
38 Sash Lift
38 Sash Pivots
38 Sash Drops
39 Sash Rollers
1   SAUCEPANS
5   Saucepan and Stewpan Digesters
43A Scale Brackets
85 SCRAPERS (and to 98E)
30 Screw, Side, & Upright Pulleys
75 Seed Cups
37 Secret Latches
41A Secure Hat Holders
74 SHEAVES (and 28A)
43 Shelf Bracket
74 Shoe Anvils
100 Shoe Bills and Pins
67 SHOE TIPS (and to 69)
29 Shower Bath Pulleys
38 Shutter Fastenings
38 Shutter Lifts
38 Shutter Screws
29A Signal Pulleys
73 SINK TRAPS
12 SIFTERS
26 Skew Butts (27 and 25)
13 Skillets
100 Slate Pegs
45A Sleeve Irons
32 Socket Castors
82 Soot Doors
73 Sough Grates
3   Soup Pots
71 Spanish Irons
72 Spanish Weights
30 Spectacle Pulleys
72 Spiking for Wood Fences
15 SPITTOONS
26 Square Butts
73 Stable Drains
41A Stable Hooks
37 Stable Latches (and 41B)
29A Stanhope Door Spring
40 Staples, for Locks (and 29A)
9   Steak Pans
28A Strop Screw Pulleys
75 Stay Pins and Spikes, for Fence
        Chains

PAGE
6   STEWPANS
3   Stock Pots
43A String Boxes
43A String Reels
38 Stubs and Plates
16 SUGAR NIPPERS
83 Supply Cisterns
40 Surplice Pins (and 25)

T.

71 TAILORS' IRONS (and 70B)
17 Table Mills
4   TEA KETTLES
5   TEA KITCHENS
77 Tea Pot Handles
74 Tea Urn Heaters
83 THREE-LEGGED POTS, or
        RINGS instead of Legs
31 Three-wheel Castors (and 25)
36 Thumb Latches
75A Tincture Presses
11 Tobacco Pots
101 Top Spikes
42A Toy Cannons
71 TOY IRONS
44 Toy Italian Irons
37 Trap Door Rings
45 Tripod Italian Irons
73B Trivets, for Grates
35 Trunk Handles
74 Tue Irons
7   TURBOT KETTLES

U.

2   Upright Pots (and 3)
30 Upright Pulleys
74 Urn Heaters
20 UMBRELLA STANDS (and
        to 24H)

V.

16 Vertical Coffee Mills

W.

84 Wafer and Waffle Irons
99 Wall Nails
10 Wash-hand Basins
81 Water Closet Castings
14 Water Jug
72 WEIGHTS, various kinds
3A Well Kettles
46 WROUGHT BOX IRONS